BERLITZ®
TRAVEL GUIDE

FRENCH RIVIERA

W9-BMD-935

With photos and maps in colour .
Plus special section of Practical
Information

Deluxe Guide
1988/1989 Edition

By the staff of Berlitz Guides

Copyright © 1978 by Berlitz Guides, a division of
Macmillan S.A., Avenue d'Ouchy 61, 1000 Lausanne 6, Switzerland.

Berlitz Trademark Reg. U.S. Patent Office and other countries.
Marca Registrada. Library of Congress Catalog Card No. 78-52518.

Printed in Hong Kong by Mandarin Offset.

How to use our guide

- All the practical information, hints and tips that you will need before and during the trip start on page 100, with a complete rundown of contents on page 104.

- For general background, see the sections The Region and its People, p. 6, and A Brief History, p. 11.

- All the sights to see are listed between pages 20 and 77. Our own choice of sights most highly recommended is pinpointed by the Berlitz traveller symbol.

- Entertainment, nightlife and all other leisure activities are described between pages 77 and 90, while information on restaurants and cuisine is to be found on pages 91 to 99.

Although we make every effort to ensure the accuracy of all the information in this book, changes occur incessantly. We cannot therefore take responsibility for facts, prices, addresses and circumstances in general that are constantly subject to alteration. Our guides are updated on a regular basis as we reprint, and we are always grateful to readers who let us know of any errors, changes or serious omissions they come across.

Text: Suzanne Patterson
Photography: Monique Jacot
Layout: Doris Haldemann
We wish to thank Mr. and Mrs. Jean Fischbacher and Bob Davis, as well as the Société des Bains de Mer in Monte Carlo and the Caves de la Madeleine, Paris, for their help in the preparation of this guide. We're especially grateful to the tourist offices of Nice, Cannes and the Alpes Maritimes for their valuable assistance.

4 Cartography: Falk-Verlag, Hamburg.

Contents

The Region and its People

The Côte d'Azur, the Riviera, Provence, the Midi—call it what you will—this is the world's dream spot. Storied, chronicled, painted, photographed, it probably has more aura and more money than any other seacoast. It could also be called the French Gold Coast, with soaring real estate prices and cost-of-living among the world's highest.

The Riviera calls up a picture of lolling millionaires, limpid sea and pink palaces of the F. Scott Fitzgerald era. From the fabled princes or rakes gambling at Monte Carlo to lissom girls basking nude at beaches near Saint-Tropez, the

Port-Grimaud, the coast's newest little Venice, is built on canals.

coast's legends are still very real. But they are not the whole story.

The term Riviera usually includes not only the Mediterranean coast but the countryside behind, extending from around Cassis to the Italian border. The ribbons of golden sand disappearing into azure sea and the sheer, rocky spectacular views of the great Corniche routes between Nice and Monte Carlo attract obvious admiration, but less widely acclaimed sights wait to be discovered by adventurous travellers.

You can explore medieval villages—many now deserted,

or nearly so—perched perilously on their peaks, or clinging to their lofty outcrops like hazardous dice-throws. Cypresses and silvery olive groves, bright mimosa and roses, the heady wafts of thyme, rosemary and sage and the *garrigues*, the almost impenetrable scrub growth, are as much a part of southern France as the blue sea. To really savour life down here try sitting in small-town squares. Take in the musically gurgling fountains and the desultory social life under the shade of outsized plane-trees, and learn how to relax.

The sun is out twice as much here as in Paris, even if out of season the climate is not always perfect. Winter has its share of cool or cold days, and any time of year the Mistral wind can come raging down the Rhône valley freshening the vivid hues of Provence, but also exhausting inhabitants and discouraging beach-goers with its incessant, irritating roar.

Given the bright colours and pervasive, luminous light, it's no wonder that artists since Fragonard have gravitated to

Early morning—the time to beat the crowds at the Baie des Anges.

the south. Monet, Matisse, Cocteau and Picasso are just a few who celebrated the Riviera in unforgettable masterpieces.

Tourism is the area's largest business but not the only one. Other industries include ship-building, perfume, ceramics, glass and ready-to-wear garments. And the agricultural sector produces magnificent fruit and vegetables, olives, olive oil and wine for domestic consumption and for export.

Unfortunately, because of its success, this is not the place to find deserted beaches. The Riviera is thickly populated. Marseilles ranks as France's second largest city, and the number of people on the coast almost doubles in the summer.

As for the natives of Provence, they have more in common with the easy-going, voluble Italians than with their cousins to the north. They speak in a drawn-out, lilting southern-French accent. There are several dialects or *patois*, difficult for outsiders to understand.

In fact, Provençal people act much like the characters in Marcel Pagnol's novels or the cinema star Fernandel. While genial smiles prevail, there is also a good deal of eyeball-rolling, shoulder-shrugging and fist-waving. But

the general mood is carefree, and you might as well sit back and forget schedules.

Just enjoy the good food and wine, the outgoing people, the beautiful scenery and sunny days that bless the French Riviera. For nowhere else will you find the marvellous blend that make this the world's most glamorous resort area.

Delights of the back country— the charming square of Saint-Paul and bright yellow hillside.

A Brief History

The attractions of the French Riviera were discovered very early on. Artefacts have been found at Beaulieu, Nice and the Grimaldi Grottoes, indicating that people lived here in Palaeolithic and Neolithic times.

More definite history begins around 1,000 B.C. with the Ligurians, far-ranging colonizers from the south-east who settled along the coast. Four centuries later, the ubiquitous

ships of Greece arrived and the Ligurians were forced to the east. These energetic Greek traders, the Phoceans, founded Marseilles, La Ciotat, Antibes and Nice. On two occasions, they called in Roman armies to help them fight the Ligurians.

Then in 125 B.C. the Romans marched in on their own account, determined to establish a passageway to their Iberian colony. They set up Provincia Narbonensis, which eventually became Provence. Among the important cities founded at this time were Narbonne, the capital, in 118 B.C., Aix in 123 B.C. and Fréjus in 49 B.C., built by Caesar as a rival to Marseilles.

The Greeks brought civilization and agriculture—the olive tree, the fig tree and grape vines—to the area; the Romans introduced their administrative systems, law and agricultural methods. Roman influence lasted for nearly six centuries; and during this period of relative peace, roads, towns and cities burgeoned all over southern France.

The Dark Ages
Christianity spread gradually throughout the Mediterranean during the first centuries A.D. In 450 the church of Provence was formally organized along

the lines of Roman administration. Then hard times followed. From the 5th to 7th centuries, successive waves of invaders swept over the country, breaking down the established order and leaving behind an utter shambles.

The Franks, who created the basis of a French state, prevailed but Provence was left more or less autonomous until the rule of Charles Martel. In several campaigns between 736 and 739 he took Avignon, Arles and Marseilles, forcefully establishing his authority over the area. Charlemagne's reign (771–814) was one of relative stability, but his heirs squabbled over the domain. In 843, the empire was divided by treaty among Charlemagne's three grandsons: Provence fell to the lot of Lothaire I. When his son Charles assumed control in 855, it became the Kingdom of Provence.

From the 8th century on, the coast was often attacked by North African Moslems, known as Moors or Saracens. In 884, they even built a mountain base at La Garde-Freinet from which they swooped down to raid and pillage neighbouring communities. Before they were driven out almost a century later by Guillaume le Libérateur, the Saracens had forced many local overlords and their followers to retreat into the hills—the origin of the perched village strongholds that dot the Midi today.

The Counts of Provence
The situation improved markedly in the 10th century. With the Saracens gone, the counts of Provence emerged as strong, independent rulers under the titular authority of the Holy Roman Empire. Trade and cultural activity revived. The 12th and 13th centuries were the heyday of the troubadours, the period when Provençal became the most important literary language of western Europe.

The counts of Barcelona gained title to Provence by a propitious marriage in 1112. One particularly able Catalonian ruler, Raimond Bérenger V, reorganized and unified the Comté of Provence. In 1246, his daughter Beatrix became the wife of Charles of Anjou (brother of Louis IX of France). The people of Provence received both commercial benefits and greater liberty from their ambitious new ruler who

La Garde-Freinet was once the base of the pillaging Saracens.

also became king of Naples and Sicily.

Avignon had its hour of glory in the 14th century. Through French influence, the bishop of Bordeaux was elected pope in 1305. The new pontiff, subservient to the kings of France, made Avignon rather than Rome his residence.

The ensuing period was a humiliating one for the Church but a golden age for Avignon. The city became a great cultural centre attracting many artists and scholars — notably Petrarch. It remained the religious capital until 1377, when Pope Gregory XI returned to Rome. But after his death, the "Great Schism" arose between Italian and French factions: there were two, and sometimes three popes (one in Avignon), each with his own College of Cardinals. The Schism did not come to an end until 1417.

Provence Becomes French

After various changes of ruling powers, the larger part of Provence (including Aix and Marseilles) came back under the control of the Dukes of Anjou. The last of them, the civic- and artistic-minded "Good King René", left his domain to his nephew, who before dying 17 months later named Louis XI, King of France, his successor. Thus Provence became part of France in 1481. Nice, however, went its separate way. It had formed an alliance with the Dukes of Savoy in 1388, and it remained Savoyard — with a few interruptions — until 1860.

Langue d'Oc

An offshoot of Latin, Provençal began to take shape in the 4th century. By the 11th, it was widely spoken in the south, carried from Nice to Bordeaux by the troubadours. These roving ambassadors went from château to château, singing the praises of idealized love. Both in style and theme, their poetry influenced the development of Western literature.

The language was known as *occitan* because *oc* rather than the northern *oïl* (which became *oui*) was the word for "yes". After the 14th century *langue d'oc* started to break down into regional dialects. Then, in 1539, Francis I decreed that French should be used in all administrative matters, and that was really the end.

Today you may hear — but certainly not understand — a bit of Niçois, Monegasque or another vestige of Provençal. Some expressions, like *lou vieux mas* (the old farmhouse), have worked themselves into everyday life.

14

The early 16th century was marked by strife between Francis I of France and Charles V, the Holy Roman Emperor. After an early victory in Milan (1515), the French monarch was driven out of Italy and imprisoned. Then Charles invaded Provence. In 1536, he took Aix and had himself crowned king of Arles before he was eventually checked at Marseilles and Arles and forced into a disastrous retreat.

Acting as go-between in 1538, Pope Paul III managed to get both sides to sign the Treaty of Nice, a precarious armistice at best. Never deigning to meet, each party convened separately with the pope in Nice. The truce didn't last.

In 1543, helped by the Turkish fleet, Francis I bombarded Nice (allied to his rival through the House of Savoy). After a valiant struggle, Nice repelled the invaders, returning to the realm of the House of Savoy.

Wars and Revolutions

Meanwhile Europe had become the scene of fierce religious conflicts caused by the rise of Protestantism. The confrontations were especially bloody in the south of France. In 1545 more than 20 "heretic" villages (north of Aix) were levelled by order of Francis I; the years following saw much violence on both sides. The Edict of Nantes in 1598 palliated the situation by granting religious freedom to Protestants (later revoked in 1685).

In the 17th century, Cardinal Richelieu, Louis XIII's all-powerful adviser, decided to reinforce the southern coast as protection against Spain. Toulon and Marseilles were converted into major ports. Measures of centralization and new taxes gave rise to much agitation and to outright rebellion, in the case of Marseilles. Louis XIV brought the troublesome city to heel in 1660, imposing additional contributions and restrictions.

Provence was the battleground during the 17th and 18th centuries for numerous disputes, both domestic and foreign. France took and lost Nice several times but did gain some additional territory from the Duke of Savoy. A veritable disaster hit Provence in 1720: 100,000 people died in a great epidemic that was carried into Marseilles on a ship from the Middle East.

Like the rest of France, Provence was profoundly affected by the revolution of 1789 and the cataclysmic upheavals that followed. Bad crops and **15** the election of a new Provençal Estates General contributed to the turbulence. Riots and massacres occurred in many places.

In the administrative re-organization of France in 1790, Provence was divided into three *départements*—Var, Basses-Alpes, Bouches-du-Rhône —and violence continued.

Widespread reaction set in in 1794. Royalist extremists initiated the White Terror in Orange, Marseilles and Aix, slaughtering their Jacobin opponents. A state of lawlessness prevailed in some areas.

Man on the way up: Napoleon as portrayed by Baron Gros in 1796.

Napoleon in the South

Profiting from the disarray, the English easily took Toulon in 1793. Napoleon Bonaparte, an obscure captain at the time, distinguished himself in the recapture of the city. Promoted to general, he launched his Italian campaign from Nice (annexed by France from 1793 to 1814) in 1796. Two years later, Toulon was the starting-point for his sensational Egyptian campaign. When Napoleon returned in 1799, he landed triumphantly at Saint-Raphaël. You can see a small pyramid there erected to his victories.

His empire was unpopular in Provence, where Royalist sentiment remained strong. Besides, the Continental blockade was disastrous for Marseilles' trade, further exacerbating ill-feeling.

Napoleon went through Saint-Raphaël again in 1814—but this time in disgrace, ignominiously escorted by Austrian and Russian troops on his way to exile on Elba. He escaped from his island prison a year later, landing at Golfe-Juan and returning to Paris via Cannes, Grasse, Digne and Gap—a road now known as the Route Napoléon.

The Revolution of 1848 took the form of uprisings all over the south of France, as peasants demanded land. They rebelled again in 1851 but were eventually quelled by government troops.

In 1860, the House of Savoy gave up Nice in return for Napoleon III's help in ousting the Austrians from the northern provinces of Italy. In a plebiscite, the Niçois overwhelmingly proclaimed their desire to join France. But Monaco stayed apart as a hereditary monarchy allied closely with France (see p. 41). In 1861, Monaco sold all rights to Menton and Roquebrune, which had also voted to join France.

Twentieth Century

Southern France was scarcely concerned in the First World War, and the population east of Nice felt more drawn to the Italians than anybody else. It couldn't escape the Second World War, however. In 1940, the Italians opened hostilities against France and succeeded in taking Menton. The Vichy government of Marshal Pétain was left to govern the rest of the area until the Germans took over at the end of 1942, with the Italians occupying the Côte d'Azur. But before the Germans arrived, the French scuttled their own fleet at **17**

Toulon, blocking that important harbour.

As the American, British and Allied forces approached from North Africa and Italy, the Germans put up blockhouses and barbed wire on the beaches; Saint-Tropez was dotted with mines and various beach obstacles. Then on August 15, 1944, the long-awaited landings began, led by General Patch's 7th Army. The Americans swarmed over the beach ot Saint-Raphaël and destroyed the blockhouses. The following day French General de Lattre de Tassigny landed with his Free French troops at Saint-Tropez. Within two weeks Provence was free.

The scars of war were quickly erased, and with the appearance of the bikini bathing costume (a Riviera original, in spite of the name), everyone took heart. Business started to skyrocket. So did a building and tourism boom, which hasn't stopped to this day.

The Follies of Fashion

The English were the first to go to the Riviera. In the latter part of the 18th century, it was considered a fine place for consumptive and other fragile beings to escape the raw English winters. Summers, on the other hand, were shunned as being unbearably hot.

The English gravitated to Nice, especially Cimiez. Cannes was "discovered" in 1834 by Lord Brougham. Finally the French joined the sun seekers, when writers like George Sand, Alexandre Dumas and Guy de Maupassant became aware of the joys of the coast. Artists, writers, musicians, aristocrats and others followed. Every night of the winter season was brilliant with masked balls and assorted diversions.

The Riviera became a mecca for the Impressionists. Renoir and Cézanne loved the colour and light, as did the artists who arrived after them — Bonnard, Matisse, Léger and Picasso, to name but a few.

Towards the end of the 19th century, it was really the playground for international "high society", where royalty kissed the hands of American heiresses and French courtesans. The Russian aristocrats were legendary, travelling in private trains with dozens of servants.

The turn of America's affluent society came in the twenties. Charmed by the scenery and the low cost of a sybaritic life, millionaires and film stars started the vogue for the French coast in the summer.

Though the tone may have changed somewhat, people from all over still flock to the Riviera attracted by the aura of glamour and the sun.

La Croisette, a favourite rendezvous for young and old at Cannes. **19**

Where to Go

♟ Nice
Pop. 360,000

Nice is like a rich dowager of simple origins who never lost her common touch. Unofficial capital of the Riviera, it is a vibrant, important city, boasting France's third largest airport, an opera house and excellent philharmonic orchestra, a university and several good museums. The city's shops, hotels and restaurants rival the world's best. However, the older quarters and their inhabitants have the theatrical, good-natured, brawling character of an Italian town.

Greeks (Phoceans) from Marseilles settled here in the 4th century B.C., and the name Nice may have come from *nike*, the Greek word for victory. Two centuries later, Romans left the seaport to fishermen and built a town on the Cimiez hill.

Nice broke away from the rest of Provence in 1388, when it was annexed by the House of Savoy. In the following century, the hill now known as Le Château supported a fortified castle, and beneath it a city grew up (now the *vieille ville*). In 1631, Nice was almost wiped out by the plague—but it survived. Bonaparte used the city as a base during his Italian campaign. It joined France officially in 1860.

Although Nice was known as a winter resort in the late 1700s, its touristic career really got underway in the next century with the arrival of the English and their queen, Victoria.

Promenade des Anglais

Any visit to Nice begins along this splendid palm-tree-lined boulevard stretching 5 kilometres from just outside the airport east along the Baie des Anges, joining up with the Quai des Etats-Unis, to Le Château, the rock that cuts Nice off from its harbour.

The Promenade des Anglais was thus named because in 1822 the philanthropic Rev. Lewis Way encouraged the English colony to pay for the widening of a miserable footpath—creating jobs for fruit-pickers who'd been thrown out of work by a disastrous frost.

You'll pass landmarks like the legendary Negresco, an imposing hotel with a rococo façade, colourful turrets and doormen dressed in operatic costumes.

Further along on the left, you'll see a pleasant flowered

park, the **Jardin Albert-Ier**, with an 18th-century Triton fountain and a modern outdoor theatre. Behind the gardens, parallel to the Promenade des Anglais, are "shopping streets", mostly reserved for pedestrian traffic.

On the other side of the park is the Place Masséna, a picturesque square of arcaded buildings in ruddy stucco, built in 1835.

La Vieille Ville

You can enter the old city from the seaside (Quai des Etats-Unis) or the Place Masséna. From this latter direction, you'll pass the **Opéra** and its elaborate 19th-century façade. On the **Cours Saleya** (the name comes from "salt", which was at one time sold in bulk here), you shouldn't miss the afternoon flower market full of the colour and scent of roses, tulips, dahlias and geraniums. The fruit and vegetable market takes place in the morning and is just as picturesque, though more aromatic, and the open square is surrounded by cheery pizza stalls, cafés and bistros.

On the quay side, the little pastel houses where fishermen used to live (mostly restaurants and art galleries now) are known as *ponchettes*, an old provençal word meaning little

rocks. Opposite is the **Miséricorde** chapel. Built by the Black Penitents (a lay sect) in 1736, it contains an attractive altarpiece by Miralhet, *La Vierge de la Miséricorde*.

Turning left at the end of the Cours Saleya, you'll enter the old world of Nice with its appetizing aromas, tiny shops spilling their wares onto the streets, excited voices talking Niçois, a form of Provençal that rolls like Italian.

Rue Droite just looks like a cramped alleyway now, but it was the main street in the Middle Ages. On the right you'll pass the heavily decorated baroque church of Saint-Jacques, modelled after Il Gesù in Rome. Set back on the left is Sainte-Réparate cathedral (1650) with its handsome 18th-century belfry.

Showcase of the old town, the **Palais Lascaris** (15, Rue Droite) is a 17th-century town house that belonged to the Lascaris family of Ventimiglia until the French Revolution. Guided tours of historical Nice begin here. Small for a palace, the building has a handsome

A superb sampling of mollusks and crustaceans served at seafood bar.

carved marble staircase and frescoed ceilings; don't miss the odd-angled carved door, built to swing shut automatically. On the ground floor is a beautifully preserved pharmacy, dating from 1738, complete with apothecary jars. The whole shop came from Besançon, a gift of the Gould family (American industrialists).

Further on you'll find Place Saint-François with its nicely proportioned, late-baroque, former town hall. Mornings, a frenetic fish market takes over the square — gleaming with red mullet, sea bass, octopus and squid and resounding with the raucous cries of the fish merchants.

On Place Garibaldi, just outside the old town, a handsome Calder stabile stands in front of the new bus station.

Le Château and the Harbour

Though you won't find anything left of Nice's stronghold of the Middle Ages, destroyed in 1706, a visit to the 300-foot summit of Le Château is pleasant nonetheless. Hardy walkers can climb the steps in 15 minutes, but a lift service also operates from the end of the Quai des Etats-Unis. Up on top
is a public park, with exotic

Two Local Heroes

ANDRÉ MASSÉNA (1756–1817) was a late-blooming military success. Born of a wine merchant's family, he went to sea and later joined the French army. But when he left after 14 years' service, he hadn't even achieved the rank of second lieutenant. During the Revolution, Masséna re-enlisted and this time proved his mettle. Napoleon called him the "spoilt child of victory" and promoted him to Marshal of France, Duke of Rivoli and Prince of Essling. Wellington considered Masséna his most formidable rival after Napoleon. His grandson, Victor, built an elaborate mansion that now houses Nice's historical museum (see p. 78).

GIUSEPPE GARIBALDI (1807–82), hero in the struggle for Italian unification, came from Nice. He was furious when House of Savoy ceded his native city to France in 1860 in return for assistance against the Austrians. An equestrian statue of him occupies the large arcaded Place Garibaldi.

pines and cacti — and a spectacular view of the colourful port on one side and the Baie des Anges on the other. The white stones you'll see are remnants of Romanesque religious buildings. Military buffs will be interested by the naval museum in the Tour Bellenda.

Filled with pleasure and merchant boats, the port is always lively — lined with cafés and restaurants, from the simplest, rough sailors' bars to elaborate restaurants.

From the northeast corner of the harbour, you can take the Boulevard Carnot to an extraordinary new museum, the **Terra Amata,** at number 25. Practically hidden under towering residential buildings, it contains a large collection of prehistoric remains found when the land was being cleared for construction. Three hundred thousand years ago, the sea reached 85 feet higher than today, and primitive men hunted on the shores which now lie under these buildings.

Shop talk is just part of the fun on pedestrian mall in Nice.

Cimiez

This hilly residential area—preferred first by the Romans, then by the 19th-century aristocrats—is dotted with ornate hotels resembling outdated stage sets. Queen Victoria's favourite hotel, the Régina, was the home of Matisse until his death in 1954. Now it has been divided up into flats and shops.

The way to Cimiez (you can take a bus from Place Masséna) passes near the important **Chagall Museum** (see p. 78). At Cimiez itself, the brick ruins of the entry to the Roman arena area are a rendezvous for young mothers and their charges.

The Villa des Arènes houses two rather dusty-looking museums. Rush through the archaeological museum (unless that subject is your passion) and enjoy the **Matisse museum** at leisure; it's a collection of the master's works, from sketches to monumental collages, including mementoes like his palette and an old shell-shaped chair from his studio.

Behind the villa, for a small fee, you can walk around the Roman ruins (2nd and 3rd centuries A.D.) which look like rubble until brought to life by a guide. The 33-foot-high walls were the *frigidarium* (cold) part of the Roman bath complex, fed by fresh streams and undoubtedly fancier than any modern sauna.

The nearby Cimiez Franciscan church is a heavy, 19th-century "Gothic" construction containing three remarkable paintings on wood by the Bréa brothers, 15th-century Niçois painters.

Nice Excursions

Nice is an excellent starting point for short tours all along the Riviera and for some out-

Wriggling whitebait fresh from the sea; below: the imposing ruins of Roman baths at Cimiez.

of-the-ordinary trips into the area behind Nice.

If you like mountain views —and are not frightened by mountain driving—take the Beuil-Valberg circuit, a day-long tour featuring the **Gorges du Cians.** Flowing down 5,250 feet to the Var, the River Cians cuts through awesome chasms of grey and red limestone rock. The road is sometimes lined with icicle walls. Stops include the old alpine town of BEUIL, the modern ski resort of VALBERG and the old fortified town of ENTREVAUX, with a Gothic church and 17th-century altarpiece.

Another spectacular excursion goes to the **Vésubie Valley**—green mountain slopes and rushing waters fed by melting snows. Visit SAINT-MARTIN-VÉSUBIE, located on a spur between two torrential streams that form the Vésubie. Nearby, at the Mercantour National Park, don't miss the beautiful **Vallée des Merveilles** (open July–October) with its prehistoric rock engravings.

The sinuous road leading up to the **Madone d'Utelle** (3,850 feet) passes by an interesting 18th-century church in UTELLE. At the summit you'll find a breathtaking view and a sanctuary founded in 850 (rebuilt **28** in 1806).

The Corniches

The pre-Alpine mountains between Nice and Menton drop to the sea in a changing panorama of spectacular scenery.

Highest views are from the route known as the **Grande Corniche,** built by Napoleon along the ancient Aurelian Way. The **Moyenne** (middle) **Corniche** offers a contrast of rocky cliffs and the sea. The **Corniche Inférieure,** or Corniche du Littoral, runs along beside the sea and can be terribly crowded in summer but some very worthwhile places are located on this road.

Six kilometres east of Nice, **Villefranche** is one of the most sheltered Mediterranean harbours, quieter since the U.S. Navy stopped using it as a base.

Clinging to a steep slope under the road, Villefranche offers instant charm, with its yellow, pink and red stucco or brick houses packed against the hill, the plunging alleyways and staircases and the covered **Rue Obscure** that snakes down to the sea. The quayside cafés are well placed for watching the pleasure boats and for a

The colourful Villefranche quay is fine for fishing or a picnic.

view of Cap Ferrat, pointing off to the left like a green finger.

On the right, below the town's old citadel (built for the Duke of Savoy in 1560), is the 14th-century Chapelle Saint-Pierre, also known as the **Cocteau chapel,** since writer-artist Jean Cocteau decorated it in 1956. The pastel, boldly outlined drawings completely fill the small vaulted chapel with scenes of fishermen, plus biblical episodes from the life of St. Peter.

A short drive around the rocky, pine-green peninsula of **Cap Ferrat** will convince you that the rich indeed appreciate privacy. The view is mostly of gates with hints of grandeur behind them. The vast, cream-coloured villa that belonged to King Leopold II of the Belgians can only be seen from afar. Somerset Maugham lived in Villa Mauresque, also rather well hidden.

The best views are from the upper levels of the **Ephrussi de Rothschild** foundation, also known as Musée Ile-de-France. Built in 1905–12 by Madame Béatrice Ephrussi, née Rothschild, the pinkish Italian-style villa is the delirious assemblage of an insatiable art collector. While you'll see a Coromandel screen and other beautiful *chi-* *noiseries*, plus examples of Renaissance, Louis XIII furniture and a few Impressionist paintings, the museum really shines in its French 18th-century pieces. The collection of Sèvres porcelain, composed of thousands of rare pieces and signed complete sets, is perhaps the largest in the world. The museum opens only in the afternoon and closes Mondays and in November.

The gardens surrounding the villa are no less extraordinary: the main one is French style, but bordered by others of worldwide inspiration.

Not far away, the modest Cap Ferrat zoo offers an unlikely contrast. Favourite with kids are the trained monkey shows *(Ecole des chimpanzés)*.

SAINT-JEAN-CAP-FERRAT is the port side of the peninsula, with a modern seaside promenade and an older fishing village; Cocteau decorated the marriage room of its small town hall.

The main thing to see in the small resort of BEAULIEU is the Villa Kérylos, a monument to the glory of Greece built at the turn of the century by scholar-musician-bibliophile Théodore Reinach.

Reinach studied and planned for years, all the while collecting artefacts. Then he commissioned an Italian architect, Pontremoli, to design a Greek mansion that would be perfect in every detail. Built out of cool marble and fruitwood, the house has a pleasant peristyle courtyard in Carrara marble and a "study" of grandiose proportions with mosaic floors. So as not to ruin the effect, Reinach even hid his upright piano behind a Greek-looking console. It is said the fanatic Graecophile occasionally dined with family and friends reclining on high couches.

Ephrussi de Rothschild museum, a pink palace on Cap Ferrat.

The Grande Corniche road goes all the way to Menton (via Roquebrune and the Vistaëro lookout). You can stop off at La Turbie, or explore the higher roads, visiting villages like PEILLE and PEILLON.

On a clear day, the **Belvédère d'Eze** (1,680 ft.) offers a panoramic view of the coast, the Tête de Chien mountain over Monte Carlo, the old perched city of Eze below and, on the right, as far as Cap d'Antibes and the Estérel mountains.

LA TURBIE's star curiosity is the **Trophée des Alpes,** a round ruin with Doric columns standing guard over Monaco. Emperor Augustus built it in 6 B.C. to celebrate victory over various battling peoples who had prevented the construction of a road between Rome and Gaul. Blown up and used as a quarry at various times, the mutilated monument has been partially restored.

Highlight off the Moyenne Corniche (best road of the three) is the village of **Eze.** It hangs at a dizzying angle above the sea—majestic and deep blue from this perspective. One of the most magnificent views on the coast.

The medieval town is closed to traffic but not tourists, who flock here in all seasons. On the site of an old château, razed in 1706 by Louis XIV, you'll find a public garden full of exotic flowers and cacti. Amble around the narrow stone streets, fully equipped with souvenir shops.

Continuing on, the Moyenne Corniche skirts around Mo-

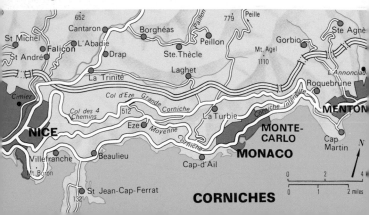

CORNICHES

naco (see p. 37). Enjoy the stunning view at CABBÉ before turning off for Roquebrune and Menton.

Instead of **Roquebrune** ("brown rock"), the town should really have been called "Roquerose"—for pink is what you see here on a sunny day (caused by reflections from the sienna-red stucco buildings along the narrow streets).

You can visit the dungeon of the fortified castle, built in the 10th century by a count of Ventimiglia to fend off the Saracens. Stony and spartan, the ruin still looks very much the fortress, with walls 6 to 12 feet thick and a bedroom furnished with a blunderbuss. A hole plunging hundreds of feet down was just what it looks like—a toilet!

Part of the Roquebrune municipality, the CAP MARTIN promontory is a millionaire's enclave, green with pine and olive trees, favoured in the last century when nobody cared much for sea-bathing (there is no beach).

Hot-point of the Riviera for climate, lukewarm for fun and games, **Menton** is a favourite

Witness to the past, a narrow medieval street in Roquebrune.

of retired people for its warmth, simplicity and two casinos (the main one is a baroque gem).

Lemons flourish in this sunny spot. In February, they even hold a lemon festival —the 15 or so tons of citrus fruits used in the décor are later sent to hospitals or made into jam. Menton is also proud of its olives and *clémentines* (a type of tangerine). It's no surprise that the natives like to tell their Adam-and-Eve legend: when they were chased from Paradise, Eve took along a lemon. After finding this new garden very like Paradise, she planted the "immortal fruit", which sprang up all over the

slopes under the greyish limestone mountains.

A long pebble beach and Promenade George V lead to a 16th-century bastion, now a **Cocteau museum;** further along is a jetty with a lighthouse and the modern Garavan harbour. You can see how the old town crowds up from the sea.

After a stop at the **Place aux Herbes,** with its arcades and three huge plane trees, you go uphill to reach the heart of the **old town.** It has a decidedly

Happily dozing in its sun-warmed setting, Menton attracts young yachtsmen and seasoned sailors.

Italian air. Here the 17th-century church of **Saint-Michel** occupies a charming square with a view right to Italy.

Cocteau painted some bold and fanciful allegorical frescoes in the marriage room of the Hôtel de Ville (town hall). The Musée Municipal contains odd bits of folklore, modern works and old bones, though not the famed pre-historic Grimaldi man once exhibited here.

Two public gardens in Menton are worth a look. The

Rocky hike around Sainte-Agnès, highest of the perched villages.

Jardin Botanique, arranged around a villa called Val Rahmeh, proves that everything can indeed grow in Menton—from a riot of roses to Mexican yucca, fuchsia and Japanese cane bamboo. More curious is the **Jardin des Colombières.** Built by writer-painter Ferdinand Bac, the Hellenic-style villa (now a modest hotel-restaurant) sits in the midst of Mediterranean lushness—with a splendid view. The terraced gardens out back are a romantic haven of flowered walks, punctuated by cypresses, ponds, fountains and statuary.

Around Menton, hikers can venture up through groves of gnarled olive trees, pine and scrub oak and finally the thick *maquis*, or bushy growth, scented with wild herbs.

Picturesque sites just a short drive away include L'Annonciade, a Capuchin monastery with a beautiful view; Sainte-Agnès, which claims to be the highest of the local perched villages; and the picturesque medieval towns of Gorbio and Castellar.

If you long for real Italian spaghetti, just cross the border to **Ventimiglia.** A visit here should include the Romanesque cathedral, the baptistery (11th century) and a walk through the old streets.

Monaco
Pop. 30,000

This fairytale princedom, an enclave rising from the rocks above the sea, is famed for its casino and wealth. Monaco owes much of its current success to dashing Prince Rainier and to the charm of the late Princess Grace.

The atmosphere here is both big city and miniature operatic. There are crowds in this paradise, with a population density comparable to Hong Kong's and cars jamming thoroughfares all over the hills (strolling is for the sturdy). But the smartly uniformed Monegasque *gendarmes* keep order, and the streets are the cleanest on the Riviera.

Don't get the idea that gambling is the only local attraction; a mere 5 per cent of the principality's revenue comes from the casino. Many other commercial and cultural activities take precedence. For one thing, Monaco is a music capital with a top European orchestra, an opera house and a music festival. Then there's the motor rally and the Grand Prix, synonymous with the name Monte Carlo, which set the sinuous streets roaring. Besides brillant galas and balls, Monaco holds a dog show, **37** flower show and TV festival. It also boasts a good soccer team and a radio station that beams all over Europe. Last but not least, philatelists know Monaco's beautiful stamps.

To clarify nomenclature: Monaco refers to the principality, geographically the historic peninsula-rock where you'll see the palace; Monte Carlo (which means Mount Charles) is the newer 19th-century area curving out east of the rock. In between lies La Condamine, a land-fill flat area, comprising the harbour and modern business district.

Monte Carlo

All roads lead to the main **casino** (and opera), introduced by a neatly tended garden-promenade. Any resemblance to the Paris Opéra is more than coincidental, since architect Charles Garnier designed both.

A busily decorated foyer with frescoes and bosomy caryatides in 19th-century style take you in to the opera. Off to the left are the gambling rooms. If you can tear your eyes away from the roulette wheels, the ornate décor here is a delight. Especially amusing is the Salon Rose, where painted, unclad nymphs float about the ceiling smoking cigarillos.

Next door stands the **Hôtel de Paris,** an equally opulent historical monument. Louis XIV's bronze horse in the entrance hall has so often been "stroked for luck" by gamblers that its extended fetlock shines like gold. The dining room on the right is an impressive though somewhat gloomy example of the heavy style of the Second Empire. The great chef Escoffier created dishes here for his celebrated clients.

Across the square, you'll find the lively Café de Paris, a crowded rendez-vous that hums with the frantic whir of slot machines, helpfully installed for the use of gambling addicts between drinks.

Nearby, Monaco's **National Museum** contains a delightful doll museum! Also known as the Musée Galéa, this whimsical spot houses a 2,000-piece collection assembled by Madeleine de Galéa. The villa-museum designed by Charles Garnier is a pink confection, perfect as a doll's house, nestled in a garden that has statues by Rodin, Maillol and Bourdelle. Exhibits include tableaux and exquisitely outfitted dolls from the 18th century to modern

Monte Carlo's star attraction—its baroque casino-opera house.

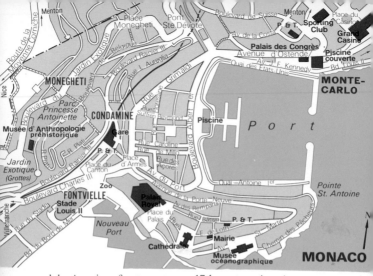

models. A series of automatons perform when the guard winds them up; there are extraordinary "acts" by mechanical card-players, acrobats, dancers and a snake-charmer — slightly spooky but quite impressive. Children love it.

The Monaco Rock

A short ride up the hill from the centre of town, you'll find the **Palais du Prince** (bus or taxi recommended; parking space is severely limited).

The Grimaldis still live here, but you can visit the palace from June to the middle of October. The tour includes a look at the magnificent

17th-century interior courtyard with its double marble staircase and painted gallery, **Galerie d'Hercule.** There are several well-maintained rooms containing priceless antiques, a gallery of mirrors, paintings by Van Loo, Brueghel and Titian, royal family portraits and the elaborate bed where the Duke of York died in 1767.

Any time of the year, at 11.55 a.m., you can watch the changing of the guard outside the palace. With fife and drums, much circumstance and little pomp, it's a good five minutes' worth of entertainment — though hardly up to Buckingham Palace standards.

The Grimaldis

Monaco's past is sensational — full of intrigues and murder in high places. By a tortuous path, it arrived at the present constitutional monarchy under the personal rule of Prince Rainier III.

The rock of Monaco was inhabited from the Stone Age onwards. In 1215, the Genoese built a fortress there, which the Guelf and Ghibelline factions disputed for the rest of the century. Finally in 1297, the Guelfs led by François Grimaldi gained the upper hand. The Grimaldi family has hung on tenaciously ever since.

Treaties with powerful neighbours assured Monaco's independence over the years (except for a French interlude from 1793 to 1814). Roquebrune and Menton broke off from the principality in 1848 and were later bought by France. Looking for a new source of revenue, Monaco's ruler, Charles III, founded the Société des Bains de Mer in 1861 to operate gambling facilities. The venture got off to a slow start, but when François Blanc, a financial and administrative wizard with a shady background, took over, business prospered. On Blanc's advice, Charles commissioned the construction of a casino and opera house.

Hotels went up, and a railway line from the rest of the coast was soon extended to Monaco. A new (though perilous) coach-road and word-of-mouth publicity brought gamblers and fun-seekers.

In spite of tricky legal tangles, Monaco has retained its independent (and tax-free!) status, with open boundaries to France, free currency exchange (French money is almost always used) and a common post-telephone system with France.

Monaco is a nice place to live but it's almost impossible to become a citizen — unless you can find some Monegasque ancestors.

The **old town** is also located on the Monaco Rock. Along the narrow pedestrian streets riddled with souvenir shops, restaurants and other tourist attractions, a gay atmosphere prevails, ringing with the Italian inflections of Monegasque *patois*.

On Rue Basse, you'll come across **L'Historial des Princes de Monaco** — a quaint wax museum assembled in 1971 by a Frenchman who likes Monaco. From the earliest Grimaldi, François, to the youngest, Princess Stéphanie, the beautifully costumed personages present a pleasant historical panorama.

41

The cathedral is a white, 19th-century neo-Romanesque monster, boasting a tryptich by Louis Bréa (right transept).

The **Musée Océanographique,** a formidable, grey-pillared construction, was founded in 1910 by Prince Albert I, who spent the better part of his time at sea. Most expensive museum to visit on the coast, it is now directed by Commandant Jacques-Yves Cousteau, the underwater explorer. In the basement aquarium, playful sea lions, jaded turtles, staring grouper fish and thousands of small incandescent fish cavort, delighting adults and children.

The cliff-hanging **Jardin Exotique** above the Condamine is worth visiting for the good view of the principality and environs. A series of stepping stones leads you through a display of exotic plants—especially fierce-looking spiny cacti in thousands of varieties, from South America and Africa.

Near the entrance is the **Anthropological Museum** (*Musée d'Anthropologie Préhistorique*), where you'll see old bones from Menton and Monaco caves, plus ancient jewellery found in the Condamine. The 250 steps down to the *grottes* will reward you with a cool promenade through lacy pinpoints of stalactites and stalagmites; but you have

Monaco is both a bustling highrise city and a seaside resort.

to walk up again to get out!

Not far off is the **Stade Louis-II,** one of Europe's biggest sports complexes, and a zoo—small, friendly but unspectacular, bar a good view.

Nice to Cannes

In all respects, this is one of the richest areas of the Riviera. The scenery can be magnificent, and art works abound both along the coast and in the villages behind.

Côte d'Antibes

Founded by the Phoceans in the 4th century B.C., **Antibes** got its name (Antipolis—the "city opposite") because it faced Nice across the Baie des Anges. The first landmark you'll see here is the imposing square fortress, **Fort Carré.** This was the French kings' stronghold against the dukes of Savoy who controlled Nice.

In 1794, Napoleon lodged his family here while supervising the coastal defence. Since he wasn't very well paid, his mother had to do her own laundry, and his sisters filched figs and artichokes from neighbouring farmers. Today the hills around Antibes are lined with glassy greenhouses; growing flowers is the main local industry.

Don't miss a tour around the ramparts, reconstructed by Vauban in the 17th century along the original medieval lines. The **Château Grimaldi,** now the Musée Picasso, is a white stone castle with a Romanesque tower built by the lords of Antibes on a Roman site. Besides many classical relics, the museum possesses a rich Picasso collection. In 1946, when the artist was having difficulty finding a place to work, the director of Antibes' museum offered him the premises as a studio. Picasso set to work among the dusty antiquities. Inspired by the classical objects around him, he completed over 145 works in a period of six months. The grateful artist gave these drawings, ceramics, paintings and other pieces from a later period to the museum.

Next to the château-museum is a 17th-century **church** with a Romanesque apse and transept and an altarpiece attributed to Louis Bréa. Behind the sunny square you'll find a maze of old streets and the covered market, colourful in the morning when it's in full swing.

Just around the bay lies the **Cap d'Antibes,** a quiet, pine-covered peninsula well endowed with big, beautiful

Watchful portrait of Picasso hangs in museum among his own works.

houses and a venerable hotel, the Eden-Roc. It served as a model for F. Scott Fitzgerald, and today you can usually see film stars and magnates lolling around its pool poised high above the sea.

The **Chapelle Notre-Dame** at LA GAROUPE is of curious composition: one nave is 13th century, the other 16th, and each is dedicated to a different madonna. They are both filled with ex-votos, all kinds of naïve art works or objects offered as prayers of thanks. Around the western side of the cape is the sandy crescent-shaped bay of JUAN-LES-PINS. The resort enjoyed its heyday in the twenties and thirties after American tycoon Frank Jay Gould built a big hotel and casino in a pinewood setting. Sleepy in winter, the town becomes rather wild in summer with a gaudy atmosphere generated by nightclubs, cafés, boutiques spilling their wares into the streets and a restless, fun-seeking crowd of young people.

The artisans' towns of Vallauris and Biot are only a few minutes' drive from Antibes. **Vallauris** is inevitably associated with Picasso, who worked here after the war, giving new impetus to a dying ceramics and pottery industry. He presented the town with the bronze statue, *Man with a Sheep*, on Place Paul-Isnard and decorated the Romanesque chapel there, now the National Picasso Museum, with the **murals** *War and Peace*.

Careful buyers still find worthwhile purchases in the ceramics shops that line Vallauris' one main street.

Perched on a cone-shaped hill, **Biot** also bulges with artisans' shops and has a restored Romanesque church (too dark most of the time to see a fine Bréa altarpiece) and a colourful 13th-century square with fountains and arcades.

Downhill, in the Biot glassworks you can see craftsmen dressed in shorts fashioning the heavy, tinted glass with minute bubbles that the town is known for.

Adjacent to Biot, the **Musée National Fernand Léger** with

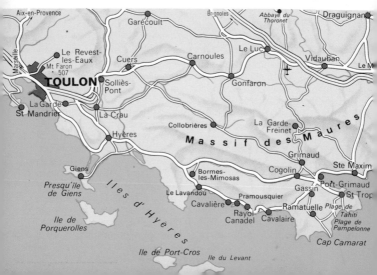

its bold façade stands out like a giant postage stamp from miles away. Light and airy, the modern structure, built and donated to France by the artist's widow, houses an incomparable collection of Léger's works — from paintings to enormous tapestries.

Children like the dolphin show at Marineland near Biot railway station, while food buffs will be interested in the gastronomic museum at VILLENEUVE-LOUBET, the birthplace of chef Auguste Escoffier.

Inland Route

Spread out over hills covered with orange and olive trees, CAGNES-SUR-MER is not one but three towns: the seaside resort of CROS-DE-CAGNES, the modern commercial section of LE LOGIS and the ancient hilltop fortress, **Haut-de-Cagnes** — the prettiest and most interesting part. Its narrow, cobbled streets corkscrew up to the **castle.** To enter, you pass through an ivy-covered, oblique-angled patio with galleries all around and a huge pepper tree in the centre. On the ground floor of the castle visit a curious museum devoted to olives — their history, cultivation, literature — probably the greatest tribute ever paid to that fruit.

Upstairs are exhibits of con-

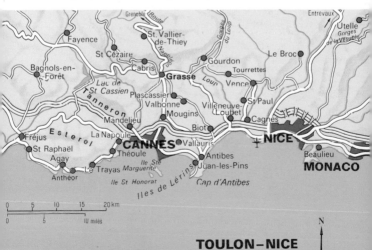

temporary art and a ceremonial hall with a 17th-century *trompe-l'œil* ceiling, *The Fall of Phaeton*. One extraordinary room contains 40 portraits of Suzy Solidor, the one-time cabaret queen, as seen by famous 20th-century painters—from a doe-eyed girl wearing a sailor suit by Van Dongen to a raffish, much older version of her wearing a matador's hat.

Renoir spent his last years (1907–19) in the villa of Les Collettes just east of Cagnes. However, there's not much left to see here besides mementoes and a few of the master's minor works.

Saint-Paul-de-Vence is another venerable bastion, built within spade-shaped walls and looming over green terraces of vineyards, bougainvillea, mimosa and cypress—plus lots of recently built villas.

The walled feudal city, entered by foot under a tower and arch with a cannon pointing right at you, was built by Francis I in the 16th century as a defence against Nice and the dukes of Savoy.

Under the big plane trees of the Place du Général-de-

Gaulle, you'll usually find a lively game of *pétanque* (or *boules*), the outdoor bowling game played with leaded balls. The Colombe d'Or restaurant across the street has an important private collection of modern painting—Matisse, Derain, Dufy, Utrillo among others.

You can make the tour of the narrow pedestrian streets in a few minutes or at a leisurely pace with stops at the Grande Fontaine and a look at the Gothic church.

On a grassy hill just outside Saint-Paul is one of the great modern art museums of the world—the **Fondation Maeght,** inaugurated in 1964 by Paris art dealer Aimé Maeght and his wife. The museum sits in a green grove of dark pines. Full of visual surprises, the brick-steel-glass construction designed by Spanish-American architect José Luis Sert is an ideal place for exploring modern art. Heralded by a black Calder stabile at the entry, the works inside include ceramics by Miró, bronze filament-figures by Giacometti, fountains and stained-glass windows by Braque—to say nothing of the paintings and lithographs by many of the great names of 20th century art. **Vence** is an ancient bishopric **49** with middle-age spread: the charming old city has been girdled by newer shops and houses. English and French artists and retired people like the bustling atmosphere, the fragrant surrounding hills and the peace that falls at night (off-season, of course!).

In the 17th century, the remarkable Antoine Godeau became bishop of Vence. A misshapen society wit, he turned to the holy orders at the age of 30, undertook restoration of the cathedral, founded new industries to give work to his parishioners and was appointed one of the first members of the august Académie Française.

Best scenic points of old Vence are the **Place du Peyra** with its gurgling fountain and friendly cafés, the cathedral (especially the arresting Romanesque belfry), and the **Place**

A ramble through the old town of Tourrettes is always rewarding; opposite: Grasse flower market.

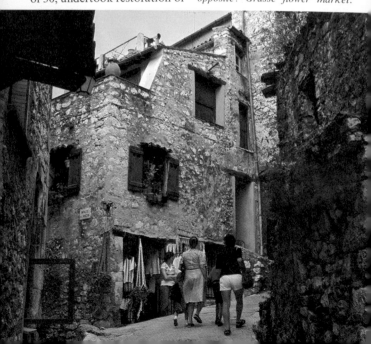

du Frêne with a centuries-old ash tree whose trunk must be at least 6 feet in diameter.

Tourists often hurry past Vence on their way to the **Chapelle du Rosaire-Henri Matisse** on the road to Saint-Jeannet (only open to the public on certain days, see p. 79). Dedicated by Matisse to the Dominican nuns who cared for him during a long illness, the chapel is the crowning achievement of the artist, then in his eighties and practically blind. The famed stained-glass windows in bold patterns of royal blue, bright green and yellow give radiant light to the simple chapel, two walls of which are decorated by powerful line-drawing figures on white faïence.

A short tour of the **Loup Valley** is worthwhile and will take you less than a day. Highlights include TOURRETTES, a charming old town popular with artisans and artists, several waterfalls (Cascade de Courmes, Cascade des Demoiselles) and the town of GOURDON, built on a steep spur 2,500 feet high. The castle here was a Saracen fort in the 9th century and contains a small medieval museum.

Grasse, the world's perfume capital, won't knock you over with heady scents; but you

can't miss the enormous signs inviting you to visit the factories.

Although the Grassois were distilling essential essences from local flowers as far back as the 13th century, the industry didn't bloom until the Medici family launched the fashion of scented gloves in the 51

16th century (Grasse made gloves as well).

Nowadays the manufacturers use at least 10,000 tons of flowers—violets (January to March), mimosa (February), daffodil (April), rose and orange-flowers and so on—to produce their essence. The gleaming brass cauldrons, alembics and other trappings displayed in the factories, though mainly for show, do give an idea of the first steps in making perfume and soap.

The high price of perfume becomes understandable when you realize it takes a ton of petals to produce 2.2 pounds of essence. The attractive soaps and scents on sale here have little to do with the sophisticated Paris-made brands, which use Grasse essences in secret formulas.

Built on a steep hill, Grasse was already renowned for its good air in the 19th century, and invalids and people on holiday flocked here. The most

charming spot in town is the friendly, crowded **Place aux Aires,** with its fountains, arcades and sculptured 18th-century façades. The morning market is a palette of brilliant colours (flowers and vegetables) under the blue shade of lotus *(micocoulier)* and plane trees.

A few blocks downhill, the Place aux Herbes has an even larger food market. Several steps away is the sober, ochre-stone **cathedral,** begun in the 12th century and restored in the 17th. Inside you'll find cradle-vaulting and a rare religious canvas by Honoré Fragonard, *The Washing of the Feet.*

The **Musée Fragonard,** on the Boulevard Fragonard, occupies the villa where the painter spent a year during the French Revolution. He brought with him a series of love-scene paintings which had been turned down by Madame du Barry. Most of the collection has ended up in the Frick Museum in New York, but the excellent, sensuous *Three Graces* remains.

The **Musée d'Art et d'Histoire de Provence** in the Rue

Perfumes come in many hues at Gourdon; right: a cool sail on artificial lake of Saint-Cassien.

Mirabeau is housed in an elegant 18th-century town house once owned by the Marquise de Cabris. Her furniture is in remarkably good condition. Among the less conventional articles on display are a nicely carved wooden bidet-chair with shell-shaped basin and a pewter bathtub on wheels.

Grasse is a good starting point for delightful side trips. Gourdon and the Loup Valley (see p. 51) are off to the northeast; to the south-west you have the Tanneron range and the man-made lake of Saint-Cassien, a popular place for windsurfing.

CABRIS (6 km. on the D4 road) commands an impressive view from its old château ruins—the Tanneron hills, the Esterel and La Napoule to the right, Mougins and the Lérins Islands to the left; and on a clear day you can even make out the hazy outline of Corsica.

Another 8 kilometres or so further on, the GROTTES DE SAINT-CÉZAIRE provide refreshing respite from the sun with stalactite shapes in extraordinary dark-red and pink colours. SAINT-CÉZAIRE itself is a peaceful, pretty town with a Romanesque chapel and a good view. You can continue north through wild, rocky limestone hills with low trees and bushes,

up to MONS (32 km. from Grasse), an ancient perched village, to the COL DE VALFERRIÈRE, and back down the Route Napoléon through SAINT-VALLIER and several splendid panoramas.

Or you may want to continue west into the Var, visiting typical towns like FAYENCE (27 km. from Grasse), BARGEMON (44 km.), DRAGUIGNAN (56 km.) and perhaps the **Abbaye du Thoronet** (two hours drive from Grasse). Lost in a beautiful landscape of reddish bauxite and green pine scrub trees, it's a cool, quiet place. The pink-stoned Thoronet, one of the three great abbeys of Provence, dates from the 12th century. It is notable for its clean-lined simplicity, its squat, colonnaded cloister and a hexagonal fountain, the *lavabo*, where the monks used to bathe.

Cannes
Pop. 68,000

During the film festival in May and the record festival (MIDEM) in January, Cannes loses its habitual cool. The rest of the year the city devotes itself to its touristic vocation—as an elegant, cosmopolitan resort in a beautiful setting, with the liveliest pleasure port on the Riviera.

The history of Cannes is linked to the two islands you can see off the coast, the Lérins. On the smaller one, St. Honorat founded a monastery in the 4th century which became a famous shrine for pilgrims. In the 10th century the Count of Antibes gave the Cannes mainland to the Lérins monks. They built ramparts to defend the lands against incursions by Moorish pirates.

By 1788, only four monks remained; the monastery was closed down and Cannes came under French rule. In 1815, Napoleon stopped there after landing at Golfe-Juan. But Cannes gave him a chilly reception; he had to move on to Grasse.

Like Nice's Promenade des Anglais, the **Croisette** is a magnificent showcase with gleaming hotels lining a flowered boulevard. The golden sand of the beach along the promenade is mainly imported from Fréjus. At one end of the Croisette lies the old port and the new **Palais des Festivals;** at the other, a second port and the Palm Beach Casino. The film festival plus multiple other festivities are held in the grand new Palais, which contains a casino as well.

Just a few blocks behind the

Cannes is "Discovered"

Cannes was just a quiet fishing village in 1834, when Lord Brougham, a leading English law reformer, had to stop over on his way to Italy because of a cholera epidemic. This chance visit turned out to be longer than expected: he built a home and returned every winter for the rest of his life.

A champion of his adopted city, Lord Brougham prodded King Louis-Philippe to provide funds for a jetty below the old town. Many English aristocrats followed Brougham to Cannes, as tourists and settlers, swelling the local population. A handsome statue of Lord Brougham, the man who "discovered" the town, presides over Prosper Mérimée Square, just across from the Palais des Festivals.

Cannes Film Festival—a field day for cinema fans and fanciers.

Croisette is the **Rue d'Antibes,** one of the coast's most glamorous shopping streets. For more down-to-earth wares—like tee-shirts, sandals, mouth-watering sausages and pastries—head for Rue Meynadier.

Looking uphill from the old port in the evening, you have a vision of the ramparts of the old town, **Le Suquet,** glowing with orange lights against the dark purple sky. You'll also see the **Tour du Suquet,** a 72-foot-high square watchtower built by the Lérins monks. It was destroyed during the Revolution, but later restored, as a favour to local fishermen who petitioned for a tall, visible navigational point. Now the white stone clock tower is a Cannes trademark.

The centre of the old town is Place de la Castre (from the Latin word for castle), a quiet, pine-shaded square. The 17th-century "Gothic" church here, rather dim inside, has several polychrome statues.

The **Musée de la Castre** (closed on Mondays) houses a quaintly eclectic assemblage of everything from an Egyptian mummy's hand to a Japanese warrior's costume and a South Pacific hut pole. The Persian objects are quite good. The donor of all this, a Dutchman named Baron Lycklama, is portrayed in an extraordinary Oriental outfit.

The view over Cannes from Le Suquet is superb. For an even more spectacular panorama, go to the **observatory** at Super-Cannes.

Iles de Lérins

One of Cannes' most refreshing diversions is an excursion to the islands. Boats leave frequently in the summer: the trip to Sainte-Marguerite takes about 15 minutes; to Saint-Honorat, 30. In season, they hold sound-and-light shows.

About a mile and a half of wooded hills, a minute "main" street lined with fishermen's houses and a couple of restaurants, **Sainte-Marguerite** is the closer and larger island. It takes its name from St. Honorat's sister who founded her own religious order.

Walk uphill to visit the old **Fort Royal,** built under Cardinal Richelieu, and enjoy a **58** marvellous view of Cannes,

Antibes and the hills. The main attraction here is the dank and smelly prison of the "Man in the Iron Mask". There's nothing to see but chains, faded ochre stone and modern graffiti, but the legend is intriguing.

Between 1687 and 1698 a masked prisoner was kept here. Actually his mask was of cloth, not iron, but he wore it constantly and nobody knows for sure who he was or why he was imprisoned. One theory identifies him as an illegitimate brother of Louis XIV; another as the larcenous ex-finance minister Fouquet.

On Sainte-Marguerite you can walk for hours among cool, fragrant woods and a grove of enormous eucalyptus trees, a Riviera staple that was first brought to the coast from Australia in the early 19th century.

The island of **Saint-Honorat,** home of the monks who governed Cannes for nearly eight centuries, is once again a monastery, run by the Cistercian Order.

Bright green and gentle with umbrella pines, roses, lavender and the monks' vineyard, it's a peaceful retreat in the off-season. Wandering around you'll come upon several small Romanesque barrel-vaulted chapels.

The most striking construction is the square, battlemented **"château"**—really a fortified dungeon. Built in the 11th century over a Roman cistern, it served as a refuge for the monks during various attacks.

The 19th-century monastery is only open for special visits on request. However, you can see the small museum and church, accompanied by a guide. Next door to the museum the monks do a brisk trade in handicrafts, lavender scent and their own liqueur—a redoubtable-looking yellowish liquid.

Around Cannes

The coast's most glorious oddity, the **Château de la Napoule** (8 km. west of Cannes), hovers in red-rock splendour over a coin-sized beach and harbour.

Here, in 1919 American sculptor Henry Clews (scion of a New York banking family) restored the medieval château with towers and battlements, endowing every possible inch with his own work. Wildly imaginative, the sculptures range from a poignant Don Quixote to pudgy grotesques of African inspiration.

The eccentric Clews, who saw himself as a latter-day Quixote and his wife as "the Virgin of La Mancha", filled his home with mottoes, ridiculing the "aberrations" of society.

The museum hours are almost as quixotic as the décor, though you can usually get in in the afternoon, except for Saturday and Sunday.

A soft and subtle backdrop of green hills characterizes the countryside between Cannes and Grasse, the *arrière-pays*.

Interesting stops include MOUGINS, a 15th-century fortified town (with a few superb restaurants); VALBONNE, with its beautiful arcaded square shaded by big elms and a brightly restored Romanesque church; and PLASCASSIER, a sleepy village on a hill.

The Esterel

Between Cannes and Saint-Raphaël lie a mass of porphyry rocks worn down and chipped by streams. This is the Esterel, now not much more than 2,000 feet at its highest, though the landscape seems abrupt and impressive. In the spring, the scrub-herb hills are golden with mimosa.

The original inland road through the Esterel was the Aurelian Way, built by the Roman emperor in the 3rd century.

These days, most people take the Côte d'Azur motorway be-   **59** tween Cannes and Saint-Raphaël, but the coastal route — the **Corniche d'Or** (the Golden Corniche) — is certainly prettier. Reddish porphyry rocks tumble into the dark blue sea making a jigsaw pattern of colours and shapes, tempting you to stop at every outcrop to admire the view.

After LA NAPOULE and then THÉOULE, with its "château" that served as a soap factory in the 18th century, you come to PORT-LA-GALÈRE, a cascade of modern houses on a flowered stony point. The Esterel is full of little fishing ports with euphonic names — LE TRAYAS, ANTHÉOR, AGAY. The **Sémaphore du Dramont,** built on the ruins of a watch-tower, offers sweeping views of the coast, and near the road is a marble monument commemorating the American landing here on August 15, 1944.

The best time to see this coast is at sunset looking east, when colours and contrasts are most flamboyant, a surrealist's dream.

Saint-Raphaël

Best known now as the railway stop for nearby Saint-Tropez, Saint-Raphaël had its heyday a century ago.

The town's centre is a palm-lined modern sea-front (the old one was destroyed during the Second World War) with an ornamental fountain and pyramid commemorating Napoleon's debarkation after the 1799 Egyptian victories.

In days gone by, there was a small holiday resort here for Romans based in Fréjus. It stood more or less on the site of the present casino — if you can imagine the clicking roulette tables replaced by luxurious tile baths and fish ponds.

The 12th-century Templars' church in the old town is surmounted with a massive watch-tower replacing the right-hand apse.

Fréjus

Little remains of the busy Roman market town of Fréjus (Forum Julii) founded in 49 B.C. The big harbour, built by Augustus into a great naval base and shipyard, has been completely filled up with silt deposits and replaced by modern Fréjus. A good part of the town was rebuilt after the 1959 catastrophe, when a dam upstream over the River Reyran broke, killing over 400 people.

Stopping point on the Esterel: splendid views at every turn.

Most impressive of the Roman vestiges is the **arena,** a restored grey-green construction which could seat 10,000 spectators—nearly as large as the arenas of Arles and Nîmes. It's closed on Tuesdays. During the season, bullfights are held here. Other Roman ruins include a theatre and big reddish arches of the aqueduct that brought water in from the River Siagnole.

Nearly razed by Saracens in the 10th century, Fréjus was revived in 990 by Bishop Riculphe, who established a fortified **episcopal city** here with a cathedral, baptistery, cloister and bishop's palace.

Apply to a side entrance for a guided tour to see the carved Renaissance doors, the baptistry and the cloisters.

One of the oldest religious buildings in France (late 4th to

Provincial Colosseum—Roman arena at Fréjus held 10,000 people.

early 5th century), the octagonal **baptistry** is punctuated by handsome black granite columns with Corinthian capitals (from the ancient Fréjus forum). The terra-cotta baptismal bowl, the original, was unearthed in the course of archaeological research.

In the **cloister,** a doubledeckered arcade surrounds a garden of roses and cypress trees. The ceiling of the upstairs arcade is decorated with some amusing 14thcentury creatures—imaginative scenes from the Apocalypse. An archaeological museum adjoining the cloister has Gallo-Roman remains.

The 10th-12th-century **cathedral,** with its "broken cradle" vaulting, exemplifies the early Gothic style of the region. It was built on the site of a Roman temple dedicated to Jupiter.

Côte des Maures

On the way to Saint-Tropez, you'll pass through the attractive little town of SAINTE-MAXIME, with a casino, a minute beach and a wide promenade. In the summer it's packed with people who would love to be in Saint-Tropez but can't find a hotel room there.

Saint-Tropez

It barely manages to keep up with its glamorous reputation: celebrity escapades, the beauty of its little port, cafés filled with fashionable people, chic boutiques and casual nudity on nearby beaches.

Brigitte Bardot avoids the crowds now, but other stars still come out at night to haunt the "in" cafés and discotheques. In Saint-Tropez more than any other place on the Riviera you feel an unspoken desire to wear the right tee-shirt, be seen with the right people, show up in certain places at certain times of day or night. The atmosphere is enlivened by clusters of motorcycles roaring by, as well as haughty mannequins and golden boys with big dogs. In winter it reverts back to an easy-going fishing town.

Saint-Tropez weathers its own snobbery while cultivating its legends. The name comes from a Roman Christian, Torpes (an officer of the capricious Nero), who was martyred in Pisa in A.D. 68. The headless body, put adrift in a small boat with a dog and a cock, came ashore in the Var region. In the local church you can see a tableau of the body drifting along with its animal companion, as well as a wide-eyed **63**

sculpture of the saint himself, neatly mustachioed, surrounded with a lacy halo, his chest covered with heart-shaped medals.

The town was battered several times by the Saracens, and recently by the German occupation and invasions of World War II. But the gallant little fishing village always managed to come back; in 1637 it routed a fleet of invading Spanish ships and still celebrates the victory in May with

the Bravade, a fête that also honours St. Tropez himself. The natives get out their muskets, don 17th and 18th-century costumes and happily fire blanks all over the place in noisy parades with fife, drums, fireworks and cannon shots from the old fort. (There is a similar but less important festival in mid-June.)

First "discovered" by the French writer Guy de Maupassant, Saint-Tropez became very fashionable in the twenties,

Market day—gossip and good humour are order of the day.

when it was visited and painted by Dunoyer de Segonzac, Bonnard, Dufy and Signac; Colette wrote reams in her villa here, La Treille Muscate.

After World War II, the town managed to put itself together again in its former style, wisely rejecting plans for modern urban development.

You can't miss the **port** with its restless crowds, shiny yachts and pastel houses with red tile roofs, most of them rebuilt in the old fishermen's style. Nearby the plane-tree-shaded **Place des Lices** is crowded with local colour: a food market takes over several mornings a week, and *pétanque* (bowls) games are the centre of interest in late afternoon.

The **Musée de l'Annonciade**, a former chapel situated on the west side of the port, houses an **65** excellent collection of Impressionist and Post-Impressionist works. Many of the artists lived in and loved Saint-Tropez. You can view paintings by Signac, Van Dongen, Dufy, Bonnard and others in rooms lit by refracted Saint-Tropez sunshine. Outside, the quay space is crowded with contemporary artists, trying their best to sell their work, which can only be called "wares" compared to the contents of the Annonciade.

A short walk behind the Quai Jean-Jaurès will take you to the old town—through an arcade by La Ponche (the old fishing port), past narrow old buildings now housing expensive hotels and boutiques, to the 17th-century **Citadel** on top of the hill.

The moat, surrounded with

Saint-Tropez: sun and games at Tahiti beach; a junior gourmet.

greenery, is living quarters for preening peacocks, a few duck and deer. The Musée de la Marine here contains souvenirs of a locally born hero, Admiral de Suffren (who took his fleet on an odyssey around the Cape of Good Hope in 1781), model ships and diving equipment.

Saint-Tropez is noted for its beaches. Nearby ones like the Plage des Graniers and the Bouillabaisse are popular with local people on weekends, but holiday visitors look down their noses at them. They drive out to Les Salins or the vast sandy crescent (6 miles long) that stretches in front of green vineyards from Tahiti beach via Pampelonne to Cap Camarat.

Smooth-sanded and bordering a clear aquamarine sea, the beaches are fully equipped in summer with all manner of huts and shacks to furnish mattresses, umbrellas and sustenance to sunbathers. Part of the beach is traditionally given over to nudists — of all shapes; other areas are more or less discreet and more or less chic; each has its own style. Every summer the beautiful people gravitate to the bar-restaurant-beach of the moment.

More Ports and Hill Towns

Saint-Tropez is surrounded by delightful spots to visit when

you've had enough of the beach scene. A short trip will take you to GASSIN and RAMATUELLE — towns with panoramic views and pleasant restaurants — and the ruins of MOULINS DE PAILLAS. They provide an introduction to the **Maures** mountains, the oldest geological mass of Provence: worn-down cristalline hills, green and covered with pines and scrub trees.

Going north into the Maures over a long road full of hairpin bends, through thick forests of **67** chestnut and cork, you come to LA GARDE-FREINET. At 1,329 feet, the town is considerably cooler than the coast. It has a natural, unspoilt charm that attracts crowd-weary Parisians. It also makes a living off the land — corks and chestnuts.

The ruins of an old fortress evoke the last stand of the marauding Saracens. For several centuries these pirates of Arab origin managed to hold out here as they pillaged the towns below — until they were thrown out in 973.

If you're pressed for time, forget La Garde-Freinet but stop at GRIMAUD — best in the late afternoon, when you can look out to the sea through the Provençal lotus trees and enjoy a drink in a local café. Grimaud was once the fiefdom of Gibalin (Ghibellin) de Grimaldi.

The fortress ruins stand up in piles of stony remnants against a grassy hill. A sign warns you not to poke around here because of the danger of falling rocks, but you can take a look at the simple, barrel-vaulted 11th-century Templars' church (restored version) and arcaded charterhouse.

Inland, the place to find an old
68 *fortress and fragrant fresh herbs.*

PORT-GRIMAUD, 6.5 kilometres downhill on the bay of Saint-Tropez, is the French modern version of Venice. Designed by François Spoerry and opened in 1964, it is a series of artificial canals built on marshland, lined with pleasant little houses and terraces painted in the same colours as Saint-Tropez.

For most French people, the Riviera stops at Saint-Tropez (some even say Saint-Raphaël), but the coast does go on. Not always the prettiest stretch, it is spoiled in parts by 20th-century concrete construction.

Still reasonably pleasant, however, are a string of small resort towns — LA CROIX-VALMER, CAVALAIRE, RAYOL and PRAMOUSQUIER — in flowered settings under the Maures hills.

LE LAVANDOU, originally a colourful spot, has suffered from urbanism, though it's still quite popular. The town has a pretty beachside promenade and is a good starting-point for excursions. Uphill, you'll find BORMES-LES-MIMOSAS, a lovely retreat that lives up to its name—blooming not only with mimosa, but oleander, roses, geraniums and bougainvillea.

Hyères is the "granny" of Mediterranean resorts. The French were coming here in the 18th century, when the English

started to winter at Nice. On the tree-shaded Place de la République, you'll see a 13th-century **church** where St. Louis, King of France, prayed after his return from a crusade in 1254; Hyères was the landing port for returning crusaders, though they disembarked at what is now the middle of town. Today modern boulevards run right over the old harbour.

Hyères is a busy city featuring an uphill market street, Rue Massillon (go in the morning

when it's in full swing), the old town, an ancient Templars' building and the Eglise Saint-Paul (a Gothic church renovated in the 16th century). From the square you have a panoramic view.

Instead of taking a noon siesta, this fisherman repairs his nets.

Iles d'Hyères

Also known as the Iles d'Or ("golden islands") because of their shiny, mica-shot rocks— sometimes mistaken for gold— they are three: Levant, Port-Cros and Porquerolles. You can easily visit them by ferry from Hyères and Le Lavandou or even from Cavalaire or Toulon.

The rocky **Ile du Levant** is France's nudist capital. You can keep your trousers on, but refrain from obvious gawking and photography: the *naturistes* don't like to be treated as curiosities. The eastern half **71** of the island is seriously off-limits — a naval base.

Next to the Levant lies the smaller **Ile de Port-Cros,** covered with steep myrtle- and heather-decked hills and an abundance of bird life. This protected national park area boasts resident flamingoes, turtle-doves, cormorants and puffins, plus rare flowers, especially orchids, and mushrooms in season (boletus and chanterelles).

The largest island, **Porquerolles** (5 miles long, 2 miles wide), is another enchanting setting, with a series of beaches along the north side (where the boat lands) and steep cliffs on the south coast. There are some excellent small beaches and coves for bathing on these islands, but you'll probably not be alone in the high season.

From Toulon to Marseilles

Toulon
Pop. 186,000
Military buffs love Toulon, France's big naval port, which reeks of maritime history. Its picturesque seafront was devastated during World War II, but even now with its modern concrete seaport blocks, it retains a certain dignity.

Toulon was pushed into prominence in the 17th century by Cardinal Richelieu, who saw the potential of a great natural harbour. Under Louis XIV, the military engineer Vauban was commissioned to fortify and enlarge the facilities.

World War II was a tragedy for the naval centre. Nearly the whole French fleet was

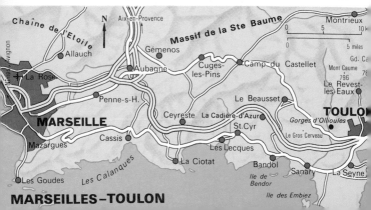

MARSEILLES–TOULON

scuttled on November 27, 1942, to keep it from falling into German hands. Two years later the port was battered by Allied troops, and then the Germans blew up their installations before leaving, wreaking more havoc. But with modern reconstruction, Toulon has regained its former importance.

Broad, busy Boulevard de Strasbourg (off Place de la Liberté) runs through the heart of Toulon, slicing the city in half. On the north is the newer, more residential area; to the south, the remains of the **old town.** Head in this direction for Place Puget, a charming Provençal square (just behind the Municipal Theatre) with a dolphin fountain and lots of greenery. Downhill is the narrow market street, Rue d'Alger, a favourite for evening strolling.

Off to the left, the cathedral, **Sainte-Marie-Majeure,** has a handsome baroque façade and belfry (18th century). Another block east is the Cours Lafayette, one of the most animated indoor-outdoor market streets in Europe, where you can buy everything from flowers to leather souvenirs. History enthusiasts can visit the nearby Musée Historique du Vieux-Toulon.

The **port** is a particularly lively part of town. See the magnificently muscled caryatids that guard the entrance to the **Musée Naval.** They look as if they were shouldering the world—and they're about all that's left of the old port. The museum (closed Tuesdays) contains some impressive boat models.

Across from the public garden in the west central part of town is the **Musée d'Art et d'Archéologie** (closed Mondays and Thursdays). It possesses a very good collection of Oriental art (Tibet, India, Japan and especially China), plus paintings from several periods and countries.

Mont Faron (1,778 feet) commands a grandiose view of Toulon, the surrounding mountains and the coast. You can get there by car via a steep, sinuous route or take a *téléphérique* from the Faron Corniche. Close to the peak is the Tour Beaumont, a fairly new war museum containing a wealth of information about the Liberation.

Inland excursions from Toulon include **Le Gros Cerveau** mountain with its magnificent panorama, the rugged **Gorges d'Ollioules,** the 16th-century castle remnants of **Evenos** and another look-out point at **Mont Caume.** If you have time to venture further north, the **Massif de la Sainte-Baume** offers the irregular hilly landscape typical of Provence, a venerable forest and a stunning view from **Saint-Pilon.**

🚶 Côte des Calanques

The limestone coastline between Toulon and Marseilles is riddled with deep, uneven inlets *(calanques)*. This stretch, backed by the green scrub growth of the *maquis*, has in-evitably spawned holiday developments. But you can still find attractive natural sites.

Well-sheltered SANARY, with sandy beaches and an old port, is the first town you come to on the Baies du Soleil (sunny bays). **Bandol** takes honours as the area's leading resort. It has a mild climate and long beach lined with housing developments. It is known for its vineyards which produce good red and white wine.

You can make a pleasant

side trip to the privately owned island of **Bendor**. This recently developed site boasts a reproduction of a Provençal village and museums devoted to the sea and to wine.

One of the world's largest shipyards, LA CIOTAT has managed to retain a small bit of its original charm. Against the background of towering cranes and steel hulls of the busy modern shipyard, the old fishing port holds out doggedly—typically Provençal with nets, small boats and colourful houses.

The port of **Cassis** may seem familiar—paintings of it by artists like Vlaminck, Matisse and Dufy hang in museums all over the world. Today you'll see the same gaily-coloured stucco houses and crisp little triangular sails bobbing on the clear blue water, with the rocks

Limestone cliffs of Calanques drop off abruptly into the sea.

of La Gardiole or the tree-covered Cap Canaille hovering in the background.

Cassis is mainly known for its incomparable shellfish, its *bouillabaisse* (fish soup) and its white wine, appreciated all over the south (but not to be confused with the *cassis,* black-currant, syrup or liqueur).

From Cassis you'll probably want to visit some *calanques,* best done in a rented boat or on a tour. The most spectacular of them all is **d'En Vau**—a mini-fjord with limpid blue-green water fingering through the rocky cliffs to a minute crescent of a white beach.

Marseilles

Though not really part of the French Riviera, this great city of one million (*Marseille* to the French) merits a visit for many reasons. France's largest port, its second largest metropolis and its oldest, Marseilles has always played a major role in the country's history.

If offers excellent shopping, an international atmosphere, big industry, interesting museums and very good food: some of the best *bouillabaisse* on the coast is to be found here, particularly around the famous Canebière area.

Be sure to wander around the old port, first used by the Phoceans in 600 B.C., and to see the impressive facilities of the modern port. You can also tour it by boat.

The Marseillaise

France's bellicose national anthem is not really a local creation. Written by an Alsatian, Rouget de Lisle, it was taken up by Marseilles revolutionaries marching to Paris in 1792. On their arrival, they caused a sensation, and the song was immediately named: *La Marseillaise*.

Maritime parking lot in Marseilles for small craft and fishing boats.

What to Do

Museums

The Riviera is studded with excellent museums (some described more fully under town headings). Schedules tend to be a bit chaotic: most museums are open mornings 9 or 10 to noon, and afternoons 2 to 6 (winter), 3 to 7 (summer).

Antibes

All the museums are closed Tuesdays and in November.

Musée Grimaldi-Picasso, Place du Château, prodigious collection of Picasso's works (see p. 44).

Musée Archéologique, Bastion Saint-André, antiquities from the region.

Musée Naval et Napoléonien, Eden-Roc Cap d'Antibes, Napoleonic souvenirs.

Beaulieu

Villa Kérylos, open afternoons only; closed Mondays, November (see p. 30).

Biot

Musée National Fernand Léger, impressive one-man retrospective; closed Tuesdays (see p. 46).

Cagnes-sur-Mer
Château-Musée, modern art works and olive museum; closed Tuesdays and October 15 to November 15 (see p. 47).

Cannes
Musée de la Castre, Le Suquet, eclectic collection; closed Monday, and November 1 to December 15.

Grasse
Musée d'Art et d'Histoire de Provence and *Musée Fragonard*, closed Saturdays and Sundays (except on first and last Sunday of each month when entrance free) and November (see p. 53–54).

La Napoule
Château (Henry Clews Foundation), impressive sculptures in a stylish setting; open in the summer 5–6 p.m., in winter 3–5 p.m. (see p. 59).

Monaco
Musée National, open every day except public holidays; *Palais du Prince*, open all day from June 1 to October 15; *Musée Océanographique*, open every day (see pp. 38, 40, 42).

Nice
All museums are closed Mondays, public holidays and in **78** November.

Musée Masséna, 35, Promenade des Anglais, an old mansion with a good collection of Empire furnishings, historical exhibits, paintings from the 15th–16th-century Nice school, Impressionist paintings.

Musée des Beaux-Arts Jules-Chéret, 33, avenue des Baumettes, outstanding Impressionist paintings and lovely pastels by Chéret, works by painter Gustav-Adolf Mossa, a symbolist whose eerie, intricate dream-fantasies deserve to be better known.

Palais Lascaris, baroque palace in the heart of old Nice (see p. 22–23).

Musée du Vieux-Logis, 59, avenue Saint-Barthélemy, historical collection featuring Gothic statuary, religious paintings and stained glass.

Musée de Malacologie, 3, cours Saleya, seashells galore.

Musée de Terra Amata, 25, boulevard Carnot, an engaging view of prehistoric man around Nice.

Musée Matisse et d'Archéologie, 164, avenue des Arènes, Cimiez (see p. 26–27).

Musée Chagall, avenue du Docteur-Ménard, biblical themes in a modern setting.

Musée International d'Art Naïf, Château Sainte-Hélène, Avenue Val Marie; entrance free.

Monumental sculpture by Léger stands near his museum in Biot.

Saint-Jean-Cap-Ferrat

Fondation Ephrussi de Rothschild, "Belle Epoque" dwelling and gardens; closed Monday and November (see p. 30).

Saint-Paul-de-Vence

Fondation Maeght, one of the world's great modern art museums, open every day (see p. 49).

Saint-Tropez

Musée de l'Annonciade, a sunny display of 20th-century paintings on the old port; closed Tuesday, November (see p. 65).

Vence

La Chapelle du Rosaire, the famous Matisse chapel; open Tuesday and Thursday 10 to 11.30 a.m. and 2.30 to 5.30 p.m. (more frequently from July to September), closed public holidays and November 1 to mid-December (see p. 51).

For Children

Besides the myriad of sporting activities, there's lots to amuse children around the Riviera. Monaco, Cap Ferrat (don't miss the afternoon monkey show here), Fréjus and Toulon all have zoos.

The Monaco Oceanographic Museum has an excellent aquarium, while Marineland between Antibes and Biot offers penguins, seals and an afternoon dolphin show.

Monaco's Musée National features beautifully dressed dolls and mechanical puppets that perform wind-up tricks. The Monaco wax museum is also a favourite with children.

Brilliant bouquet crowns every important festival on the Riviera.

Festivals and Other Events

The Riviera's calendar is filled with festivals and religious pageants (especially around Lent, Easter and Christmas), plus major artistic and sporting events. Here are just a few of the outstanding ones:

January
Monte Carlo. Automobile Rally: the final leg of the 4,500-kilometre race roars through the city.
Cannes. MIDEM, international recording and music-publishing fair.

February
Nice. The Carnival fills the streets with floats, girls and gaiety in the two weeks preceding Shrove Tuesday.
Cannes. The mimosa festival celebrates nature.
Menton. During the Lemon Festival the town takes on a golden glow with citrus mosaics everywhere and parades.

March-April
Vence. Battle of Flowers, Provençal dancing (Easter).

April
Monte Carlo. Tennis Championships.

May
Cannes. The International Film Festival stirs frenzy for a few weeks.
Saint-Tropez. The Bravade (see p. 64), is a costumed, noisy event commemorating local victories, May 16-18.
Monaco. The Grand Prix motor race.
Grasse. Rose Festival.

June
Antibes. Festival of St. Peter, sailors' religious celebration (last Sunday in June).
Nice. Festival of Sacred Music.
Saint Tropez. Second Bravade (June 15).

July
July 14, Bastille Day and National Day. Celebrations with fireworks in all towns and villages.
Antibes/Juan-les-Pins. Jazz Festival.
Monaco. Firework Festival.
Nice (Cimiez). Jazz Festival.

August
Menton. International Chamber Music Festival.
Roquebrune. Passion procession through streets of old town (August 5).

October
Cannes. VIDCOM, international video fair.

Shopping

Most shops and department stores are open from 8 or 9 a.m. to noon and from 2 to 7 p.m., Tuesday to Saturday (many stores close Monday). But hours can be casual. In the summer, small shops often close for longer periods in the middle of the day, but stay open later in the evening for the tourist trade. They may also open on Sundays.

Best Buys

The coast is a mouth-watering bazaar. You can find the best of everything French—jewellery, couturier clothing, silverware, crystal and even furs. In Nice (Rue de France), Cannes (Rue d'Antibes) and Monte Carlo (around the casino), the shopping areas are on a par with Paris.

In the mini-luxury category, good buys include silk scarves, perfumes, liqueurs and even scented soaps. Sportswear is highly recommended, especially for women. The latest thing is always displayed in little boutiques and aggressively brushes your nose on the quayside at Saint-Tropez, where you can hardly go through the yards of tee-shirts without purchasing something.

Arts and Crafts

You'll see some beautiful pottery, glazed stoneware and ceramic work, particularly around Vallauris, Saint-Paul-de-Vence and Biot. Anything from simple ashtrays to entire dinner sets—plain, flowery, contemporary abstract, even some original Picasso designs.

The heavy, bubbled Biot glass-work in subtle colours fits well in a country-home setting.

Semi-precious stones, often set in jewellery, are abundant in shop windows. You'll

What to buy? Wooden antiques or an abstract print made yesterday.

frequently see olive-wood tables, stools, salad sets and bracelets—especially in the little towns behind Cannes.

The famous, attractively flowered Provençal cotton is ubiquitous; you can purchase it in bolts or made up into cushions, carryall bags, small shoulder bags, skirts or quilts.

Antiques and Art

You'll find old Provençal tables and commodes, brass clocks and candlesticks, copper cooking utensils, rare and common china patterns and plenty of "kitsch". Alas, most of the real bargains have already been snatched up.

If you're looking for art works, you'll find endless possibilities at all prices. There are hundreds of galleries selling paintings and sculptures by famous and local names: around the ports, painters turn out their rendition of the scene and sell at whatever price they can get.

Souvenirs

There's no lack in this area. Looking for a picture of the port of Cannes on a fringed satin flag, an ash-tray with the local château on it? Almost

Olives galore on market day in Place des Lices, Saint-Tropez.

anything decorated with portraits of the royal family of Monaco? Your wishes will be easily gratified.

For philatelists, there are the beautifully printed Monaco stamps; for children, old favourites like sea-shell jewellery and traditionally costumed dolls.

Shopping Tips
If you have the time, compare prices in different shops before buying. You can always try to bargain at stands or small shops, but it rarely works, especially when a price tag is attached. Sometimes, though, you'll receive a special discount with a big purchase.

If you're returning home to a non-Common Market country, ask about the possibility of a refund of the value-added tax (TVA) on larger purchases. You must fill out a form, give a copy to the customs when leaving France and later receive your refund at home. (Beware, however, of bank clearance charges on foreign cheques.)

Shops with "duty-free" signs in the windows often give the TVA refund even on small purchases. The international airport is a good place to purchase duty-free items, especially liquor and perfumes.

Sports and Games

The Riviera's climate makes it ideal for outdoor sports, and facilities are generally first-rate.

Swimming
In the new official classification of beaches by cleanliness, the Côte d'Azur does well; of its 143 beaches, only 6 are "C"-grade (usable), all the others being "A"- or "B"-grade (impeccable or virtually pollution-free).

Beach concessionaires charge entry and/or changing-room fees at many bathing areas. You can also indulge yourself a little and rent a mattress (practically indispensable on some of the stony beaches). But of course, there are also free—if not always spic and span—public beaches. The other trick is a fee for parking. If you prefer a pool, there are many of them charging a small fee for entry.

Windsurfing
Windsurfing, or sailboarding, is one of the coast's fastest-growing sports. It is also one of the most difficult. Courses are given, and boards (*planche à voile*) can be hired in all the major resorts.

Water-skiing

Ski nautique exists at all the larger beaches (Nice, Cannes, Antibes and so on). Real daredevils go for kite-skiing.

Scuba Diving, Snorkelling

There are diving centres at Antibes, Cagnes, Cannes, Monte Carlo and Nice. Equipment may be hired and instruction arranged at centres in these localities.

Fishing

The piscine population of the Mediterranean is suffering from over-fishing and pollution. But you can spend a few pleasant hours with baited hook around the coast or take a day-tour on a fishing boat. Real sportsmen like to angle for trout in the mountain streams. Inquire about licence regulations.

Boating and Sailing

The coast is lined with first-class yacht facilities. If you require the best of everything but haven't brought your own boat, you can hire a 30-metre vessel with a ten-man crew and enjoy the "the life of Riley." Smaller boats, of course, are

The exuberance of scuba divers contrasts with the quiet joys of angling in a mountain stream.

also available for those with more modest requirements and tighter budgets. For an idea of what it might cost, see p. 103. Cannes and Antibes are the biggest rental centres.

Tennis

You find tennis courts almost everywhere along the coast. The proper attire and payment of an hourly court fee will admit you to most clubs. In summer you may have to book a day ahead.

Golf

The best in France—with scenic 18-hole courses at Biot, Mandelieu-La Napoule, Mougins, Valbonne (all clustered around Cannes), Monte Carlo (Mont-Agel), and a few 9-hole courses. You can hire clubs, though it's advisable to bring your own shoes and golf balls, as these are expensive in France.

Anyone can take a crack at it.

Horse-riding

There are lots of possibilities for riding, often "ranch" style in the country behind the coast.

Skiing

About two hours from the coast are 11 winter sports areas, some very well developed. Best-known are Isola 2000 (they teach the new graduated short-ski method there), Auron and Valberg.

Other Activities

You can play the local *pétanque* (or *boules*) if the natives will initiate you to this bowling game; but every sport is available somewhere—from regular bowling, judo and archery to table tennis. If you're feeling fit, hire a bicycle and pedal around the hills alongside the fanatics practising for semi- or professional races. The Riviera's modern racecourse is at Cros-de-Cagnes, near the Nice airport.

Nightlife

The Riviera is a night-crawler's dream. From the very first seaside aperitif to well after midnight or even till dawn, nocturnal activity is hectic. Some people can hardly drag themselves to the beach the next day. Possibilities range from "pub" crawling around some of the dock areas (Nice, Toulon) to the most elegant balls in the world, particularly at Monte Carlo.

Cultural Activities

On the dignified side, the coast offers the best in music and ballet. Monte Carlo's opera house features brilliant opera, concerts, ballet and theatre the year round; summer concerts in the palace courtyard are particularly popular (try to book in advance). Ticket prices for concerts and opera vary considerably.

Menton has a famous music festival in August; Nice, its own opera house with good theatre in the winter; Toulon, a municipal theatre that also presents concerts and ballet. The latest films are shown in French or dubbed in French.

Nightclubs and Discotheques

For slick floorshows or elegant dining and dancing, go to Nice, Monte Carlo or Cannes. As you would expect, the disco-theque scene is frenetic but you can get in almost anywhere. (For an idea of nightclub and discotheque prices, see p. 103.) Monte Carlo has the **89**

Well-heeled visitors enjoy sumptuous show at Monte Carlo casino.

most elegant discos, Saint-Tropez the prettiest clientele, and in between you'll find everything, with a particularly rowdy ambiance at Juan-les-Pins in summer. Dine late, because discos don't start to warm up till 11 p.m. or so.

Casinos

The tense atmosphere may not be apparent in the streets, but for some here gambling is a way of life. Monte Carlo started the ball rolling in 1860, and the other towns joined the profitable bandwagon 50 years later.

Now at least 20 casinos operate between Menton and Sainte-Maxime.

You'll find every game going —from the non-stop slot machines to baccarat. The casinos usually open sometime after 3 p.m. (hours vary) and stay open till the last discouraged customer quits, but for early birds, Monte Carlo's main casino opens at 10 a.m.

Entry prices vary from place to place, but entrance to Monte Carlo casino is free. Most establishments ask to see your passport.

Wining and Dining

Wandering through the streets of a southern French town, you can often guess what's cooking for dinner. Marvellous aromas — of fresh rosemary or thyme, all-pervading garlic, fragrant olive oil, the smoky smell of charcoal-broiled meat or fish — waft through the air. Add to that images of the plump and juicy tomatoes, glistening green and red peppers, dark purple aubergines, silvery sardines, all fresh from the marketplace, and you'll be ready to sit down to eat.

French cooking reaches great peaks in Provence*. Some of the country's best restaurants here offer exquisite (and expensive) food in incomparable settings. But food can also be deliciously simple with robust flavours. When you see *à la provençale* on a menu, you can be fairly sure garlic, tomato and herbs are part of the recipe. And don't shy away from garlic and onions: they're eminently appropriate in this climate.

---

*For a comprehensive glossary of French culinary terms and how to order wine, ask your bookshop for the Berlitz EUROPEAN MENU READER.

Soup and Salad

Pistou is practically a whole meal — a thick vegetable soup made with beans, onions or leeks, fresh herbs, especially basil, and usually garlic, topped with freshly grated cheese.

Soupe de poisson can also fill you up for hours. Made with available fish leftovers, tomato, saffron, garlic and onions, it's served with generous garnishings of toast rounds, grated cheese and *rouille*, a hot tomato-garlic-flavoured mayonnaise. *Bourride* is thicker and richer, with lots of fish ground up in it.

Speaking of garlic, try a bracing *aïoli* (when you don't have any important social engagements). You dip boiled fish, potatoes, green beans and so on in the heavily perfumed mayonnaise.

The renowned *salade niçoise* can be a treat. Essential ingredients include tomato, anchovies, radishes, green peppers, olives, sometimes cucumbers and artichoke hearts, well doused in a vinaigrette dressing. Tuna, celery, green beans, hard-boiled egg quarters and a few lettuce leaves (the latter anathema to the purists) may complete the picture.

Endless mixed salads are offered, many with ham and cheese or seafood. *Salade anti-*

Bouillabaisse

It's only fish stew, but the mystique surrounding it is substantial enough to fill a Proustian novel. Every chef has his own idea: some say it's heresy to include spiny lobster and that mussels are only for Parisians. Marseilles chefs are appalled by their Toulon confreres' addition of potatoes.

The important thing is really the fresh local seafood — with fascinating names like *rascasse*, *baudroie*, *chapon* and *Saint-Pierre*. These can be translated but mean next to nothing away from the Mediterranean. The fish are served in their own broth highly flavoured with wine, cayenne and saffron, and accompanied by crunchy croutons and garlicky red-hot *rouille*.

boise usually combines cooked diced fish and anchovy fillets with green peppers, beetroot, rice and capers with vinaigrette dressing. *Crudités*, a raw vegetable salad, makes a nice light first course.

Fish

On the Riviera, the aristocrat of fish is the *loup de mer* (sea bass), best prepared with fennel, flamed. *Daurade*, a tender white fish (gilt-head or sea bream), costs less; it's usually grilled or baked with onion, tomato and lemon juice and a dash of wine, occasionally with garlic and a *pastis* (anis) flavouring. *Rouget* (red mullet) may be served grilled or *en papillotte* (baked in foil with lemon wedges).

The grilled *scampi* (prawns) you'll see on menus everywhere can be good, but they're invariably imported and frozen. *Langouste*, or spiny lobster, costs a king's ransom. It's eaten cold with mayonnaise or hot in a tomato-and-cognac-flavoured sauce (*à l'américaine*).

Mussels (*moules*) are popular *à la marinière* (in white wine), in soup or with savoury stuffings. A lowly but tempting gourmandise is *friture de mer*, crisp-fried small fish to be eaten like chips.

Meat and Poultry

Steak turns up in various fashions, but the good cuts (*entrecôte*, *côte de bœuf*, *faux-filet*, *filet*) are as tasty charcoal-broiled with fresh herbs as with sauces. *Saignant* means rare; *bleu*, almost raw; *à point*, medium done.

Mougins—one of the places to find the best in French cuisine.

Lamb is succulent in the spring; you'll most often see *gigot d'agneau* or *côtes d'agneau grillées aux herbes* (leg of lamb or grilled chops with herbs), which the French serve medium rare. *Brochettes*, or skewered kebabs, can be delicious, though the quality depends on the meat chosen by the chef.

Daube de bœuf is a traditional beef stew particularly good in Nice. With its aromatic brown, wine-flavoured mushroom sauce, accompanied by freshly made noodles *(pâtes fraîches)*, it can be memorable. *Estouffade*, a variation on the theme, adds black olives to the sauce.

Veal is often of Italian inspiration, as in breaded-fried *esca-*

Relaxed aperitif hour in Menton on the lively Place aux Herbes.

lopes milanaises (scaloppini). But *alouettes sans têtes* are not "headless larks" as the translation would imply: they're small rolled veal cutlets with stuffing (veal birds).

Even tripe-haters are converted by the Niçois version of this dish *(tripes niçoises):* a superb concoction simmered in olive oil, white wine, tomato, onion, garlic and herbs.

Pieds et paquets, a Marseilles speciality, consists of stuffed tripe and sheeps' trotters cooked with bacon, onion, carrot rounds, white wine, garlic and sometimes tomato.

Chickens are frequently spit-roasted with herbs *(poulet rôti aux herbes)* ; *poulet niçoise* is a local fricassee made with white wine, stock, herbs, tomatoes and black olives. Rabbit *(lapin)* can be quite tender, like chicken, and might be served in a mustard sauce or *à la provençale*.

In season (autumn/winter), the menu may list partridge *(perdreau)*, pigeon or quail *(caille)* often served with a grape sauce *(aux raisins)*, or boar *(marcassin or sanglier)*.

Pasta and Vegetables

The Italian influence is strong around Menton and Nice, becoming less so as you go west. You'll often find superb pasta —ravioli, cannelloni, fettuccine, lasagne—rivalling Italy's best.

But the glory of southern France is its fresh vegetables. *Ratatouille* — the celebrated vegetable stew made with tomatoes, onions, aubergine (eggplant), marrow (zucchini) and green peppers—practically stands as a meal in itself, either hot or cold. You'll also find delicious stuffed aubergines, marrow and tomatoes well seasoned with local herbs.

Asparagus *(asperges)* are superb warm with melted butter or hollandaise sauce or cold with *vinaigrette*. Artichokes receive the same treatment or may appear with meat or herb stuffings.

Cheese and Dessert

In the south you can usually eat classics from the 300-odd varieties of French cheese. But don't miss out on the regionally made goat or sheeps'-milk cheeses *(fromages de chèvre, de brebis)*. A few good names: *tomme de Sospel, tomme de chèvre de montagne, brousse de la Vésubie, cabécou, poivre d'âne*.

For dessert, nothing can rival the local fruits in season. Savour the fat, dark-red strawberries (April–Oct.) dipped in *crème fraîche* (a slightly acid **95** double cream). Melons of all kinds (from Cavaillon, near Aix, they're renowned) taste sweeter than usual. Figs and peaches are equally good. Ices are refreshing, especially the fruit *sorbets*. You can satisfy a sweet tooth with all kinds of fruit tarts and local pastries: *ganses* (small fried cakes topped with sugar), *pignons* (buttery *croissants* with pine-nuts) and the famed *tarte tropézienne* of Saint-Tropez—a rich yellow cake with custard filling and coarse-sugar topping.

Quick Snacks

Cafés serve hearty sandwiches on long chunks of French bread (pâté, ham or cheese). Thin-sliced sandwich bread *(pain de mie)* is used for the delicious *croque-monsieur* (toasted ham-and-cheese sandwich). Omelettes are always reliable fare.

Tian is a local term vaguely covering warm or cold stuffed pastry or omelettes sold by street vendors and in some restaurants. The filling is usually an egg-custard, green vegetable mixture. *Tourtes* are pastry turnovers with similar vegetable stuffings.

Another popular local item (great at the beach) is *pan bagnat*—essentially a huge round sandwich filled with to-matoes, hard-boiled egg, olives, anchovies, and sliced onions, moistened with olive oil.

Also noteworthy are the excellent thin-crusted pizzas (all flavours) and *pissaladière:* a savoury tart with a topping of onion, anchovies, black olives and sometimes tomatoes.

Aperitifs and Wine

You can find the world's most sophisticated cocktails in the big hotel bars down here. If you order a martini, specify *un dry* or you might get Martini, the sweet Italian vermouth. Every little bar-café sells scotch, various imported and domestic beers, many non-alcoholic drinks. A very refreshing drink is *citron pressé* (fresh-squeezed lemon juice).

The number one local drink, of course, is *pastis*. This anise-flavoured yellow liquid turns milky when you add water—very refreshing on a warm day.

Vintage wines from all over France are available in the better restaurants, but for daily fare stick to the local product—white, red and especially rosé.

The best regional wines bear an *appellation contrôlée* (A.C.) label, guaranteeing place of origin and government-controlled quality. Four areas are given these labels: La Palette, Cassis, Bandol and Bellet.

La Palette (grown at Meyreuil, near Aix) comes from country thick with pines or herbs whose fragrances are said to permeate the wines. They exist in red and white (most notable — *Château Simone*). Cassis produces a fine red wine, but the flowery-light white wine is a special treat, particularly with shellfish.

Near Toulon, Bandol wine grows in a particularly favoured setting, producing some whites and lots of fruity rosés and reds, the latter particularly good; look for *Domaine des Tempiers*. Bellet is the fourth A.C. area, on precariously sloped vineyards above Nice, producing white, red and rosé wines.

Further down the official scale, wines marked V.D.Q.S. *(vin délimité de qualité supérieure)* appear all over the south.

Mid-morning snack in old Nice: socca, an outsized fried pancake.

Wine Guidelines

The fresh, slightly fruity qualities of Provençal white wine make it the perfect accompaniment to fish and shellfish. Sometimes the wines lack acidity because of the constant sunshine.

Rosé is much-maligned by wine snobs, who treat it as a poor compromise between white and red. But in Provence, it's another matter; even connoisseurs enjoy a well-chilled bottle with meals (particularly chicken or fish dishes) or as an aperitif. Rosés with the V.D.Q.S. label are reliably good; Tavel and Lirac, grown near Avignon, are famous.

The colour of rosé is important: it should be light to rosy *pink*, not orange, which shows it has oxidized prematurely.

Red wines are gaining in both virtue and renown in the south. The A.C. areas now produce honourable reds, some to be drunk quite young and fresh (preferably cool), others age gracefully. *Château Vignelaure*, grown northeast of Aix, is a special case.

Don't be surprised by the lack of vintage year on the labels of wine from Provence. Most are meant to be served very young (often within the year) and don't benefit from ageing.

To Help You Order...

Do you have a table?
Do you have a set-price menu?

Avez-vous une table?
Avez-vous un menu à prix fixe?

I'd like a/an/some...

J'aimerais...

beer	**une bière**	menu	**la carte**
butter	**du beurre**	milk	**du lait**
bread	**du pain**	mineral water	**de l'eau**
coffee	**un café**		**minérale**
dessert	**un dessert**	potatoes	**des pommes**
egg	**un œuf**		**de terre**
fish	**du poisson**	salad	**une salade**
fruit	**un fruit**	sandwich	**un sandwich**
glass	**un verre**	soup	**de la soupe**
ice-cream	**une glace**	sugar	**du sucre**
lemon	**du citron**	tea	**du thé**
meat	**de la viande**	wine	**du vin**

... and Read the Menu

agneau	lamb	langouste	spiny lobster
ail	garlic	langoustine	prawn
anchois	anchovy	langue	tongue
artichaut	artichoke	lapin	rabbit
asperges	asparagus	lièvre	hare
aubergine	eggplant	loup de mer	sea-bass
bifteck	steak	macédoine	fruit salad
bœuf	beef	de fruits	
caille	quail	médaillon	tenderloin
calmar	squid	moules	mussels
canard, caneton	duck	moutarde	mustard
cervelle	brains	mulet	grey mullet
chèvre, cabri	goat	navets	turnips
chou	cabbage	nouilles	noodles
chou-fleur	cauliflower	oignons	onions
choux de	brussels sprouts	oseille	sorrel
Bruxelles		petits pois	peas
concombre	cucumber	pintade	guinea fowl
côte, côtelette	chop, cutlet	poisson	fish
courgettes	baby marrow	poireaux	leeks
	(zucchini)	pomme	apple
coquelet	baby chicken	porc	pork
coquilles	scallops	poulet	chicken
Saint-Jacques		prunes	plums
crevettes	shrimps	radis	radishes
daurade	gilt-head (fish)	raisins	grapes
écrevisse	crayfish	ris de veau	sweetbreads
endive	chicory (endive)	riz	rice
épinards	spinach	rognons	kidneys
fenouil	fennel	rouget	red mullet
fèves	broad beans	St. Pierre	John Dory (fish)
flageolets	dried beans	saucisse/	sausage/dried
foie	liver	saucisson	sausage
fraises	strawberries	sorbet	water-ice
framboises	raspberries		(sherbet)
fruits de mer	seafood	thon	tunny (tuna)
gigot (d'agneau)	leg (of lamb)	truffes	truffles
glace	ice, ice-cream	veau	veal
haricots verts	string beans	volaille	chicken
jambon	ham		

99

How to Get There

The ever-changing air fares and airline regulations are complicated even for seasoned travellers. A reliable travel agent will be able to suggest a plan best suited to your timetable and budget.

When planning your trip, consult the Blueprint section in this book (pages 104 to 125), especially for ENTRY AND CUSTOMS FORMALITIES and HOTELS AND ACCOMMODATION. If looked through in advance, this section can help you prepare for your visit to the French Riviera.

BY AIR

Scheduled flights

The main international airport serving the French Riviera is Nice-Côte d'Azur (see p. 105), which is linked frequently to many European and North African cities. However, most intercontinental flights use Paris as gateway city to France.

Charter flights and package tours

From the U.K. and Ireland: Most tour organizers use scheduled airlines. although some charter flights are available in the summer. Self-catering is popular, and there is a wide choice of accommodation available.

Most travel agents recommend cancellation insurance which prevents loosing money in case illness or accident forces you to cancel your holiday.

From North America: Paris–Riviera package deals are frequently offered by tour organizers. Check the newspapers for the latest possibilities. There are charter flights available directly to the Riviera, or to many convenient gateway cities in Europe. Some companies also have "Discover France" bus vacations.

From Australia and New Zealand: There are no package tours to the French Riviera. Travel either by independent arrangement (the usual direct economy flight to Paris with unrestricted stopovers, or fly through another European gateway city with connections to Nice) or go on an air-and-car-hire arrangement.

BY ROAD

From Paris you can follow the A-6/A-7/A-8 *autoroutes* (motorways/expressways). Via Lyons, Orange, Aix-en-Provence, you reach Fréjus

(870 km./540 miles), Cannes (900 km./560 miles), Nice (940 km./585 miles). Motoring is also easy on the secondary roads in France which, though longer than the *autoroutes,* offer good scenery and are toll-free. From Paris, you can also put your car on a train *(train autos couchette* or *service autos express).*

BY RAIL

Express trains operate from Paris to the Riviera (see also p. 120). Senior citizens can obtain a RES-*Rail Europ Senior Card*-which allows a 50% reduction on all participating railways, including the French National Railways-S.N.C.F. Anyone under 26 years of age can purchase an *Inter-Rail Card* which allows one month's unlimited 2nd-class travel. People living outside Europe and North Africa can purchase a *Eurailpass* for unlimited rail travel in 16 European countries including France. This pass must be obtained before leaving home. The S.N.C.F.'s *France Vacance Special Ticket* is available to non-French residents for unlimited 1st and 2nd-class travel over the entire S.N.C.F. network for any 8 days within one month.

When to Go

July and August are the peak summer months when the crowds are drawn to France's sunniest beaches. These are the months when the climate is at its best, though spring and fall offer many days of mild weather with fewer visitors.

You may want to plan your holiday around one of the many events on the Riviera, such as Cannes' annual film festival in May.

Following are some monthly average temperatures:

		J	F	M	A	M	J	J	A	S	O	N	D
Air temperature	C	9	9	11	13	17	20	23	22	20	17	12	9
	F	48	48	52	55	63	68	73	72	68	63	54	48
Sea temperature	C	13	13	13	15	17	21	24	25	23	20	17	14
	F	55	55	55	59	63	70	75	77	73	68	63	57

France: Facts and Figures

Geography: Area 547,000 square kilometres (213,000 square miles). Largest country in Western Europe, France shares frontiers with Belgium, Luxembourg, West Germany, Switzerland, Italy and Spain. Its highest point is Mont Blanc, Western Europe's tallest peak, at 4,800 metres (15,800 feet) above sea level. Four major rivers crisscross the country: the Seine, the Loire, the Garonne and the Rhône; and Le Havre, Nantes, Bordeaux and Marseilles, France's four leading ports, lie at the mouths of these rivers.

Population: 55 million, of which about 4½ million are foreigners. 80% live in urban areas. Density: about 100 per square kilometre, or 255 per square mile.

Major cities: Paris (2.3 million, greater urban area 9 million), Marseilles (900,000), Lyons (450,000), Toulouse (350,000), Strasbourg (250,000).

Government: Republic, multi-party centralized democracy, headed by a president elected for seven years by universal suffrage. The Parliament consists of two houses, the National Assembly with 491 deputies and the Senate with 322 members. The country is divided into 95 *départements* (plus five overseas departments).

Economy: France is a major industrial country; the main industries are metal, machinery, shipbuilding, textiles, electrical and electronic equipment, clothing. Major exports: transport equipment, iron and steel products, textiles and clothing, agricultural products.

Religion: About 90% Catholic.

Language: French. Minorities speak Basque, Breton, Catalan, etc.

French Riviera: The Côte d'Azur forms an administrative region with Provence, and belongs within the Alpes-Maritimes and Var *départements*. The capital of Alpes-Maritimes (area: 4,300 square km./1,600 square miles) is Nice, with a population of about 360,000; the Var (area: 6,000 square km./2,300 square miles) has Toulon as its main city (about 185,000 inhabitants), France's main naval port in the Mediterranean.

Planning Your Budget

The following are some prices in French francs (F). However, they must be regarded as approximate; inflation in France, as elsewhere, rises steadily.

Baby-sitters. 30–50 F per hour, 150–200 F per day.

Bicycle and moped rental. Bicycle 50–65 F per day, moped 65–100 F, deposit minimum 500 F.

Boat rental. Motor boat 800–1,500 F per day, sailing boat (medium) 2,500 F.

Camping. 50–100 F for four persons with tent, 40–100 F with caravan (trailer).

Car hire (international company). *Renault Super 5 GL* 162 F per day, 2.28 F per km., 1,932 F per week with unlimited mileage. *Renault 11 TL* 183 F per day, 2.77 F per km., 2,247 F per week with unlimited mileage. *Renault 25 GTS* 295 F per day, 3.56 F per km., 4,704 F per week with unlimited mileage. Add 33.33% tax.

Cigarettes. French 4.50–7 F per packet of 20, foreign 7–13 F, cigars 17–48 F per piece.

Entertainment. Cinema 30–35 F, admission to discotheque 40–90 F, Casino admission 55 F, cabaret 150–350 F.

Guides. 500–700 F for half day, 70 F for each additional hour.

Hairdressers. *Woman's* haircut 80 F and up, blow-dry/shampoo and set 90 F and up, manicure 50 F and up. *Man's* haircut 80–180 F.

Hotels (per double room). ****L 600–2,500 F, **** 500–1,200 F, *** 300–500 F, ** 200–300 F, * 100–250 F. **Youth hostel** 30–35 F.

Meals and drinks. Continental breakfast 15–17 F, tourist menu 60–100 F, lunch/dinner in fairly good establishment 120–250 F, coffee 5.50–10 F, whisky or cocktail 25–60 F, beer/soft drink 8–16 F, cognac 27–60 F, bottle of wine 40 F and up.

Museums. 5–15 F.

Sports. Windsurf board about 50 F an hour, 1,500 F a week, instruction (with equipment, one week) 500–700 F, water skiing (6 minutes) 80 F, tennis 60 F an hour for a court, golf 180–210 F per day.

BLUEPRINT for a Perfect Trip

An A-Z Summary of Practical Information and Facts

Contents

A star (*) following an entry indicates that relevant prices are to be found on page 103.

Listed after most entries is the appropriate French translation usually in the singular, plus a number of phrases that may come in handy during your stay in France.

AIRPORT *(aéroport)*. The Nice-Côte d'Azur international airport (7 km. from Nice) is used by 20 airlines serving over 40 foreign destinations. Facilities include a currency-exchange bank, restaurants, bars, post office and car-rental agency as well as souvenir and duty-free shops. An airline bus leaves every 30 minutes for Nice, and another to Cannes stops at Antibes and Juan-les-Pins. A helicopter service connects the airport with Monaco.

The Marseilles-Marignane airport has direct connections with French and major European cities, Corsica and North Africa.

Where's the bus for...? **D'où part le bus pour...?**

A

BABY-SITTERS* *(baby-sitter, garde d'enfants)*. The larger towns and cities have baby-sitter services that advertise in the local papers. The best system is to first ask your hotel to help you find a sitter. You may be able to engage a hotel maid to "look in" from time to time.

Can you get me a baby-sitter for tonight? **Pouvez-vous me trouver une garde d'enfants pour ce soir?**

B

BICYCLE and MOTORCYCLE RENTAL* *(location de bicyclettes/de motocyclettes)*. It's possible to hire bicycles, mopeds, called *vélomoteurs,* motorcycles and scooters in most towns of the French Riviera. Be prepared to lay out a deposit.

Minimum age to ride a moped is 14; for scooters from 50 to 125 cc., 16 years; over 125 cc. it's 18. Crash-helmets are obligatory. Enquire about rentals at your hotel or the local tourist office *(syndicat d'initiative)*.

CAMPING* *(camping)*. Camping is extremely popular and very well organized in the South of France. There are over 300 officially recognized sites in the Alpes-Maritimes and the Var, most of them offering attractive locations and good facilities. These sites are classified from one to four stars depending on their amenities.

C

C

A *camping interdit* notice means the site is forbidden to campers, and the sign isn't a joke. You can always try to obtain an owner's permission to camp on private property in the region, but your chances are not very good.

Excellent booklets, such as *Camping—Côte d'Azur* (Menton to Cannes) can be obtained through the French Tourist Office in your country (see TOURIST INFORMATION OFFICES). For the Var region, write to Promo-Var, Conseil Général du Var, 1, bd Foch, 83300 Draguignan.

In the summer season, it's important to book in advance.

May we camp here, please?	**Pouvons-nous camper ici, s'il vous plaît?**

CAR HIRE* *(location de voitures)*. All major car-hire firms in France handle French-made cars and occasionally foreign makes. Locally based firms generally charge less than the international companies but give little or no choice of where you can return the car.

To hire a car you must produce a valid driving licence (held for at least one year) and your passport. Some firms set a minimum age at 21, others 25. Holders of major credit cards are normally exempt from deposit payments, otherwise you must pay a substantial (refundable) deposit for a car. Third-party insurance is usually automatically included, and with an extra fee per day you can obtain full insurance coverage.

I'd like to hire a car tomorrow.	**Je voudrais louer une voiture demain.**
for one day/a week	**pour une journée/une semaine**
Please include full insurance.	**Avec assurance tous risques, s'il vous plaît.**

CIGARETTES, CIGARS, TOBACCO* *(cigarettes; cigares; tabac)*. Tobacco is a state monopoly in France, and the best place to buy your cigarettes is at an official *débit de tabac* (licensed tobacconist's). There are plenty of these—cafés and bars—bearing the conspicuous double red cone.

French cigarettes include brands with dark or light tobacco, with or without filter. Dozens of foreign brands are also available at higher prices. Pipe tobacco comes in a variety of cuts, from sweet to strong.

A pack of.../A box of matches, please.	**Un paquet de.../Une boîte d'allumettes, s'il vous plaît.**
filter-tipped/without filter	**avec/sans filtre**
light/dark tobacco	**du tabac blond/brun**

CLOTHING *(habillement)*. From May to October you can usually count on mild to hot weather and light summer clothing is best. On the other hand, be sure to take a warm jacket or wrap for cool evenings, and you'll appreciate a raincoat in the low season, even in late spring. Light wool clothing and an overcoat are necessary in the winter.

Anything goes on the Riviera, but each town has its code. Complete nudity is tolerated on some beaches (notably around Saint-Tropez and on the Ile du Levant); topless sunbathing is permitted in most places.

At night, *tenue correcte* is required in casinos — that is, a jacket and tie for men, dresses or neat slacks for women. When visiting churches, respectable clothing should be worn.

COMMUNICATIONS

Post Office *(poste)*. You can identify French post offices by a sign with a stylized blue bird and/or the words *Postes et Télécommunications* or P & T. In cities the main post office is open from 8 a.m. to 5 p.m., Monday to Friday, and 8 a.m. to noon on Saturdays. In smaller towns the hours are from 8.30 a.m. to noon, and 2.30 to 5 or 6 p.m., Monday to Friday; 8 a.m. to noon on Saturdays.

In addition to normal mail service, you can make local or long-distance telephone calls, send telegrams and receive or send money at any time at the post office.

Note: You can also buy stamps at a tobacconist's.

Mail *(courrier)*. If you don't know ahead of time where you're staying, you can have your mail addressed to *poste restante* (general delivery) in any town. Towns with more than one post office keep mail at the main post office. Take your passport with you for identification.

Telegrams *(télégramme)*. All local post offices accept telegrams, domestic or overseas. You may also dictate a telegram over the telephone (dial 36.55).

Telephone *(téléphone)*. International or long-distance calls can be made from phone boxes, but if you need assistance in placing the call go to the post office or ask at your hotel. If you want to make a reverse-charge (collect) call, ask for *un appel en PCV* (pronounced: pay-say-vay). For a personal (person-to-person) call, specify *un appel avec préavis pour...* (naming the party you want to talk to).

Local calls can also be made from cafés, where you might have to buy a *jeton* (token) to put into the phone.

For long-distance calls within France, there are no area codes (just dial the 8-digit number of the person you want to call), *except* when

C telephoning from Paris or the Paris region to the provinces (dial 16 and wait for the dialling tone, then dial the 8-digit number of the subscriber) and from the provinces to Paris or the Paris region (dial 16, wait for the dialling tone, then dial 1 followed by the 8-digit number). If you need the assistance of an operator, dial 36.10.

To ring abroad from France, dial 19 followed, after the change of tone, by the country's number (listed in all boxes), the area code and the subscriber's number. If direct dialling is not available to that country or if you don't know the telephone number of the subscriber, dial 19 and wait for the tone, then dial 33 followed by the code number of the country in question to reach the operator (UK 44, U.S.A. and Canada 1). If you do not know the number of the country, call the international information, 19.33.33.

It's cheaper to make long-distance trunk calls after 8 p.m.

express (special delivery)	**exprès**
airmail	**par avion**
registered	**recommandé**
A stamp for this letter/ postcard, please	**Un timbre pour cette lettre/ carte postale, s'il vous plaît.**
I want to send a telegram to...	**J'aimerais envoyer un télégramme à...**
Have you any mail for...?	**Avez-vous du courrier pour...?**

COMPLAINTS *(réclamation)*

Hotels and restaurants. Complaints should be referred to the owner or manager of the establishment in question. If you fail to obtain on-the-spot satisfaction for your complaint, you can refer the matter to the nearest police station *(commissariat de police)*. If they cannot help, apply to the regional administration offices *préfecture* or *sous-préfecture*), asking for the *service du tourisme*.

Bad merchandise; car repairs. Complain at once to the proprietor or manager. In the event of gross abuse, register your complaint at the local *commissariat*. For complaints about cars or car repairs, members of automobile associations can consult the Touring Club de France.

I'd like to make a complaint.	**J'ai une réclamation à faire.**

CONSULATES *(consulat)*. Most consulates are open, Monday to Friday, from 9 or 10 a.m. to 4 or 5 p.m. with an hour or so off for lunch.
108 Schedules may change with the season, so it's best to call in advance.

Australia: (embassy) 4, rue Jean Rey, 75015 Paris; tel. 16~(1) 15.75.62.00

Canada: 24, avenue du Prado, Marseilles 6ᵉ; tel. 91.37.19.37

Eire: 71, boulevard Poincaré, Juan-les-Pins; tel. 93.61.08.85

United Kingdom: 24, avenue du Prado, Marseilles 6ᵉ; tel. 91.53.43.32

U.S.A.: 9, rue Armeny, Marseille 6ᵉ; tel. 91.33.78.33
36, rue Maréchal Joffre, 06000 Nice; tel. 93.88.89.55

CONVERTER CHARTS. For fluid and distance measures, see pages 111-112. France uses the metric system.

Temperature

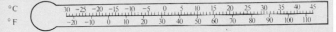

Length

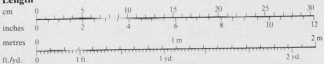

Weight

grams | 0 | 100 | 200 | 300 | 400 | 500 | 600 | 700 | 800 | 900 | 1 kg

ounces | 0 | 4 | 8 | 12 | 1 lb. | 20 | 24 | 28 | 2 lb.

COURTESIES. See also MEETING PEOPLE. The sunny climate of southern France makes for a good-natured but impetuous temperament. Though you'll hear lots of shouting, it's usually high-spirited discussion rather than real argument, and the shopkeepers and restaurant personnel are far more relaxed than in Paris.

In restaurants and cafés, *garçon* is the customary way to call a waiter (*mademoiselle* for a waitress), or you can simply say *s'il vous plaît*. The *maître d'hôtel* (headwaiter) and *sommelier* (wine steward) are addressed as *monsieur*.

French people kiss or shake hands when greeting each other or saying goodbye. When you're introduced to someone or meeting a friend you're expected to shake hands at least. Close friends are kissed on both cheeks.

C If you stop a policeman or passerby to ask for directions, start with *excusez-moi, Monsieur/Madame*. Use your French, no matter how faulty, unless the person you're speaking to seems impatient and speaks your language well. Your effort will be appreciated.

CRIME and THEFT *(délit; vol)*. If you have items of real value, keep them in the hotel safe and obtain a receipt for them; it's a good idea to leave large amounts of money and even your passport there as well.

Another wise precaution is to keep any valuables out of sight especially when you leave your car. Any loss or theft should be reported at once to the nearest *commissariat de police* or *gendarmerie* (see POLICE).

D **DRIVING IN FRANCE.** To take a car into France, you will need:

- A valid driving licence
- Car registration papers
- Insurance coverage (the green card is no longer obligatory but comprehensive coverage is advisable)
- A red warning triangle and a set of spare bulbs

Drivers and front-seat passengers are required by law to wear seat belts. Children under 10 may not travel in the front (unless the car has no back seat). Driving on a provisional licence is not permitted in France. Minimum age is 18.

Driving conditions: The rules are the same as elsewhere on the Continent —drive on the right, overtake on the left, yield right of way to all vehicles coming from the right (except on roundabouts/traffic circles), unless otherwise indicated.

Speed limits in force: on dry roads, 130 kph on toll motorways (expressways), 110 kph on dual carriageways (divided highways), 90 kph on all other roads, and 45 to 60 kph in built-up areas. When roads are wet, all limits are reduced by 10 kph. The word *rappel* means a restriction is continued. Fines for exceeding the speed limits are payable on the spot.

The French style of driving can be terrifying if you're not used to it, with plenty of speed and daring overtaking. Stick to your own pace and keep a safe distance between yourself and the vehicle in front.

Road conditions: French roads are designated by an A, standing for *autoroute* (motorway); an N for national highways; a D for *départementale*, or regional roads; or a V for local roads *(chemins vicinaux)*. In recent years, road surfaces have been greatly improved. The *nationales,* or major highways, are good on the whole but often not as wide as they could be, especially at the time when most French people go on holiday: the 1st and 15th of July, the 1st and 15th of August and the 1st of September.

The motorways are excellent and owned by public companies which usually charge tolls according to vehicle size and distance travelled. All amenities (restaurants, toilets, service stations, etc.) are available, plus orange S.O.S. telephones every 2 kilometres.

Many tourists like to travel on secondary roads at a more leisurely pace with better views. Sometimes you'll find alternative routes *(itinéraires bis)* sign-posted along the way by emerald-green arrows.

Parking: In town centres, most street parking is metered. In blue zones (parking spaces marked with a blue line) you must display a *disque de stationnement* or parking clock (obtainable from petrol stations or stationers), which you set to show when you arrived and when you must leave. Some streets have alternate parking on either side of the street according to which half of the month it is (the dates are marked on the signs).

Breakdowns: Towing and on-the-spot repairs can be made by local garages, and spare parts are readily available for European cars. It's wise to take out some form of internationally valid breakdown insurance before leaving home, and always ask for an estimate *before* undertaking repairs.

Traffic police: The *Garde Mobile* patrols the roads and motorways in cars or on powerful motorcycles. Always in pairs, they are courteous and helpful but extremely severe on lawbreakers and have authority to fine offenders on the spot.

Fuel and oil: Fuel (gas) is available in super (98 octane), normal (90 octane), lead-free (95 octane) and diesel *(gas-oil)*. All grades of motor oil are on sale. It's usual to tip service-station attendants for any additional services rendered.

Fluid measures

imp. gals.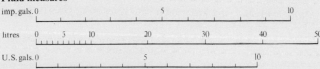

litres

U.S. gals.

D Distance

```
km    0    1    2    3    4    5    6         8         10        12        14        16
      |----|----|----|----|----|----|---------|---------|---------|---------|---------|
miles 0   ½    1   1½   2         3         4         5    6    7    8    9    10
```

Road signs: Most road signs are the standard pictographs used throughout Europe, but you may encounter these written signs as well:

Accotements non stabilisés	Soft shoulders
Chaussée déformée	Bad road surface
Déviation	Diversion (detour)
Douane	Customs
Péage	Toll
Priorité à droite	Yield to traffic from right
Ralentir	Slow
Sauf riverains	Entry prohibited except for inhabitants of street
Serrez à droite/gauche	Keep right/left
Stationnement interdit	No parking

(international) driving licence	**permis de conduire (international)**
car registration papers	**carte grise**
Are we on the right road for...?	**Sommes-nous sur la route de...?**
Fill the tank, please	**Le plein, s'il vous plaît.**
lead-free/normal/super	**sans plomb/normale/super**
Check the oil/tires/battery.	**Veuillez contrôler l'huile/ les pneus/la batterie**
I've had a breakdown.	**Ma voiture est en panne.**
There's been an accident.	**Il y a eu un accident.**

DRUGS. The possession, use and distribution of drugs are criminal offences. Prison sentences for offenders can be extremely severe, and suspects may have to wait a considerable time for trial—in jail.

E ELECTRIC CURRENT.

220-volt, 50-cycle A.C. is now almost universal, though 110 volts may still be encountered. British and American visitors using electric appliances should remember to buy a Continental adaptor plug before leaving home. They can also be bought in some electric supply shops *(magasins d'électricité)* or *drogueries.*

What's the voltage—110 or 220?	**Quel est le voltage – cent dix ou deux cent vingt?**
an adaptor plug/a battery	**une prise de raccordement/une pile**

EMERGENCIES *(urgence)*. For real emergencies you can get assistance anywhere in France by dialling the number 17 for the police *(Police-Secours)*; call number 18 for the fire brigade *(pompiers)* which also comes for such emergencies as drowning. For less pressing problems, see separate entries in this section such as CONSULATES, MEDICAL CARE, POLICE, etc.

Though we hope you'll never need them, here are a few key words you might like to learn in advance:

Careful!	**Attention!**	Help!	**Au secours!**
Fire!	**Au feu!**	Police!	**Police!**

ENTRY FORMALITIES and CUSTOMS *(douane)*. Visitors from EEC countries need only a valid passport to enter France. Travellers from other countries should check with the French consulate to see if they need a visa. Though European and North American residents are not subject to any health requirements, visitors from further afield may require a smallpox vaccination. Check with your travel agent before departure.

The following chart shows what main items you may take into France:

Into:	Cigarettes		Cigars		Tobacco	Spirits		Wine
France 1)	200	or	50	or	250 g.	1 l.	and	2 l.
2)	300	or	75	or	400 g.	1½ l.	and	5 l.
3)	400	or	100	or	500 g.	1 l.	and	2 l.
Canada	200	and	50	and	900 g.	1.1 l.	or	1.1 l.
Eire 1)	200	or	50	or	250 g.	1 l.	and	2 l.
2)	300	or	75	or	400 g.	1½ l.	and	5 l.
U.K. 1)	200	or	50	or	250 g.	1 l.	and	2 l.
2)	300	or	75	or	400 g.	1½ l.	and	2 l.
U.S.A.	200	and	100	and	4)	1 l.	or	1 l.

1) If arriving from EEC countries with duty-free items or from other European countries.
2) If arriving from EEC countries with non-duty free items.
3) Residents outside Europe.
4) A reasonable quantity.

E **Currency restrictions:** There's no limit on the importation of French francs or foreign currencies or traveller's cheques. Unless a declaration was made on entry, non-residents are only allowed to reconvert up to 12,000 French francs into foreign currencies when leaving the country.

F **FOREST FIRES.** Every summer, alas, they occur, more or less serious, more or less destructive. Do your part in preventing them: put out cigarettes carefully, do not light fires, and be especially careful if using a grill or primus stove on a picnic. Only a spark does it, and they catch on in no time.

G **GUIDES and INTERPRETERS*** *(guide; interprète)*. Local *syndicats d'initiative* (see TOURIST INFORMATION OFFICES) can supply or direct you to qualified official guides and interpreters if you want a personally conducted tour or any linguistic assistance. Guides engaged for a whole day should be offered lunch.

Bus companies from Nice and Cannes also offer many guided tours. It's customary to tip the guide.

We'd like an English-speaking guide.	**Nous aimerions un guide parlant anglais.**
I need an English interpreter.	**J'ai besoin d'un interprète anglais.**

H **HAIRDRESSERS* and BARBERS** *(coiffeur)*. Prices vary widely according to the class of establishment, but rates are often displayed in the window.

Tipping: Most establishments include *service* in the price, but it's customary to give a little something to the person who washes your hair, and a small tip to the stylist.

haircut	**coupe**
simple cut	**coupe simple**
shampoo and set	**shampooing et mise en plis**
blow-dry	**un brushing**
a colour chart	**un nuancier**
a colour rinse/hair-dye	**un rinçage/une teinture**
Not too much off (here).	**Pas trop court (ici).**
A little more off (here).	**Un peu plus court (ici).**

HOTELS and ACCOMMODATION* *(hôtel; logement)*. See also CAMPING and YOUTH HOSTELS. France offers a huge variety of hotel accommodation to suit every taste and pocket.

Hotels are officially classified into five categories by the Commissariat Central du Tourisme. Room prices, fixed according to amenities, size and to the hotel's star rating, must be posted visibly at reception desks and behind each room door. Hotels marked *NN (Nouvelles Normes)* have recently been reclassified and correspond to current standards of comfort.

Note: Hôtel de Ville is not a hotel, but the town hall.

Other accommodation: This can run from the relatively modest *gîte* and *logis de France* to luxurious settings like the *château-hôtel* and *relais de campagne*, where prices can be very high.

House rental: Tourist offices can recommend agencies with complete lists of available houses and apartments to let. In full season, you should book well ahead.

a double/single room with/without bath	**une chambre à deux lits/à un lit avec/sans bains**
What's the rate per night?	**Quel est le prix pour une nuit?**
Must I take meals?	**Est-ce que la pension est obligatoire?**
I'm looking for a flat to rent for a month.	**Je cherche un appartement à louer pour un mois.**

LANGUAGE. Real southerners have a charming, droll accent, drawing out their syllables in a way you don't hear elsewhere. The usual nasal French "en" ending becomes a hard "ng" *(chien* sounds like *chieng)*.

In addition, you'll hear all sorts of rolling, vaguely Italianate dialects, especially Niçois and Monegasque. See also the box on page 14.

The Berlitz phrase book FRENCH FOR TRAVELLERS covers almost all situations you're likely to encounter in your travels in France. In addition, the Berlitz French-English/English-French pocket dictionary contains a 12,500 word glossary of each language, plus a menu-reader supplement.

Good morning/Good afternoon	**Bonjour**
Good afternoon/Good evening	**Bonsoir**
Please	**S'il vous plaît**
Thank you	**Merci**
You're welcome	**Je vous en prie**
Goodbye	**Au revoir**

H

L

115

L **LAUNDRY and DRY-CLEANING** *(blanchisserie; teinturerie, nettoyage à sec)*. You'll still see some women in the Midi beating their laundry against the stone in the public fountain *lavoirs*. But modern facilities are growing fast.

If your hotel will not take care of laundry or cleaning, you can have clothes cleaned quickly and cheaply in chain dry-cleaners (not recommended, however, for fragile fabrics or difficult spots). Better care takes longer and is more expensive; prices vary according to fabric and cut.

LOST PROPERTY *(objets trouvés)*; **LOST CHILDREN.** Check first at your hotel desk and if you have no success there report the loss to the nearest *commissariat de police* or *gendarmerie* (see POLICE).

Restaurant and café personnel are quite honest about keeping objects forgotten or lost until the owner reclaims them, or in the case of wallets, turning them over to the police.

If you lose a child, you'll find people very helpful. It should be reported to any policeman *(agent de police)* on duty or the nearest *commissariat* or *gendarmerie*. In any case, don't let young children out of your sight in crowded places.

I've lost my child/wallet/handbag/passport.	**J'ai perdu mon enfant/portefeuille/sac/passeport.**

M **MAPS** *(carte; plan)*. Various detailed topographical and road maps exist for motorists and hikers. Particularly useful is Michelin's No. 84, and the detailed map of the Alpes-Maritimes, No. 195. Falk-Verlag, who provided the maps for this guide, publishes a map of France.

Do you have a map of the city/of the region?	**Avez-vous un plan de la ville/une carte de la région?**

MEDICAL CARE. See also EMERGENCIES. To be at ease, make sure your health insurance policy covers any illness or accident while on holiday. If not, ask your insurance representative, automobile association or travel agent for details of special travel insurance.

You'll find well-trained doctors and specialists in the south of France. If you're taken ill or have a toothache, consult your hotel receptionist, who can probably recommend an English-speaking doctor or dentist. In Cannes, the Sunnybank Anglo-American Hospital is staffed by British nurses:

116 133, avenue du Petit-Juan; tel. 93.68.29.96

Visitors from EEC countries with corresponding health insurance facilities are entitled to medical and hospital treatment under the French social security system. Before leaving home, make sure you find out about the appropriate form(s) required to obtain this benefit in case of need. Doctors who belong to the French social security system (*médecins conventionnés*) charge the minimum.

Chemists' (*pharmacie*) with green crosses are helpful in dealing with minor ailments or in finding a nurse (*infirmière*) if you need injections or other special care.

Health (*santé*). The "tourist's complaint" that hits many travellers is not due to drinking tap water, which is safe in towns all over France. Fatigue, too much sun, change of diet and over-indulgence are the main causes of most minor complaints. Be careful about over-eating and, especially, drinking. French mineral water is a good thirst quencher and helps to digest meals. Serious gastro-intestinal problems lasting more than a day or two should be looked after by a doctor.

Where's the chemist on duty?	**Où est la pharmacie de garde?**
I need a doctor.	**Il me faut un médecin.**
a dentist	**un dentiste**
an upset stomach	**mal à l'estomac**
a fever	**de la fièvre**
sunburn	**un coup de soleil**
I've a pain here.	**J'ai mal ici.**

MEETING PEOPLE. See also Courtesies. The French Riviera has been for many years a very cosmopolitan and popular resort area, not only for foreigners but for the northern French themselves. Something of a blasé attitude towards tourists may be met with in the over-frequented spots, while off the beaten track spontaneous warmth and kindness are as alive as ever. This natural friendliness on the part of girls, however, should not be taken as an invitation to forego the normal approach procedures. Do not consider a topless beauty an easy mark; she may prefer to stay alone or with her companions. As for French men, you will find them slightly less brash than other southern Europeans.

MONEY MATTERS

Currency (*monnaie*). For currency restrictions, see Entry Formalities and Customs. The *franc*, France's monetary unit (abbreviated F or FF) is divided into 100 *centimes*. Current coins include 5-, 10-, 20- and 50- **117**

M centime pieces as well as 1-, 2-, 5- and 10-franc pieces. Banknotes come in denominations of 20, 50, 100, 200 and 500 francs.

Many French people still like to express prices in "old" francs (*anciens francs*) — although the system changed 20 years ago: 100 of them equal 1 "new" franc. In shops, however, only new francs are referred to.

Banks and Currency-Exchange Offices (*banques; bureau de change*). Hours may vary, but most banks are open Monday to Friday from 8.30 or 9.30 a.m. to noon and 1.30 to 5 p.m. Some currency-exchange offices operate on Saturdays as well. At Monte Carlo, a *bureau de change* opposite the Casino is open every day.

Your hotel will usually change currency or traveller's cheques into francs, but the rate is not favourable—nor is it in shops and casinos where traveller's cheques are often accepted. Always take your passport along when you go to change money.

Credit Cards (*carte de crédit*). Most hotels, smarter restaurants, some boutiques, car-hire firms and tourist-related businesses in towns accept certain credit cards.

Traveller's cheques (*chèque de voyage*). Hotels, travel agents and many shops accept them, although the exchange rate is invariably better at a bank. Don't forget to take your passport when going to cash a traveller's cheque. Eurocheques are also accepted.

Prices (*prix*). The cost of living on the Riviera is generally high, but it is possible to have a good time on a budget if you choose carefully. (The further you get away from the coast, the more likely you are to find reasonably priced hotels and restaurants.)

Official prices are always posted prominently in public establishments, including cafés, bars, hotels and restaurants.

Could you give me some (small) change?	**Pouvez-vous me donner de la (petite) monnaie?**
I want to change some pounds/dollars.	**Je voudrais changer des livres sterling/des dollars.**
Do you accept traveller's cheques?	**Acceptez-vous les chèques de voyage?**
Can I pay with this credit card?	**Puis-je payer avec cette carte de crédit?**

N **NEWSPAPERS and MAGAZINES** (*journal; revue*). In addition to French national and local papers, most towns also have British newspapers for sale and the Paris-based *International Herald Tribune*, usually on publication day.

Magazines in many languages are available at larger news-stands.

Have you any English-language newspapers?	**Avez-vous des journaux en anglais?**

PETS *(animal domestique)*. If you want to bring your pet dog or cat along, you'll need a health and rabies inoculation certificate for the animal to enter the country. Many hotels and restaurants allow pets, but check first.

PHOTOGRAPHY *(photographie)*. The coast is a photographer's dream, with plenty of light, varied scenery and colours of every intensity from soft pastel shades to the most vibrant hues. Certain museums will give you permission to photograph inside.

All popular film makes and sizes are available in France. Rapid development is possible, but quite expensive.

I'd like a film for this camera.	**J'aimerais un film pour cet appareil.**
a black-and-white film	**un film noir et blanc**
a film for colour prints	**un film couleurs**
a colour-slide film	**un film de diapositives**
How long will it take to develop this film?	**Combien de temps faut-il pour développer ce film?**
Can I take a picture of you?	**Puis-je vous prendre en photo?**

POLICE *(police)*. In cities and larger towns you'll see the blue-uniformed *police municipale;* they are the local police force who keep order, investigate crime and direct traffic. Outside of the main towns are the *gendarmes*—they wear blue trousers and black jackets with white belts and are also responsible for traffic and crime investigation.

The C.R.S. police *(Compagnies Républicaines de Sécurité)* are a national security force responsible to the Ministry of the Interior and are called in for emergencies and special occasions. The *Garde Mobile,* or *Police de la Route,* patrol the roads.

In case of need, dial 17 anywhere in France for police help.

Where's the nearest police station?	**Où est le poste de police le plus proche?**

P PUBLIC HOLIDAYS *(jours férié)*

January 1	*Jour de l'An*	New Year's Day
May 1	*Fête du Travail*	Labour Day
May 8	*Fête de la Libération*	Victory Day (1945)
July 14	*Fête Nationale*	Bastille Day
August 15	*Assomption*	Assumption
November 1	*Toussaint*	All Saints' Day
November 11	*Anniversaire de l'Armistice*	Armistice Day
December 25	*Noël*	Christmas Day
Movable dates:	*Lundi de Pâques*	Easter Monday
	Ascension	Ascension
	Lundi de Pentecôte	Whit Monday

These are the national French holidays. See page 81 for details of local celebrations and events.

PUBLIC TRANSPORT

Buses *(autobus, autocar)*. Larger towns and cities like Cannes, Nice, Toulon and Monte Carlo have urban bus services — a particularly good way to get around. Inter-city bus services all along the coast and into the hinterland are efficient, comfortable, inexpensive and fairly frequent.

Taxis *(taxi)*. Taxis are clearly marked and available in all the larger towns. If the cab is unmetered, or you have a fair distance to go, ask the fare beforehand.

Trains *(train)*. The French National Railways (S.N.C.F.) operate a widespread network. Services are fast, punctual and comfortable. In season, at least ten trains a day (car train and TGV—*train à grande vitesse*) run from Paris' Gare de Lyon to Nice, and there is also a daily sleeper which carries cars. A major line links Marseilles and Menton along the Mediterranean coast. An old-fashioned steam train on the Nice–Digne line makes pleasant tours of the Provence countryside in season.

Trains are also a good way of getting around the coast quickly and cheaply in the height of summer traffic. The train ride from Menton to Nice, for example, lasts half an hour; by car or bus the same trip may take you an hour or more.

S.N.C.F. offer various categories of ticket, like Billet Touristique, Billet de Groupes, Billet de Famille, France-Vacances, etc. Inquire at the

nearest tourist office or railway information counter. Eurailpasses and
Inter-rail cards are valid in France (see p. 101).

(see p. 101)

When's the next bus/train to...?	**Quand part le prochain bus/ train pour...?**
When's the best train to...?	**A quelle heure part le meilleur train pour...?**
single (one-way)	**aller simple**
return (round-trip)	**aller et retour**
first/second class	**première/deuxième classe**
I'd like to make seat reservations.	**J'aimerais réserver des places.**

RADIO and TV *(radio; télévision).* There are three main TV channels in
France. Some hotels have television lounges; a few have TV in the
rooms. All programmes (except for a few late films) are in French.
Monte Carlo television can also be picked up in most places along the
coast.

You can easily tune in to BBC programmes on either short- or
medium-wave radios. In summer the French radio broadcasts news and
information in English. Local newspapers have the details. Radio 104
FM transmits in English all day.

RELIGIOUS SERVICES. France is a predominantly Roman Catholic
country. Ask your hotel receptionist or the local tourist office for
information about the location and times of services in English. There
are English-speaking Protestant churches and synagogues in Cannes,
Menton, Monaco, Nice and Saint-Raphaël. Non-Catholic services are
called *cultes.*

Where is the Protestant church/ synagogue?	**Où se trouve l'église protestante/ la synagogue?**

TIME DIFFERENCES. France follows Greenwich Mean Time + 1,
and in spring the clocks are put forward one hour. If your country does
the same, the time difference remains constant for most of the year.

Los Angeles	Chicago	New York	London	Nice
3 a.m.	5 a.m.	6 a.m.	11 a.m.	**noon**

What time is it? **Quelle heure est-il?**

T **TIPPING.** A 10 to 15% service charge is generally included automatically in hotel and restaurant bills. Rounding off the overall bill helps round off friendships with waiters, too. It is also in order to hand the bellboys, doormen, filling station attendants, etc., a coin or two for their service.

The chart below gives some suggestions as to what to leave.

Hotel porter, per bag	4–5 F
Hotel maid, per week	20–40 F
Lavatory attendant	2 F
Waiter	5–10% (optional)
Taxi driver	10–15%
Hairdresser/Barber	15% (gen. incl.)
Tour guide	10%

TOILETS *(toilettes).* Clean public conveniences are still not all that common in France, and the stand-up toilet facilities can be rather harrowing. If there is no light-switch, the light will usually go on when you lock the door. Three-star W.C.'s do exist, mostly in better hotels and restaurants.

Café facilities are generally free, but you should order at least a coffee if you use the toilet. A saucer with small change on it means that a tip is expected. The women's toilets may be marked *Dames;* the men's either *Messieurs* or *Hommes.*

Where are the toilets, please? **Où sont les toilettes, s'il vous plaît?**

TOURIST INFORMATION OFFICES *(office du tourisme).* French national tourist offices can help you plan your holiday and will supply you with a wide range of colourful, informative brochures and maps.

Some addresses:

Canada: 1840 Ouest, rue Sherbrooke, Montreal H3H 1E4, P.Q.; tel. (514) 931-3855
1 Dundas St. W, Suite 2405, P.O. Box 8, Toronto, Ont. M5G 1Z3

122 **United Kingdom:** 178, Piccadilly, London W1V OAL; tel. (01) 493-6594

U.S.A. 645 N. Michigan Ave., Suite 430, Chicago IL 60611; tel.: (312) 337-6301
9401 Wilshire Blvd., Room 840, Beverly Hills CA 90212; tel.: (213) 271-6665
610 5th Ave., New York NY 10020; tel.: (212) 757-1125

On the spot:

Cannes:	Office du Tourisme, Palais des Festivals, Esplanade Président Georges Pompidou, La Croisette; tel. 93.39.24.53
Marseilles:	Office Municipal du Tourisme, 4, La Canebière; tel. 91.54.91.11
Monaco:	Direction du Tourisme et des Congrès, 2a, boulevard des Moulins; tel. 93.30.87.01
Nice:	Office du Tourisme, 5, avenue Gustave V; tel. 93.87.60.60; and at the airport (parking Ferber) Syndicat d'Initiative, central railway station

Local tourist information offices *(syndicat d'initiative)* are invaluable sources of information (from maps to hotel lists and other miscellaneous items) in all French towns. They are usually found near the town's centre and often have a branch at the railway station. Opening hours vary, but the general rule is 8.30 or 9 a.m. to noon and from 2 to 6 or 7 p.m., every day except Sunday.

Where's the tourist office, please?   **Où est le syndicat d'initiative, s'il vous plaît?**

WATER *(eau)*. Tap water is safe throughout the country, except when marked *eau non potable* (not safe for drinking). A wide variety of mineral water can be found on sale everywhere.

a bottle of mineral water   **une bouteille d'eau minérale**
  fizzy/still   **gazeuse/non gazeuse**
Is this drinking water?   **Est-ce de l'eau potable?**

YOUTH HOSTELS *(auberge de jeunesse)*. Your national youth hostel association can give you all the details, or contact the
Fédération Unie des Auberges de Jeunesse, 6, rue Mesnil, 75116 Paris; tel. 16~(1) 42.61.84.03

DAYS OF THE WEEK

Sunday	**dimanche**	Thursday	**jeudi**
Monday	**lundi**	Friday	**vendredi**
Tuesday	**mardi**	Saturday	**samedi**
Wednesday	**mercredi**		

MONTHS

January	**janvier**	July	**juillet**
February	**février**	August	**août**
March	**mars**	September	**septembre**
April	**avril**	October	**octobre**
May	**mai**	November	**novembre**
June	**juin**	December	**décembre**

NUMBERS

0	**zéro**	19	**dix-neuf**
1	**un, une**	20	**vingt**
2	**deux**	21	**vingt et un**
3	**trois**	22	**vingt-deux**
4	**quatre**	23	**vingt-trois**
5	**cinq**	30	**trente**
6	**six**	40	**quarante**
7	**sept**	50	**cinquante**
8	**huit**	60	**soixante**
9	**neuf**	70	**soixante-dix**
10	**dix**	71	**soixante et onze**
11	**onze**	80	**quatre-vingts**
12	**douze**	90	**quatre-vingt-dix**
13	**treize**	100	**cent**
14	**quatorze**	101	**cent un**
15	**quinze**	126	**cent vingt-six**
16	**seize**	200	**deux cents**
17	**dix-sept**	300	**trois cents**
18	**dix-huit**	1000	**mille**

SOME USEFUL EXPRESSIONS

yes/no	oui/non
please/thank you	s'il vous plaît/merci
excuse me	excusez-moi
you're welcome	je vous en prie
where/when/how	où/quand/comment
how long/how far	combien de temps/à quelle distance
yesterday/today/tomorrow	hier/aujourd'hui/demain
day/week/month/year	jour/semaine/mois/année
left/right	gauche/droite
up/down	en haut/en bas
good/bad	bon/mauvais
big/small	grand/petit
cheap/expensive	bon marché/cher
hot/cold	chaud/froid
old/new	vieux/neuf
open/closed	ouvert/fermé
here/there	ici/là
free (vacant)/occupied	libre/occupé
early/late	tôt/tard
easy/difficult	facile/difficile

Does anyone here speak English?	Y a-t-il quelqu'un ici qui parle anglais?
What does this mean?	Que signifie ceci?
I don't understand.	Je ne comprends pas.
Please write it down.	Ecrivez-le-moi, s'il vous plaît.
Is there an admission charge?	Faut-il payer pour entrer?
Waiter/Waitress!	S'il vous plaît!
I'd like...	J'aimerais...
How much is that?	C'est combien?
Have you something less expensive?	Avez-vous quelque chose de moins cher?
What time is it?	Quelle heure est-il?
Help me please.	Aidez-moi, s'il vous plaît.

Index

An asterisk (*) next to a page number indicates a map reference. For sites and town names starting with an article (le, la, les, l') see the basic word. For index to Practical Information, see p. 104.

INDEX

Selection of French Riviera Hotels and Restaurants

Where do you start? Choosing a hotel or restaurant in a place you're not familiar with can be daunting. To help you find your way amid the bewildering variety, we have made a selection from the *Red Guide to France 1987* published by Michelin, the recognized authority on gastronomy and accommodation throughout Europe.

Our own Berlitz criteria have been price and location. In the hotel section, for a double room with bath but without breakfast, Higher-priced means above 900 F, Medium-priced 400–900 F, Lower-priced below 400 F. As to restaurants, for a meal consisting of a starter, a main course and a dessert, Higher-priced means above 250 F, Medium-priced 150–250 F, Lower-priced below 150 F. $$$ stands for Higher-priced, $$ for Medium-priced and $ for Lower-priced. Special features where applicable are also given. Most hotels and restaurants close down a fortnight or a month per year and many restaurants have a regular weekly closing day (or days). Both a check to make certain that they are open and advance reservations are advisable. Prices for French Riviera hotels and restaurants generally include a service charge.

For a wider choice of hotels and restaurants, we strongly recommend you obtain the authoritative Michelin *Red Guide to France,* which gives a comprehensive and reliable picture of the situation throughout the country.

ANTIBES

Hotels

Bleu Marine $
rue des 4 Chemins
06600 Antibes
Tel. 93 74 84 84
18 rooms. View. No restaurant.

du Cap d'Antibes $$$
bd Kennedy
06600 Antibes
Tel. 93 61 39 01; tlx. 470763
*100 rooms. Pleasant, luxury hotel
with large flowered garden giving
onto the sea. Outdoor pool.
Private beach. Tennis court.*

La Gardiole $$
chemin La Garoupe
06600 Antibes
Tel. 93 61 35 03
*21 rooms. Quiet situation. Garden.
Outdoor dining.*

Josse $
8 bd James Wyllie
06600 Antibes
Tel. 93 61 47 24
24 rooms. View. Outdoor dining.

Mas Djoliba $$
29 av. Provence
06600 Antibes
Tel. 93 34 02 48; tlx. 461686
*14 rooms. Quiet position. Pleasant
garden. Outdoor swimming pool.*

Royal Hotel $
bd Mar.-Leclerc
06600 Antibes
Tel. 93 34 03 09
*43 rooms. View. Beach with bath-
ing facilities. Outdoor dining.*

Restaurants

Bacon $$$
bd Bacon
06600 Antibes
Tel. 93 61 50 02
*Notably good cuisine. View of the
Baie des Anges. Outdoor dining.*

Du Bastion $
1 av. Gén.-Maizière
06600 Antibes
Tel. 93 34 13 88
Outdoor dining.

Le Cabestan $$
bd Garoupe
06600 Antibes
Tel. 93 61 77 70
View. Outdoor dining.

L'Écurie Royale $$
33 rue Vauban
06600 Antibes
Tel. 93 34 76 20
Notably good cuisine.

La Marguerite $$
11 rue Sadi Carnot
06600 Antibes
Tel. 93 34 08 27

BEAULIEU-SUR-MER

Hotels

Métropole $$$
bd Mar.-Leclerc
06310 Beaulieu-sur-Mer
Tel. 93 01 00 08; tlx. 470304
*53 rooms. Quiet situation. Large
terrace overlooking the sea.
Garden. Outdoor swimming pool.
Beach with bathing facilities.
Notably good cuisine.*

La Réserve $$$
bd Mar.-Leclerc
06310 Beaulieu-sur-Mer
Tel. 93 01 00 01; tlx. 470301
47 rooms. Quiet situation. Pleasant, luxuriously appointed hotel on seafront. View. Outdoor swimming pool. Garden. Outdoor dining.

La Résidence $$
9 bis av. Albert-1er
06310 Beaulieu-sur-Mer
Tel. 93 01 06 02
21 rooms. Quiet situation. Garden. No restaurant.

BIOT

Restaurants

Les Terraillers $
06410 Biot
Tel. 93 65 01 59
Situated in a 16th-century former pottery.

BORMES-LES-MIMOSAS

Hotels

Paradis Hotel $
Mont des Roses
83230 Bormes-les-Mimosas
Tel. 94 71 06 85
20 rooms. Quiet hotel. View. Garden. No restaurant.

Safari Hotel $$
rte Stade
83230 Bormes-les-Mimosas
Tel. 94 71 09 83; tlx. 404603

33 rooms. Quiet hotel. View of the bay and islands. Outdoor swimming pool. Garden. Hotel tennis court.

Restaurants

La Cassole $$
ruelle Moulin
83230 Bormes-les-Mimosas
Tel. 94 71 14 86

Tonnelle des Délices $$
place Gambetta
83230 Bormes-les-Mimosas
Tel. 94 71 34 84

CAGNES-SUR-MER

Hotels

Le Cagnard $$
rue Pontis-Long (Haut-de-Cagnes)
06800 Cagnes-sur-Mer
Tel. 93 20 73 21; tlx. 462223
10 rooms. Pleasant hotel in quiet situation. View. Notably good cuisine. Outdoor dining.

Les Collettes $
av. Collettes
06800 Cagnes-sur-Mer
Tel. 93 20 80 66
13 rooms. Quiet position. View. No restaurant.

Tiercé Hotel $
33 bd Kennedy
06800 Cagnes-sur-Mer
Tel. 93 20 02 09
23 rooms. View. No restaurant.

4

Restaurants

Le Neptune $
bd Plage
06800 Cagnes-sur-Mer
Tel. 93 20 10 59
View. Outdoor dining.

Peintres $
71 montée Bourgade (Haut de Cagnes)
06800 Cagnes-sur-Mer
Tel. 93 20 83 08

La Réserve $$
91 bd Plage
06800 Cagnes-sur-Mer
Tel. 93 31 00 17
Notably good cuisine. Reservation essential.

Villa du Cros $$
Port du Cros
06800 Cagnes-sur-Mer
Tel. 93 07 57 83

CANNES

Hotels

Beau Séjour $$
5 rue Fauvettes
06400 Cannes
Tel. 93 39 63 00; tlx. 470975
46 rooms. Outdoor swimming pool. Garden.

Carlton $$$
58 bd Croisette
06400 Cannes
Tel. 93 68 91 68; tlx. 470720
295 rooms. Pleasant, luxury hotel. View. Beach with bathing facilities. La Côte restaurant.

Corona $
55 rue d'Antibes
06400 Cannes
Tel. 93 39 69 85
20 rooms. No restaurant.

La Madone $$
5 av. Justinia
06400 Cannes
Tel. 93 43 57 87
22 rooms. Cosy establishment. Quiet situation. Garden. No restaurant.

Majestic $$$
bd Croisette
06400 Cannes
Tel. 93 68 91 00; tlx. 470787
262 rooms. Pleasant, luxury hotel. View. Outdoor swimming pool. Beach with bathing facilities. Garden. Outdoor dining.

Martinez $$$
73 bd Croisette
06400 Cannes
Tel. 93 68 91 91; tlx. 470708
421 rooms. Pleasant, luxury hotel. View. Outdoor swimming pool. Beach with bathing facilities. Garden. Hotel tennis court. Outdoor dining. L'Orangeraie restaurant.

Molière $
5 rue Molière
06400 Cannes
Tel. 93 38 16 16
34 rooms. Garden. No restaurant.

Les Orangers $$
1 rue des Orangers
06400 Cannes
Tel. 93 39 99 92; tlx 470873
45 rooms. View. Outdoor swimming pool. Outdoor dining.

Paris $$
34 bd d'Alsace
06400 Cannes
Tel. 93 38 30 89; tlx. 470995
*48 rooms. Outdoor swimming
pool. Garden. No restaurant.*

Provence $
9 rue Molière
06400 Cannes
Tel. 93 38 44 35
30 rooms. Outdoor dining.

Restaurants

Blue Bar $$
ancien Palais des Festivals
06400 Cannes
Tel. 93 39 03 04
Outdoor dining.

Caveau Provençal $
45 rue Félix-Faure
06400 Cannes
Tel. 93 39 06 33
View. Outdoor dining.

La Croisette $
15 rue Cdt-André
06400 Cannes
Tel. 93 39 86 06

Le Festival $$
52 bd Croisette
06400 Cannes
Tel. 93 38 04 81
Outdoor dining.

Au Mal Assis $
15 quai St-Pierre
06400 Cannes
Tel. 93 39 13 38
View. Outdoor dining.

Le Monaco $
15 rue 24-août
06400 Cannes
Tel. 93 38 37 76

La Palme d'Or $$$
73 bd Croisette
06400 Cannes
Tel. 92 98 30 18
Notably good cuisine.

Royal Gray $$$
2 rue des Etats-Unis
06400 Cannes
Tel. 93 68 54 54; tlx. 470744
*Excellent cuisine. Outdoor dining.
Elegant contemporary decor.*

CAVALIÈRE

Hotels

Le Club $$$
83980 Le Lavandou
Tel. 94 05 80 14; tlx. 420317
*32 rooms. Pleasant, elegant hotel
beside the sea. View. Tennis court.
Outdoor swimming pool. Beach
with bathing facilities.
Garden. Notably good cuisine.
Outdoor dining.*

ÈZE

Hotels

Hermitage du Col d'Èze $
06360 Eze-Village
Tel. 93 41 00 68
14 rooms. View.

Restaurants

Château de la Chèvre d'Or $$$
rue Barri
06360 Èze-Village
Tel. 93 41 12 12
*Pleasant restaurant with notably
good cuisine. Overlooking the sea.
Outdoor swimming pool.*

Le Grill du Château $$
06360 Èze-Village
Tel. 93 41 00 17
View. Outdoor dining.

FAYENCE

Hotels

Moulin de la Camandoule $
83440 Fayence
Tel. 94 76 00 84
*11 rooms. Pleasant hotel in a
former oil mill. Garden. Outdoor
swimming pool. Outdoor dining.*

Restaurants

France $
place République
83440 Fayence
Tel. 94 76 00 14
*Outdoor dining. Reservation
essential.*

GRASSE

Hotels

Panorama $
2 place Cours
06130 Grasse
Tel. 93 36 80 80; tlx. 970908
36 rooms. No restaurant.

GRIMAUD

Hotels

La Boulangerie $$
83360 Grimaud
Tel. 94 43 23 16
*10 rooms. Quiet hotel. View.
Garden. Outdoor swimming pool.
Hotel tennis court. Outdoor
dining.*

Coteau Fleuri $
83360 Grimaud
Tel. 94 43 20 17
*14 rooms. Quiet hotel. View.
Garden.*

Restaurants

Café de France $
83360 Grimaud
Tel. 94 43 20 05
Outdoor dining.

JUAN-LES-PINS

Hotels

Alexandra $
rue Pauline
06160 Juan-les-Pins
Tel. 93 61 01 36
*20 rooms. Beach with bathing
facilities.*

Juana $$$
la Pinède av. G.-Gallice
06160 Juan-les-Pins
Tel. 93 61 08 70, tlx. 470778
*50 rooms. Pleasant hotel in quiet
situation. Outdoor swimming pool.
Private beach. Outdoor dining.
La Terrasse restaurant.*

Juan Beach $
5 rue Oratoire
06160 Juan-les-Pins
Tel. 93 61 02 89
30 rooms. Quiet situation. Beach with bathing facilities. Garden. Outdoor dining.

Mimosas $
rue Pauline
06160 Juan-les-Pins
Tel. 93 61 04 16
34 rooms. Quiet hotel in a park. Swimming pool. No restaurant.

Restaurants

Auberge de l'Esterel $$
21 rue des Iles
06160 Juan-les-Pins
Tel. 93 61 08 67
Outdoor dining. Garden.

Le Perroquet $
av. G.-Gallice
06160 Juan-les-Pins
Tel. 93 61 02 20

MENTON

Hotels

Aiglon $
7 av. Madone
06500 Menton
Tel. 93 57 55 55
32 rooms. Outdoor swimming pool. Garden. No restaurant.

Méditerranée $
5 rue République
06500 Menton
Tel. 93 28 25 25; tlx. 461361
90 rooms.

Pin Doré $
16 av. F.-Faure
06500 Menton
Tel. 93 28 31 00
42 rooms. View. Outdoor swimming pool. Garden. No restaurant.

Princess et Richmond $$
617 prom. Soleil
06500 Menton
Tel. 93 35 80 20
43 rooms. View. No restaurant.

Viking $
2 av. Gén.-de-Gaulle
06500 Menton
Tel. 93 57 95 85
36 rooms. View. Outdoor swimming pool.

Restaurants

Chez Mireille-l'Ermitage $$
prom. Soleil
06500 Menton
Tel. 93 35 77 23
View. Outdoor dining.

Paris-Palace $
2 av. F.-Faure
06500 Menton
Tel. 93 35 86 66
View. Outdoor dining.

MIRAMAR

Hotels

St-Christophe $$
06590 Théoule
Tel. 93 75 41 36; tlx. 470078
40 rooms. Pleasant hotel. View. Beautiful garden. Outdoor swimming pool. Private beach.

Tour de l'Esquillon $$
06590 Théoule
Tel. 93 75 41 51
25 rooms. Pleasant hotel. Access to beach with bathing facilities by private cable car. Beautiful garden. Stunning view over sea.

Restaurants

Père Pascal $
06590 Théoule
Tel. 93 75 40 11
View. Outdoor dining.

MONACO

Hotels

Balmoral $$
12 av. Costa
98000 Monaco
Tel. 93 50 62 37; tlx. 479436
68 rooms. Quiet situation. View. No restaurant.

Hermitage $$$
square Beaumarchais
98000 Monaco
Tel. 93 50 67 31; tlx. 479432
220 rooms. Pleasant hotel. View. Indoor swimming pool. Baroque-style dining room. Outdoor dining.

Paris $$$
place Casino
98000 Monaco
Tel. 93 50 80 80; tlx. 469925
206 rooms. Pleasant, luxury hotel. View. Indoor swimming pool. Garden. Notably good cuisine. Louis XV restaurant. Grill. Outdoor dining.

Terminus $
9 av. Prince Pierre
98000 La Condamine
Tel. 93 30 20 70
54 rooms.

Restaurants

Polpetta $
6 av. Roqueville
98000 Monaco
Tel. 93 50 67 84
Outdoor dining.

du Port $$
quai Albert Ier
98000 Monaco
Tel. 93 50 77 21
View. Outdoor dining. Italian cuisine.

MOUGINS

Hotels

Clos des Boyères $$
chemin de la Chapelle
06250 Mougins
Tel. 93 90 01 58
22 rooms. Bungalows in a park. Outdoor swimming pool. Hotel tennis court. Outdoor dining.

Mas Candille $$
06250 Mougins
Tel. 93 90 00 85; tlx. 462131
24 rooms. Quiet situation. View. Terraced garden. Outdoor swimming pool. Outdoor dining.

Restaurants

Le Bistrot $
06250 Mougins
Tel. 93 75 78 34

Ferme de Mougins $$$
St-Basile
06250 Mougins
Tel. 93 90 03 74; tlx. 970643
Pleasant restaurant. Outdoor dining. Garden.

Feu Follet $
place Mairie
06250 Mougins
Tel. 93 90 15 78
Outdoor dining.

Moulin de Mougins $$$
Notre-Dame-de-Vie
06250 Mougins
Tel. 93 75 78 24; tlx. 970732
Superb cuisine. Outdoor dining.

Relais à Mougins $$$
place Mairie
06250 Mougins
Tel. 93 90 03 47
Notably good cuisine. Outdoor dining. Reservation essential.

Aux Trois Etages $
06250 Mougins
Tel. 93 90 01 46
Outdoor dining.

LA NAPOULE

Hotels

La Calanque $
bd de la Mer
06210 Mandelieu-La Napoule
Tel. 93 49 95 11
18 rooms. View. Outdoor dining.

Ermitage du Riou $$$
06210 Mandelieu-La Napoule
Tel. 93 49 95 56; tlx. 470071
40 rooms. Pleasant hotel. View. Outdoor swimming pool. Garden. Outdoor dining. Lamparo restaurant.

Restaurants

Brocherie II $$
06210 Mandelieu-La Napoule
Tel. 93 49 80 73
View. Outdoor dining.

NICE

Hotels

Durante $
16 av. Durante
06000 Nice
Tel. 93 88 84 40
26 rooms. Quiet hotel. Garden. No restaurant.

Georges $
3 rue. H.-Cordier
06000 Nice
Tel. 93 86 23 41
18 rooms. Quiet situation. No restaurant.

Grand Hotel Aston $$
12 av. F.-Faure
06000 Nice
Tel. 93 80 62 52; tlx. 470290
157 rooms. Terrace on roof. Outdoor dining.

Harvey $
18 av. de Suède
06000 Nice
Tel. 93 88 73 73
58 rooms. No restaurant.

Méridien $$$
1 prom. des Anglais
06000 Nice
Tel. 93 82 25 25; tlx. 470361
297 rooms. View of the bay. Outdoor swimming pool on the roof. Outdoor dining.

Négresco $$$
37 prom. des Anglais
06000 Nice
Tel. 93 88 39 51; tlx. 460040
140 rooms. Pleasant, luxury hotel. View. 16th- and 18th-century, Empire, Napoleon III period rooms and public rooms. La Rotonde restaurant. Chantecler restaurant.

New York $
44 av. Mar.-Foch
06000 Nice
Tel. 93 92 04 19; tlx. 470215
52 rooms. No restaurant.

La Pérouse $$
11 quai Rauba-Capeu
06000 Nice
Tel. 93 62 34 63; tlx. 461411
63 rooms. Quiet hotel. View of Nice and the Promenade des Anglais. Outdoor swimming pool.

Plaza $$
12 av. Verdun
06000 Nice
Tel. 93 87 80 41; tlx. 460979
187 rooms. View. Terrace on roof.

Sofitel Splendid $$
50 bd Victor-Hugo
06000 Nice
Tel. 93 88 69 54; tlx. 460938
116 rooms. View over the town. Outdoor swimming pool on 8th floor.

Suisse $
15 quai Rauba-Capeu
06300 Nice
Tel. 93 62 33 00
40 rooms. View. No restaurant.

Victoria $$
33 bd V.-Hugo
06000 Nice
Tel. 93 88 39 60; tlx. 461337
39 rooms. Garden. No restaurant.

Restaurants

Ane Rouge $$$
7 quai Deux-Emmanuel
06300 Nice
Tel. 93 89 49 63
Notably good cuisine.

Bon Coin Breton $
5 rue Blacas
06000 Nice
Tel. 93 85 17 01

Chantecler $$$
37 prom. des Anglais
06000 Nice
Tel. 93 88 39 51
Excellent cuisine.

Les Dents de la Mer $$
2 rue St-François-de-Paule
06300 Nice
Tel. 93 80 99 16
Seafood specialities.

Florian $$
22 rue A.-Karr
06000 Nice
Tel. 93 88 86 60

Gérard Ferri $$
56 bd Jean-Jaurès
06000 Nice
Tel. 93 80 42 40

Gourmet Lorrain $$
7 av. Santa-Fior
06100 Nice
Tel. 93 84 90 78

Aux Gourmets $
12 rue Dante
06000 Nice
Tel. 93 96 83 53

La Merenda $
4 rue Terrasse
06300 Nice
Niçoise cuisine.

Rivoli $
9 rue Rivoli
06000 Nice
Tel. 93 88 12 62

PORT GRIMAUD

Hotels

Giraglia $$$
83310 Cogolin
Tel. 94 56 31 33; tlx. 470494
*48 rooms. Quiet hotel. View of
the bay. Outdoor swimming pool.
Beach with bathing facilities.
Outdoor dining.*

Restaurants

La Tartane $
83310 Cogolin
Tel. 94 56 38 32
Outdoor dining.

RAMATUELLE

Hotels

Le Baou $$
83350 Ramatuelle
Tel. 94 79 20 48; tlx. 462152
*35 rooms. Pleasant hotel in quiet
situation. Exceptional sea view.
Outdoor swimming pool. Outdoor
dining.*

ROQUEBRUNE-CAP-MARTIN

Hotels

Vista Palace $$$
Grande Corniche
06190 Roquebrune-Cap-Martin
Tel. 93 35 01 50; tlx. 461021
*60 rooms. Pleasant hotel. View
over Monaco. Outdoor swimming
pool. Garden.*

Westminster $
14 av. L.-Laurens
06190 Roquebrune-Cap-Martin
Tel. 93 35 00 68
31 rooms. View. Garden.

Restaurants

Au Grand Inquisiteur $
rue Château
06190 Roquebrune-Cap-Martin
Tel. 93 35 05 37
*Country-style interior. Reserva-
tion essential.*

Hippocampe $$$
av. W.-Churchill
06190 Roquebrune-Cap-Martin
Tel. 93 35 81 91

Notably good cuisine. View of the bay and coast. Outdoor dining. Reservation essential.

Roquebrune $$$
100 av. J.-Jaurès
06190 Roquebrune-Cap-Martin
Tel. 93 35 00 16
Notably good cuisine. View. Outdoor dining. Reservation essential.

ST-JEAN-CAP-FERRAT

Hotels

Brise Marine $$
av. J.-Mermoz
06230 St-Jean-Cap-Ferrat
Tel. 93 76 04 36
15 rooms. Quiet situation. View of the headland and bay. Garden. Outdoor dining.

Grand Hotel du Cap-Ferrat $$$
bd Gén.-de-Gaulle
06230 St-Jean-Cap-Ferrat
Tel. 93 76 00 21; tlx. 470184
60 rooms. Pleasant, luxury hotel in quiet situation. View. Large park. Hotel tennis court. Outdoor swimming pool beside the sea. Beach with bathing facilities. Private cable car. Outdoor dining. Le Faradol restaurant.

Voile d'Or $$$
06230 St-Jean-Cap-Ferrat
Tel. 93 01 13 13; tlx. 470317
50 rooms. Pleasant hotel in quiet situation. View of the port and bay. Outdoor swimming pool. Notably good cuisine. Outdoor dining.

Restaurants

Petit Trianon $$$
bd Gén.-de-Gaulle
06230 St-Jean-Cap-Ferrat
Tel. 93 76 05 06
Notably good cuisine. Pergola.

Le Sloop $$
06230 St-Jean-Cap-Ferrat
Tel. 93 01 48 63
View. Outdoor dining.

ST-PAUL

Hotels

Climat de France $
06570 St-Paul
Tel. 93 32 94 24
22 rooms. View. Outdoor swimming pool. Outdoor dining.

La Colombe d'Or $$
06570 St-Paul
Tel. 93 32 80 02; tlx. 970607
16 rooms. Pleasant hotel. Old-Provence style. Modern paintings. Outdoor swimming pool and Roman garden. Outdoor dining.

Le Hameau $
06570 St-Paul
Tel. 93 32 80 24
14 rooms. Pleasant hotel. View. Terraced garden. No restaurant.

Mas d'Artigny $$$
06570 St-Paul
Tel. 93 32 84 54; tlx. 470601
52 rooms. Luxury establishment in quiet situation. View. Outdoor swimming pool. Hotel tennis court. Park. Notably good cuisine.

13

Orangers $$
06570 St-Paul
Tel. 93 32 80 95
*9 rooms. Pleasant hotel in quiet
situation. View. Beautiful garden.
No restaurant.*

La Voile d'Or $$
1 bd Gén.-de-Gaulle
83700 St-Raphaël
Tel. 94 95 17 04
View.

ST-RAPHAËL

Hotels

La Chêneraie $
83700 St-Raphaël
Tel. 94 52 08 02
*10 rooms. Quiet situation. View.
Park. Outdoor dining.*

Golf Hotel de Valescure $$
close to Valescure golf course
83700 St-Raphaël
Tel. 94 82 40 31; tlx. 461085
*40 rooms. Pleasant hotel in quiet
situation. View. Park. Outdoor
swimming pool. Hotel tennis
courts. Outdoor dining.*

San Pedro $$
close to Valescure golf course
av. Colonel Brooke
83700 St-Raphaël
Tel. 94 52 10 24
*28 rooms. Pleasant hotel in quiet
situation. Park. Outdoor swimming pool.*

Restaurants

Pastorel $
54 rue Liberté
83700 St-Raphaël
Tel. 94 95 02 36

ST-TROPEZ

Hotels

Byblos $$$
av. P.-Signac
83990 St-Tropez
Tel. 94 97 00 04; tlx. 470235
*70 rooms. Quiet situation.
Richly furnished Provençal-style
establishment. View. Outdoor
swimming pool. Garden. Outdoor
dining. La Braiserie restaurant.*

Deï Marres $$
83350 Ramatuelle
Tel. 94 97 26 68
*25 rooms. Quiet situation. View.
Outdoor swimming pool. Garden.
Hotel tennis court. No restaurant.*

Lou Cagnard $
av. P.-Roussel
83990 St-Tropez
Tel. 94 97 04 24
*19 rooms. Quiet situation. Garden.
No restaurant.*

Lou Troupelen $
chemin des Vendanges
83990 St-Tropez
Tel. 94 97 44 88
*44 rooms. Quiet situation.
Garden. No restaurant.*

Mas de Chastelas $$$
83990 St-Tropez
Tel. 94 56 09 11; tlx. 462393
21 rooms. Pleasant hotel in quiet situation. View. Park. Old silkworm workshop among the vineyards. Outdoor swimming pool. Hotel tennis court. Outdoor dining.

Résidence de la Pinède $$$
83990 St-Tropez
Tel. 94 97 04 21; tlx. 470489
40 rooms. Pleasant hotel in quiet situation. View. Outdoor swimming pool. Beach with bathing facilities. Outdoor dining.

La Tartane $$
rte des Salins
83990 St-Tropez
Tel. 94 97 21 23
12 rooms. Quiet situation. View. Pleasant garden. Outdoor swimming pool.

Restaurants

Bistrot des Lices $$
3 place des Lices
83990 St-Tropez
Tel. 94 97 29 00
Outdoor dining.

Le Chabichou $$$
av. Foch
83990 St-Tropez
Tel. 94 54 80 00
Pleasant restaurant with notably good cuisine.

Le Girelier $$
83990 St-Tropez
Tel. 94 97 03 87
View. Outdoor dining.

Laetitia-La Frégate $
52 rue Allard
89330 St-Tropez
Tel. 94 97 04 02
Outdoor dining.

Leï Mouscardïn $$$
83990 St-Tropez
Tel. 94 97 01 53
View of the bay.

STE-MAXIME

Hotels

Belle Aurore $$$
La Croisette
83120 Ste-Maxime
Tel. 94 96 02 45
17 rooms. On seafront. View. Beach with bathing facilities. Outdoor swimming pool.

Calidianus $
83120 Ste-Maxime
Tel. 94 96 23 21
27 rooms. Pleasant hotel in quiet situation. View. Outdoor swimming pool. Garden. Hotel tennis court. No restaurant.

«Croisette» Résidence $
bd Romarins
83120 Ste-Maxime
Tel. 94 96 17 75
20 rooms. Quiet situation. View. Garden. No restaurant.

Poste $$
7 bd F.-Mistral
83120 Ste-Maxime
Tel. 94 96 18 33
24 rooms. Outdoor swimming pool. Outdoor dining.

Le Revest $
48 av. J.-Jaurès
83120 Ste-Maxime
Tel. 94 96 19 60
*26 rooms. Outdoor swimming
pool.*

Restaurants

L'Esquinade $$
83120 Ste-Maxime
Tel. 94 96 01 65
*Outdoor dining. Seafood speciali-
ties.*

La Gruppi $
av. Ch.-de-Gaulle
83120 Ste-Maxime
Tel. 94 96 03 61
*View. Outdoor dining. Seafood
specialities.*

Sans Souci $
rue Paul-Bert
83120 Ste-Maxime
Tel. 94 96 18 26
Outdoor dining.

VENCE

Hotels

**Château du Domaine
St-Martin $$$**
06140 Vence
Tel. 93 58 02 02; tlx. 470282
*15 rooms. Pleasant, luxury hotel
in quiet situation. View of Vence
and coastline. Park. Outdoor
swimming pool. Hotel tennis
court. Outdoor dining.*

Floréal $
440 av. Rhin et Danube
06140 Vence
Tel. 93 58 64 40; tlx. 461613
*43 rooms. Outdoor swimming
pool. Garden. No restaurant.*

Miramar $
plateau St-Michel
06140 Vence
Tel. 93 58 01 32
*17 rooms. Quiet situation. View.
Garden. No restaurant.*

VILLEFRANCHE

Hotels

Vauban $$
11 av. Gén.-de-Gaulle
06230 Villefranche
Tel. 93 01 71 20
*12 rooms. Louis XV decor.
Pleasant garden. No restaurant.*

Versailles $$
av. Princesse-Grace
06230 Villefranche
Tel. 93 01 89 56; tlx. 970433
*43 rooms. View of the roadstead.
Outdoor swimming pool. Outdoor
dining.*

Restaurants

Le Massoury $$$
av. Léopold II
06230 Villefranche
Tel. 93 01 03 66
*Pleasant restaurant. View of the
roadstead. Outdoor dining.*

Say BERLITZ®

... and most people think of outstanding language schools. But Berlitz has also become the world's leading publisher of books for travellers – Travel Guides, Phrase Books, Dictionaries – plus Cassettes and Self-teaching courses.

Informative, accurate, up-to-date, Books from Berlitz are written with freshness and style. They also slip easily into pocket or purse – no need for bulky, old-fashioned volumes.

Join the millions who know how to travel. Whether for fun or business, put Berlitz in your pocket.

BERLITZ®

Leader in
Books and Cassettes
for Travellers

A Macmillan Company

BERLITZ® Books for travellers

TRAVEL GUIDES

They fit your pocket in both size and price. Modern, up-to-date, Berlitz gets all the information you need into 128 lively pages with colour maps and photos throughout. What to see and do, where to shop, what to eat and drink, how to save.

ASIA, MIDDLE EAST	China (256 pages) Hong Kong India (256 pages) Japan (256 pages) Nepal* Singapore Sri Lanka Thailand Egypt Jerusalem and the Holy Land Saudi Arabia
AUSTRAL-ASIA	Australia (256 pages) New Zealand
BRITISH ISLES	Channel Islands London Ireland Oxford and Stratford Scotland
BELGIUM	Brussels

AFRICA   Kenya
Morocco
South Africa
Tunisia

*in preparation

PHRASE BOOKS

World's bestselling phrase books feature all the expressions and vocabulary you'll need, and pronunciation throughout. 192 pages, 2 colours.

Arabic	Hebrew	Russian
Chinese	Hungarian	Serbo-Croatian
Danish	Italian	Spanish (Castilian)
Dutch	Japanese	Spanish (Lat. Am.)
Finnish	Korean	Swahili
French	Norwegian	Swedish
German	Polish	Turkish
Greek	Portuguese	European Phrase Book
		European Menu Reader

FRANCE	Brittany			Costa Brava
	France (256 pages)			Costa del Sol and Andalusia
	French Riviera			Ibiza and Formentera
	Loire Valley			Madrid
	Normandy			Majorca and Minorca
	Paris		EASTERN	Budapest
GERMANY	Berlin		EUROPE	Dubrovnik and Southern
	Munich			Dalmatia
	The Rhine Valley			Hungary (192 pages)
AUSTRIA	Tyrol			Istria and Croatian Coast
and	Vienna			Moscow & Leningrad
SWITZER-	Switzerland (192 pages)			Split and Dalmatia
LAND				Yugoslavia (256 pages)
GREECE,	Athens		NORTH	U.S.A. (256 pages)
CYPRUS &	Corfu		AMERICA	California
TURKEY	Crete			Florida
	Rhodes			Hawaii
	Greek Islands of the Aegean			Miami
	Peloponnese			New York
	Salonica and Northern Greece			Canada (256 pages)
	Cyprus			Toronto
	Istanbul/Aegean Coast			Montreal
	Turkey (192 pages)		CARIBBEAN,	Puerto Rico
ITALY and	Florence		LATIN	Virgin Islands
MALTA	Italian Adriatic		AMERICA	Bahamas
	Italian Riviera			Bermuda
	Italy (256 pages)			French West Indies
	Rome			Jamaica
	Sicily			Southern Caribbean
	Venice			Mexico City
	Malta			Brazil (Highlights of)
NETHER-	Amsterdam			Rio de Janeiro
LANDS and	Copenhagen		EUROPE	Business Travel Guide –
SCANDI-	Helsinki			Europe (368 pages)
NAVIA	Oslo and Bergen			Pocket guide to Europe
	Stockholm			(480 pages)
PORTUGAL	Algarve			Cities of Europe (504 pages)
	Lisbon		CRUISE	Caribbean cruise guide
	Madeira		GUIDES	(368 pages)
SPAIN	Barcelona and Costa Dorada			Alaska cruise guide (168 p.)
	Canary Islands			Handbook to Cruising (240 p.)
	Costa Blanca			

Most titles with British and U.S. destinations are available in French, German, Spanish and as many as 7 other languages.

DICTIONARIES

Bilingual with 12,500 concepts each way. Highly practical for travellers, with pronunciation shown plus menu reader, basic expressions and useful information. Over 330 pages.

Danish	Finnish	German	Norwegian	Spanish
Dutch	French	Italian	Portuguese	Swedish

Berlitz Books, a world of information in your pocket!
At all leading bookshops and airport newsstands.

BERLITZ CASSETTEPAKS

Together in one set, a phrase book and a hi-fi cassette.
Here are just those expressions you need for your trip,
plus a chance to improve your accent. Simply listen and
repeat! Available in 24 different languages.
Each cassettepak includes a script giving tips on pronunciation and the complete text of the dual-language
recording.

The most popular Berlitz cassettepaks have been completely revised and brought up to date with a 90-minute
cassette and a newly revised phrase book containing a
2000 word dictionary, plus expanded colour coding
and menu reader.

BERLITZ® GOES VIDEO – *FOR LANGUAGES*

Here's a brand new 90-minute video from Berlitz for learning key words and phrases for your trip. It's easy and fun. Berlitz language video combines computer graphics with live action and freeze frames. You see on your own TV screen the type of dialogue you will encounter abroad. You practice conversation by responding to questions put to you in the privacy of your own living room.

Shot on location for accuracy and realism, Berlitz gently leads you through travel situations towards language proficiency. Available from video stores and selected bookstores and Berlitz Language Centers everywhere.

To order by credit card, call 1-800-228-2028 Ext. 35.
Coming soon to the U.K.

BERLITZ®
GUIDES

BERLITZ® GOES VIDEO – *FOR TRAVEL*

Travel Tips from Berlitz – now an invaluable part of the informative and colourful videocassette series of more than 50 popular destinations produced by Travelview International. Ideal for planning a trip or as a souvenir of your visit, Travelview videos provide 40 to 60 minutes of valuable information including a destination briefing, a Reference Guide to local hotels and tourist attractions plus practical Travel Tips from Berlitz.

Available from leading travel agencies and video stores everywhere in the U.S.A. and Canada or call 1-800-325-3108 (Texas, call (713) 975-7077; 1-800 661 9269 in Canada). Coming soon to the U.K.

Travelview
INTERNATIONAL
5630 Beverly Hill
Houston, Texas 77057

BERLITZ® NEW, REVISED!

FRENCH
for travellers

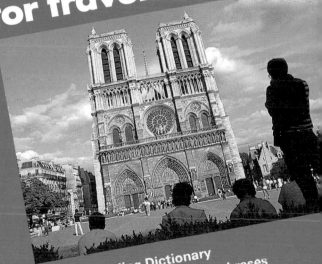

- Now including Dictionary
- 2400 useful words – 1200 phrases
- World's bestselling Phrase Book series

Quick reference page *Expressions indispensables*

Good morning/Good afternoon.	**Bonjour.**	bawngzhoor
Please ...	**S'il vous plaît ...**	seel voo pleh
Thank you.	**Merci.**	mehrssee
Yes/No.	**Oui/Non.**	wee/nawng
Excuse me.	**Excusez-moi.**	ehkkewzay mwah
Do you speak English?	**Parlez-vous anglais?**	pahrlay voo ahnggleh
Where can I find/ buy/hire (rent) ...?	**Où puis-je trouver/ acheter/louer ...?**	oo pweezh troovay/ ahshertay/looay
Where is ...?	**Où est ...?**	oo eh
How far?	**A quelle distance?**	ah kehl deestahngss
How long?	**Combien de temps?**	kawngbyang der tahng
How much is it?	**Combien est-ce?**	kawngbyang ehss
Waiter/Waitress, please.	**Garçon/Mademoi- selle, s'il vous plaît!**	gahrsawng/mahdmwahzehl seel voo pleh
I'd like ...	**Je voudrais ...**	zher voodreh
What does this mean?	**Que veut dire ceci?**	ker vur deer serssee
I don't understand.	**Je ne comprends pas.**	zher ner kwangprahng pah
When does ... open/ close?	**A quelle heure ouvre/ferme ...?**	ah kehl urr oovr/fehrm
What time is it?	**Quelle heure est-il?**	kehl urr ehteel
Do you mind if I smoke?	**Est-ce que ça vous dérange que je fume?**	ehss ker sah voo day- rahngzh ker zher fewm
Would you mind not smoking, please.	**Pouvez-vous renon- cer à fumer, s'il vous plaît.**	poovay voo rernawngssay ah fewmay seel voo pleh.
It's not permitted here.	**C'est interdit ici.**	seh angtehrdee eessee
Where are the toilets?	**Où sont les toilettes?**	oo sawng lay twahleht
Help me, please.	**Aidez-moi, s'il vous plaît.**	ehday mwah seel voo pleh
Where is the ... consulate?	**Où est le consulat ...?**	oo eh ler kawngsewlah
American British Canadian	**américain britannique canadien**	ahmayreekang breetahneek kahnahdyang

BERLITZ®

FRENCH
for travellers

By the staff of Berlitz Guides

How best to use this phrase book

● We suggest that you start with the **Guide to pronunciation** (pp. 6–9), then go on to **Some basic expressions** (pp. 10–15). This gives you not only a minimum vocabulary, but also helps you get used to pronouncing the language. The phonetic transcription throughout the book enables you to pronounce every word correctly.

● Consult the **Contents** pages (3–5) for the section you need. In each chapter you'll find travel facts, hints and useful information. Simple phrases are followed by a list of words applicable to the situation.

● Separate, detailed contents lists are included at the beginning of the extensive **Eating out** and **Shopping guide** sections (Menus, p. 39, Shops and services, p. 97).

● If you want to find out how to say something in French, your fastest look-up is via the **Dictionary** section (pp. 164–189). This not only gives you the word, but is also cross-referenced to its use in a phrase on a specific page.

● If you wish to learn more about constructing sentences, check the **Basic grammar** (pp. 159–163).

● Note the **colour margins** are indexed in French and English to help both listener and speaker. And, in addition, there is also an **index in French** for the use of your listener.

● Throughout the book, this symbol ☛ suggests phrases your listener can use to answer you. If you still can't understand, hand this phrase book to the French-speaker to encourage pointing to an appropriate answer. The English translation for you is just alongside the French.

Contents

4

Acknowledgments
We are particularly grateful to Gérard Chaillon for his help in the preparation of this book, and to Dr. T.J.A. Bennett who devised the phonetic transcription

Guide to pronunciation

This and the following chapter are intended to make you familiar with the phonetic transcription we devised and to help you get used to the sounds of French.

As a minimum vocabulary for your trip, we've selected a number of basic words and phrases under the title "Some basic expressions" (pages 10–15).

An outline of the spelling and sounds of French

You'll find the pronunciation of the French letters and sounds explained below, as well as the symbols we're using for them in the transcriptions. Note that French has some diacritical marks—accents on letters, the cedilla—which we don't have in English.

The imitated pronunciation should be read as if it were English except for any special rules set out below. It is based on Standard British pronunciation, though we have tried to take into account General American pronunciation as well. Of course, the sounds of any two languages are never exactly the same; but if you follow carefully the indications supplied here, you'll have no difficulty in reading our transcriptions in such a way as to make yourself understood.

Consonants

Letter	Approximate pronunciation	Symbol	Example
b, c, d, f, k, l, m, n, p, s, t, v, x, z	as in English		
ch	like **sh** in **shut**	sh	**chercher** shehrshay

ç	like s in sit	s	**ça**	sah
g	1) before **e, i, y,** like s in pleasure	zh	**manger**	mahngzhay
	2) before **a, o, u,** like g in **go**	g	**garçon**	gahrsawng
gn	like **ni** in onion	ñ	**ligne**	leeñ
h	always silent		**homme**	om
j	like s in pleasure	zh	**jamais**	zhahmeh
qu	like k in kill	k	**qui**	kee
r	rolled in the back of the mouth, rather like gargling	r	**rouge**	roozh
w	usually like v in voice	v	**wagon**	vahgawng

Vowels

a, à or **â**	between the **a** in hat and the **a** in father	ah	**mari**	mahree
é, er, ez	like **a** in late, but a pure vowel, not a diphthong	ay	**été**	aytay
è, ê, e	like **e** in get	eh	**même**	mehm
e	sometimes (when at the end of a syllable or of a one-syllable word), like **er** in other (quite short)	er*	**je**	zher
i	like **ee** in meet	ee	**il**	eel
o	generally like **o** in hot but sometimes like **o** in wrote	o/ oa	**donner** **rose**	donnay roaz
ô	like **o** in wrote	oa	**Rhône**	roan
u	no equivalent in English. Round your lips and try to say **ee**; this should sound more or less correct	ew	**cru**	krew

---

* The **r** should not be pronounced when reading this transcription.

Sounds spelt with two or more letters

ai, ay	can be pronounced as **a** in late	ay	**j'ai**	zhay
aient, ais, ait, aî	like **e** in get	eh	**chaîne**	shehn
(e)au	similar to **o** in wrote	oa	**chaud**	shoa
ei	like **e** in get	eh	**peine**	pehn
eu	like **ur** in fur, but with lips rounded, not spread	ur*	**peu**	pur
oi	like **w** followed by the **a** in hat	wah	**moi**	mwah
ou	like **oo** in look	oo	**nouveau**	noovoa
ui	approximately like **wee** in between	wee	**traduire**	trahdweer

Nasal sounds

The following sounds are pronounced through the mouth and the nose at the same time.

an	something like **arn** in tarnish	ahng	**tante**	tahngt
en	generally like the previous sound	ahng	**enchanté**	ahngshahngtay
ien	sounds like **yan** in yank	yang	**bien**	byang
in, ain	approximately like **ang** in rang	ang	**instant**	angstahng
on	approximately like **ong** in song	awng	**maison**	mayzawng
un	approximately like **ang** in rang	ang	**brun**	brang

---

* The **r** should not be pronounced when reading this transcription.

Liaison

Normally, the final consonants are not pronounced in French. However, when a word ending in a consonant is followed by one beginning with a vowel, they are often run together, and the consonant is pronounced as if it began the following word. For instance, **nous** *(we)* is pronounced **noo**, but, in the sentence **"Nous avons un enfant"** *(We have a child)*, the **s** of **nous** is pronounced, and the sentence sounds something like: **noo zahvawng zang nahngfahng**. Another example: **"comment"** is pronounced **kommahng**, but the **t** is pronounced in **"Comment allez-vous?"** *(How are you)*, which sounds something like: **kommahng tahlay voo.**

Stress

Unlike English, all syllables in French have more or less the same degree of stress (loudness), although in some short and common words the vowel "e" tends to be pronounced only very weakly. For French ears, there is a slightly heavier stress on the last syllable of a word-group, but as this is a fine distinction, stress has not been indicated in the transcription of this book. Each syllable should be pronounced with equal stress.

Pronunciation of the French alphabet							
A	ah	**H**	ahsh	**O**	oa	**V**	vay
B	bay	**I**	ee	**P**	pay	**W**	doobler vay
C	say	**J**	zhee	**Q**	kew	**X**	eex
D	day	**K**	kah	**R**	ehr	**Y**	ee grehk
E	er	**L**	ehl	**S**	ehss	**Z**	zehd
F	ehf	**M**	ehm	**T**	tay		
G	zhay	**N**	ehn	**U**	ew		

Some basic expressions

Yes.	**Oui.**	wee
No.	**Non.**	nawng
Please.	**S'il vous plaît.**	seel voo pleh
Thank you.	**Merci.**	mehrsee
Thank you very much.	**Merci beaucoup.**	mehrsee boakoo
You're welcome.	**De rien.**	der ryang
That's all right/ Don't mention it.	**Il n'y a pas de quoi.**	eel nee ah pah der kwah

Greetings *Salutations*

Good morning.	**Bonjour.**	bawngzhoor
Good afternoon.	**Bonjour.**	bawngzhoor
Good evening.	**Bonsoir.**	bawngsswahr
Good night.	**Bonne nuit.**	bon nwee
Good-bye.	**Au revoir.**	oa rervwahr
See you later.	**A tout à l'heure.**	ah too tah lurr
This is Mr./Mrs./ Miss ...	**Je vous présente Monsieur/Madame/ Mademoiselle ...**	zher voo prayzahngt mursyur/mahdahm/ mahdmwahzehl
How do you do? (Pleased to meet you.)	**Enchanté(e).***	ahngshahngtay
How are you?	**Comment allez-vous?**	kommahng tahlay voo
Very well, thanks. And you?	**Très bien, merci. Et vous?**	treh byang mehrsee. ay voo

---

* The final -e in the written form shows that the writer is a woman. Pronunciation remains the same, however, whether the speaker is a man or a woman.

How's life?	**Comment ça va?**	kommahng sah vah
Fine.	**Bien.**	byang
I beg your pardon?	**Pardon?**	pahrdawng
Excuse me. (May I get past?)	**Excusez-moi!/ Pardon!**	ehxkewzay mwah/ pahrdawng
Sorry!	**Désolé(e).**	dayzolay

Questions   *Questions*

Where?	**Où?**	oo
How?	**Comment?**	kommahng
When?	**Quand?**	kahng
What?	**Quoi?**	kwah
Why?	**Pourquoi?**	poorkwah
Who?	**Qui?**	kee
Which?	**Lequel/Laquelle?**	lerkehl/lahkehl
Where is ...?	**Où est/ Où se trouve ...?**	oo eh/oo ser troov
Where are ...?	**Où sont/ Où se trouvent ...?**	oo sawng/oo ser troov
Where can I find/ get ...?	**Où puis-je trouver ...?**	oo pweezh troovay
How far?	**A quelle distance?**	ah kehl deestahngss
How long?	**Combien de temps?**	kawngbyang der tahng
How much/ How many?	**Combien?**	kawngbyang
How much does this cost?	**Combien coûte ceci?**	kawngbyang koot serssee
When does ... open/ close?	**A quelle heure ouvre/ ferme ...?**	ah kehl urr oovr/fehrm
What do you call this/that in French?	**Comment appelle-t-on ceci/cela en français?**	kommahng tahpehl tawng serssee/serlah ahng frahngsseh
What does this/that mean?	**Que veut dire ceci/ cela?**	ker vur deer serssee/ serlah

Do you speak ...? *Parlez-vous ...?*

Do you speak English?	**Parlez-vous anglais?**	pahrlay voo ahnggleh
Is there anyone here who speaks English?	**Y a-t-il quelqu'un qui parle anglais ici?**	ee ahteel kehlkang kee pahrl ahnggleh eessee
I don't speak (much) French.	**Je ne parle pas (bien) français.**	zher ner pahrl pah (byang) frahngsseh
Could you speak more slowly?	**Pourriez-vous parler plus lentement?**	pooryay voo pahrlay plew lahngtermahng
Could you repeat that?	**Pourriez-vous répéter?**	pooryay voo raypaytay
Could you spell it?	**Pourriez-vous me l'épeler?**	pooryay voo mer layperlay
Please write it down.	**Ecrivez-le, s'il vous plaît.**	aykreevay ler seel voo pleh
Can you translate this for me?	**Pouvez-vous me traduire ceci?**	poovay voo mer trahdweer serssee
Can you translate this for us?	**Pouvez-vous nous traduire ceci?**	poovay voo noo trahdweer serssee
Please point to the word/phrase/sentence in the book.	**Montrez-moi le mot/l'expression/la phrase dans ce livre, s'il vous plaît.**	mawngtray mwah ler moa/lehprehssyawng/lah frahz dahng ler leevr seel voo pleh
Just a minute. I'll see if I can find it in this book.	**Un instant. Je vais voir si je la trouve dans ce livre.**	ang nangstahng. zher vay vwahr see zher lah troov dahng ser leevr
I understand.	**Je comprends.**	zher kawngprahng
I don't understand.	**Je ne comprends pas.**	zher ner kawngprahng pah
Do you understand?	**Comprenez-vous?**	kawngprernay voo

Can/May ...? *Puis-je ...?*

Can I have ...?	**Puis-je avoir ...?**	pweezh ahvwahr
Can we have ...?	**Pouvons-nous avoir ...?**	poovawng noo ahvwahr
Can you show me ...?	**Pouvez-vous m'indiquer ...?**	poovay voo mangdeekay

I can't.	**Je ne peux pas.**	zher ner pur pah
Can you tell me...?	**Pouvez-vous me dire ...?**	poovay voo mer deer
Can you help me?	**Pouvez-vous m'aider?**	poovay voo mehday
Can I help you?	**Puis-je vous aider?**	pweezh voo zehday
Can you direct me to ...?	**Pouvez-vous m'indiquer la direction de ...?**	poovay voo mangdeekay lah deerehkssyawng der

Wanting ... *Je voudrais ...*

I'd like ...	**Je voudrais ...**	zher voodreh
We'd like ...	**Nous voudrions ...**	noo voodreeyawng
What do you want?	**Que désirez-vous?**	ker dayzeeray voo
Give me ...	**Donnez-moi ...**	donnay mwah
Give it to me.	**Donnez-le-moi.**	donnay ler mwah
Bring me ...	**Apportez-moi ...**	ahportay mwah
Bring it to me.	**Apportez-le-moi.**	ahportay ler mwah
Show me ...	**Montrez-moi ...**	mawngtray mwah
Show it to me.	**Montrez-le-moi.**	mawngtray ler mwah
I'm looking for ...	**Je cherche ...**	zher shehrsh
I'm hungry.	**J'ai faim.**	zhay fang
I'm thirsty.	**J'ai soif.**	zhay swahf
I'm tired.	**Je suis fatigué(e).**	zher swee fahteegay
I'm lost.	**Je me suis perdu(e).**	zher mer swee pehrdew
It's important.	**C'est important.**	seh tangportahng
It's urgent.	**C'est urgent.**	seh tewrzhahng
Hurry up!	**Dépêchez-vous.**	daypehshay voo

It is/There is ... *C'est/Il y a ...*

It is ...	**C'est ...**	seh
Is it ...?	**Est-ce ...?**	ehss
It isn't ...	**Ce n'est pas ...**	ser neh pah

Here it is.	**Le voici/La voici.**	ler vwahssee/lah vwahssee
Here they are.	**Les voici.**	lay vwahssee
There it is.	**Le voilà/La voilà.**	ler vwahlah/lah vwahlah
There they are.	**Les voilà.**	lay vwahlah
There is/There are ...	**Il y a ...**	eel ee ah
Is there/Are there ...?	**Y a-t-il ...?**	ee ahteel
There isn't/aren't ...	**Il n'y a pas ...**	eel nee ah pah
There isn't/aren't any.	**Il n'y en a pas.**	eel nee ahng nah pah

It's ...   *C'est ...*

big/small	**grand/petit***	grahng/pertee
quick/slow	**rapide/lent**	rahpeed/lahng
hot/cold	**chaud/froid**	shoa/frwah
full/empty	**plein/vide**	plang/veed
easy/difficult	**facile/difficile**	fahsseel/deefeesseel
heavy/light	**lourd/léger**	loor/layzhay
open/shut	**ouvert/fermé**	oovehr/fehrmay
right/wrong	**juste/faux**	zhewst/foa
old/new	**ancien/nouveau (nouvelle)**	ahngssyang/noovoa (noovehl)
old/young	**vieux (vieille)/jeune**	vyur (vyehy)/zhurn
next/last	**prochain/dernier**	proshang/dehrnyay
beautiful/ugly	**beau (belle)/laid**	boa (behl)/leh
free (vacant)/ occupied	**libre/occupé**	leebr/okkewpay
good/bad	**bon/mauvais**	bawng/moaveh
better/worse	**meilleur/pire**	mehyurr/peer
early/late	**tôt/tard**	toa/tahr
cheap/expensive	**bon marché/cher**	bawng mahrshay/shehr
near/far	**près/loin**	preh/lwang
here/there	**ici/là**	eessee/lah

Quantities   *Quantités*

a little/a lot	**un peu/beaucoup**	ang pur/boakoo
few/a few	**peu de/quelques**	pur der/kehlker
much	**beaucoup**	boakoo

---

* For feminine and plural forms, see grammar section page 160 (adjectives).

many	**beaucoup de**	boakoo der
more/less	**plus/moins**	plew(ss)/mwang
more than/less than	**plus que/moins que**	plewss ker/mwang ker
enough/too	**assez/trop**	ahssay/troa
some/any	**de, de la, du, des**	der der lah dew day

A few more useful words   *Autres mots utiles*

at	**à**	ah
on	**sur**	sewr
in	**dans**	dahng
to	**à**	ah
after	**après**	ahpreh
before (time)	**avant**	ahvahng
before (place)	**devant**	dervahng
for	**pour**	poor
from	**de**	der
with/without	**avec/sans**	ahvehk/sahng
through	**à travers**	ah trahvehr
towards	**vers**	vehr
until	**jusqu'à**	zhewskah
during	**pendant**	pahngdahng
next to	**à côté de**	ah koatay der
near	**près de**	preh der
behind	**derrière**	dehryehr
between	**entre**	ahngtr
since	**depuis**	derpwee
above	**au-dessus (de)**	oa derssew (der)
below	**au-dessous (de)**	oa derssoo (der)
under	**sous**	soo
inside/outside	**dedans/dehors**	derdahng/deror
up/upstairs	**en haut**	ahng oa
down/downstairs	**en bas**	ahng bah
and	**et**	ay
or	**ou**	oo
not	**ne ... pas**	ner ... pah
never	**ne ... jamais**	ner ... zhahmeh
nothing	**rien**	ryang
none	**aucun, aucune**	oakang oakewn
very	**très**	treh
too (also)	**aussi**	oassee
yet	**encore**	ahngkor
soon	**bientôt**	byangtoa
now	**maintenant**	mangternahng
then	**ensuite**	ahngssweet
perhaps	**peut-être**	purtehtr

Arrival

CONTRÔLE DES PASSEPORTS
PASSPORT CONTROL

Here's my passport.	**Voici mon passeport.**	vwahssee mawng pahsspor
I'll be staying ...	**Je resterai ...**	zher rehsterray
a few days	**quelques jours**	kehlker zhoor
a week	**une semaine**	ewn sermehn
a month	**un mois**	ang mwah
I don't know yet.	**Je ne sais pas encore.**	zher ner seh pah zahngkor
I'm here on holiday.	**Je suis en vacances.**	zher swee zahng vahkahngss
I'm here on business.	**Je suis en voyage d'affaires.**	zher swee zahng vwahyahzh dahfehr
I'm just passing through.	**Je suis de passage.**	zher swee der pahssahzh

If things become difficult:

I'm sorry, I don't understand.	**Excusez-moi, je ne comprends pas.**	ehxkewzay mwah zher ner kawngprahng pah
Is there anyone here who speaks English?	**Y a-t-il quelqu'un qui parle anglais?**	ee ahteel kehlkang kee pahrl ahnggleh

---

DOUANE
CUSTOMS

After collecting your baggage at the airport (*l'aéroport* – lahayropor) you have a choice: follow the green arrow if you have nothing to declare. Or leave via a doorway marked with a red arrow if you have items to declare.

articles à déclarer
goods to declare

rien à déclarer
nothing to declare

The chart below shows what you can bring in duty-free (visitors from overseas are allowed greater concessions as regards duty-free cigarettes and tobacco).*

	Cigarettes	Cigars	Tobacco	Spirits (liquor)	Wine
France ⎱ Belgium ⎰	¹300 or ²200 or	75 or 50 or	400 gr. 250 gr.	1 ½ l. and 1 l. and	5 l. 2 l.
Switzerland	200 or	50 or	250 gr.	1 l. and	2 l.

¹Visitors arriving from EEC countries with non-tax-free items
²Visitors arriving from EEC countries with tax-free items

I've nothing to declare.	Je n'ai rien à déclarer.	zher nay ryang nah dayklahray
I've ...	J'ai ...	zhay
a carton of cigarettes	une cartouche de cigarettes	ewn kahrtoosh der seegahreht
a bottle of whisky	une bouteille de whisky	ewn bootehy der whisky
It's for my personal use.	C'est pour mon usage personnel.	seh poor mawng newzahzh pehrsonnehl

---

Votre passeport, s'il vous plaît.	Your passport, please.
Avez-vous quelque chose à déclarer?	Do you have anything to declare?
Pouvez-vous ouvrir ce sac?	Please open this bag.
Il y a des droits de douane sur cet article.	You'll have to pay duty on this.
Avez-vous d'autres bagages?	Do you have any more luggage?

---

* All allowances subject to change without notice.

Baggage—Porter *Bagages – Porteur*

These days porters are only available at airports or the railway stations of large cities. Where no porters are available you'll find luggage trolleys for the use of the passengers.

Porter!	**Porteur!**	porturr
Please take (this/my) ...	**Prenez ..., s'il vous plaît.**	prernay ... seel voo pleh
luggage	**mes bagages**	may bahgahzh
suitcase	**ma valise**	mah vahleez
(travelling) bag	**mon sac (de voyage)**	mawng sahk (der vwahyahzh)
That's mine.	**C'est à moi.**	seh tah mwah
Take this luggage ...	**Portez ces bagages ...**	portay say bahgahzh
to the bus	**à l'arrêt du bus**	ah lahreh dew bewss
to the luggage lockers	**à la consigne automatique**	ah lah kawngseeñ oatomahteek
How much is that?	**C'est combien?**	seh kawngbyang
There's one piece missing.	**Il en manque un/une.**	eel ahng mahngk ang/ewn
Where are the luggage trolleys (carts)?	**Où sont les chariots à bagages?**	oo sawng lay shahryoa ah bahgahzh

Changing money *Change*

Where's the currency exchange office?	**Où se trouve le bureau de change?**	oo ser troov ler bewroa der shahngzh
Can you change these traveller's cheques (checks)?	**Pouvez-vous changer ces chèques de voyage?**	poovay voo shahngzhay say shehk der vwahyahzh
I want to change some dollars/pounds.	**Je voudrais changer des dollars/livres.**	zher voodreh shahngzhay day dollahr/leevr
Can you change this into ...?	**Pouvez-vous changer ceci en ...?**	poovay voo shahngszhay serssee ahng
Belgian francs	**francs belges**	frahng behlzh
French francs	**francs français**	frahng frahngsseh
Swiss francs	**francs suisses**	frahng sweess
What's the exchange rate?	**Quel est le cours du change?**	kehl eh ler koor dew shahngzh

BANK – CURRENCY, see page 129

Where is ...?   *Où est ...?*

Where is the ...?	**Où est ...?**	oo eh
booking office	**le bureau de réservation**	ler bewroa der rayzehrvahssyawng
car hire	**l'agence de location de voitures**	lahzhahngss der lokahssyawng der vwahtewr
duty-free shop	**le magasin hors-taxe**	ler mahgahzang or tahks
newsstand	**le kiosque à journaux**	ler kyosk ah zhoornoa
restaurant	**le restaurant**	ler rehstoarahng
How do I get to ...?	**Comment puis-je aller à ...?**	kommahng pweezh ahlay ah
Is there a bus into town?	**Y a-t-il un bus pour aller en ville?**	ee ahteel ang bewss poor ahlay ahng veel
Where can I get a taxi?	**Où puis-je trouver un taxi?**	oo pweezh troovay ang taxi
Where can I hire a car?	**Où puis-je louer une voiture?**	oo pweezh looay ewn vwahtewr

Hotel reservation   *Réservation d'hôtel*

Do you have a hotel guide?	**Avez-vous un guide des hôtels?**	ahvay voo ang geed day zoatehl
Could you reserve a room for me at a hotel/boarding house?	**Pourriez-vous me réserver une chambre dans un hôtel/une pension?**	pooryay voo mer rayzehrvay ewn shahngbr dahng zang noatehl/zewn pahngssyawng
in the centre	**dans le centre**	dahng ler sahngtr
near the railway station	**près de la gare**	preh der lah gahr
a single room	**une chambre pour une personne**	ewn shahngbr poor ewn pehrson
a double room	**une chambre pour deux personnes**	ewn shahngbr poor dur pehrson
not too expensive	**pas trop chère**	pah troa shehr
Where is the hotel/boarding house?	**Où est l'hôtel/la pension?**	oo eh loatehl/lah pahngssyawng
Do you have a street map?	**Avez-vous un plan de ville?**	ahvay voo ang plahng der veel

HOTEL/ACCOMMODATION, see page 22

Car hire (rental) *Location de voitures*

To hire a car you must produce a valid driving licence (held for at least one year) and your passport. Some firms set a minimum age at 21, other 25. Holders of major credit cards are normally exempt from deposit payments, otherwise you must pay a substantial (refundable) deposit for a car. Third-party insurance is usually automatically included.

I'd like to hire (rent) a car.	**Je voudrais louer une voiture.**	zher voodreh looay ewn vwahtewr
small car	**une petite voiture**	ewn perteet vwahtewr
medium-sized car	**une voiture moyenne**	ewn vwahtewr mwahyehn
large car	**une grande voiture**	ewn grahngd vwahtewr
automatic car	**une voiture automatique**	ewn vwahtewr oatomahteek
I'd like it for a day/ a week.	**Je l'utiliserai un jour/ une semaine.**	zher lewteeleezerray ang zhoor/ewn sermehn
Are there any week-end arrangements?	**Existe-t-il des forfaits de fin de semaine?**	ehxeest teel day forfeh der fang der sermehn
Do you have any special rates?	**Proposez-vous des tarifs spéciaux?**	propoazay voo day tahreef spayssyoa
What's the charge per day/week?	**Quel est le tarif par jour/semaine?**	kehl eh ler tahreef pahr zhoor/sermehn
Is mileage included?	**Le kilométrage est-il compris?**	ler keeloamehtrahzh ehteel kawngpree
What's the charge per kilometre?	**Quel est le tarif par kilomètre?**	kehl eh ler tahreef pahr keeloamehtr
I want to hire the car here and leave it in ...	**Je voudrais prendre la voiture ici et la rendre à ...**	zher voodreh prahngdr lah vwahtewr eessee ay lah rahngdr ah
I want full insurance.	**Je voudrais une assurance tous risques.**	zher voodreh zewn ahssewrahngss too reesk
What's the deposit?	**A combien s'élève la caution?**	ah kawngbyang saylehv lah koassyawng
I've a credit card.	**J'ai une carte de crédit.**	zhay ewn kahrt der kraydee
Here's my driving licence	**Voici mon permis de conduire.**	vwahssee mawng pehrmee der kawngdweer

CAR, see page 75

Taxi *Taxi*

Taxis are clearly marked and available in all the larger towns. If the cab is unmetered, or you have a fair distance to go, ask the fare beforehand. Special rates for night journeys, baggage etc. should be posted on an official fare chart.

Where can I get a taxi?	Où puis-je trouver un taxi?	oo pweezh troovay ang tahksee
Please get me a taxi.	Appelez-moi un taxi, s'il vous plaît.	ahperlay mwah ang tahksee seel voo pleh
What's the fare to ...?	Quel est le tarif pour ...?	kehl eh ler tahreef poor
How far is it to ...?	A quelle distance se trouve ...?	ah kehl deestahngss ser troov
Take me to ...	Conduisez-moi ...	kawngdweezay mwah
this address	à cette adresse	ah seht ahdrehss
the airport	à l'aéroport	ah lahayropor
the town centre	au centre de la ville	oa sahngtr der lah veel
the ... Hotel	à l'hôtel ...	ah loatehl
the railway station	à la gare	ah lah gahr
Turn ... at the next corner.	Tournez ... au prochain coin de rue.	toornay ... oa proshang kwang der rew
left/right	à gauche/à droite	ah goash/ah drwaht
Go straight ahead.	Tout droit.	too drwah
Please stop here.	Arrêtez-vous ici, s'il vous plaît.	ahrehtay voo eessee seel voo pleh
I'm in a hurry.	Je suis pressé(e).	zher swee prehssay
Could you drive more slowly?	Pourriez-vous conduire moins vite, s'il vous plaît?	pooryay voo kawngdweer mwang veet seel voo pleh
Could you help me carry my luggage?	Pouvez-vous m'aider à porter mes bagages, s'il vous plaît?	poovay voo mehday ah portay may bahgahzh seel voo pleh
Could you wait for me?	Pourriez-vous m'attendre?	pooryay voo mahtahngdr
I'll be back in 10 minutes.	Je serai de retour dans 10 minutes.	zher serray der rertoor dahng 10 meenewt

TIPPING, see inside back-cover

Hotel—Other accommodation

Early reservation and confirmation are essential in most major tourist centres during the high season. Most towns and arrival points have a tourist information office (*le syndicat d'initiative*—ler sangdeekah deeneessyahteev), and that's the place to go if you're stuck without a room.

Hôtel
(oatehl)

Hotels are officially classified into five categories by the *Direction du Tourisme*. Room prices, fixed according to amenities, size and to the hotel's star rating, must be posted visibly at reception desks and behind each room door. *Hôtel garni* means that only a room and breakfast are offered.

Note: Hôtel de Ville is not a hotel, but the town hall.

Château-Hôtel
(shahtoa oatehl)

A chain of castles and mansions covering all of France and offering many tempting possibilities. All are four-star establishments.

Relais de campagne
(rerleh der kahngpahñ)

A similar chain offering a wider variety of hotels in country settings, from two- to four-star establishments. Some are genuine, old-time stagecoach inns. Both *châteaux-hôtels* and *relais* are listed jointly in a free booklet published annually.

**Logis de France/
Auberge rurale**
(lozhee der frahngss/
oabehrzh rewrahl)

Government-sponsored hotels, often on the outskirts or outside of towns. *Logis de France* are in the one- and two-star bracket; *auberges rurales* are three- or four-star establishments.

Motel
(motehl)

Motels are being increasingly found near motorways (expressways) and other major roads.

Auberge
(oabehrzh)

A country inn providing simple accommodation at economical boarding rates.

Pension
(pahngssyawng)

Boarding house offering full or half board.

**Auberge de
jeunesse**
(oabehrzh der
zhurnehss)

Youth hostel; in season, some local student associations operate dormitories to accommodate the influx of foreign students.

Checking in—Reception *A la réception*

My name is ...	Je m'appelle ...	zher mahpehl
I've a reservation.	J'ai fait réserver.	zhay feh rayzehrvay
We've reserved two rooms, a single and a double.	Nous avons réservé deux chambres – une pour une personne, et l'autre pour deux.	noo zahvawng rayzehrvay dur shahngbr – ewn poor ewn pehrson ay loatr poor dur
Here's the confirmation.	Voici la confirmation.	vwahssee lah kawngfeermahssyawng
Do you have any vacancies?	Avez-vous des chambres disponibles?	ahvay voo day shahngbr deesponeebl
I'd like a ... room ...	Je voudrais une chambre ...	zher voodreh ewn shahngbr
single	pour une personne	poor ewn pehrson
double	pour deux personnes	poor dur pehrson
with twin beds	avec des lits jumeaux	ahvehk day lee zhewmoa
with a double bed	avec un grand lit	ahvehk ang grahng lee
with a bath	avec salle de bains	ahvehk sahl der bang
with a shower	avec douche	ahvehk doosh
with a balcony	avec balcon	ahvehk bahlkawng
with a view	avec vue	ahvehk vew
We'd like a room ...	Nous voudrions une chambre ...	noo voodreeyawng ewn shahngbr
in the front	qui donne sur la rue	kee don sewr lah rew
at the back	qui donne sur la cour	kee don sewr lah koor
facing the sea	qui donne sur la mer	kee don sewr lah mehr
It must be quiet.	Une chambre tranquille.	ewn shahngbr trahngkeel
Is there ...?	Y a-t-il ...?	ee ahteel
air conditioning	la climatisation	lah kleemahteezahssyawng
heating	le chauffage	ler shoafahzh
a radio/television in the room	un poste de radio/ télévision dans la chambre	ang post der rahdyoa/ taylayveezyawng dahng lah shahngbr
a laundry service	une blanchisserie	ewn blahngsheesserree
room service	le service d'étage	ler sehrveess daytahzh
hot water	l'eau chaude	loa shoad
running water	l'eau courante	loa koorahngt
a private toilet	des toilettes privées	day twahleht preevay

CHECKING OUT, see page 31

| Could you put an extra bed in the room? | Pourriez-vous installer un autre lit dans la chambre? | pooryay voo angstahllay ang noatr lee dahng lah shahngbr |

How much? *Combien?*

What's the price ...?	Quel est le prix ...?	kehl eh ler pree
per night	par nuit	pahr nwee
per week	par semaine	pahr sermehn
for bed and breakfast	avec petit déjeuner	ahvehk pertee dayzhurnay
excluding meals	sans les repas	sahng lay rerpah
for full board (A.P.)	en pension complète	ahng pahngssyawng kawngpleht
for half board (M.A.P.)	en demi-pension	ahng dermee pahngssyawng

Does that include ...?	Ce prix comprend-il ...?	ser pree kawngprahng teel
breakfast	le petit déjeuner	ler pertee dayzhurnay
service	le service	ler sehrveess
value-added tax (VAT)*	la T.V.A.	lah tay-vay-ah

Is there any reduction for children?	Y a-t-il une réduction pour les enfants?	ee ahteel ewn raydewksyawng poor lay zahngfahng
Do you charge for the baby?	Faut-il payer pour le bébé?	footeel pehyay poor ler baybay
That's too expensive.	C'est trop cher.	seh troa shehr
Haven't you anything cheaper?	N'avez-vous rien de meilleur marché?	nahvay voo ryang der mehyurr mahrshay

How long? *Combien de temps?*

We'll be staying ...	Nous resterons ...	noo rehsterrawng
overnight only	juste cette nuit	zhewst seht nwee
a few days	quelques jours	kehlker zhoor
a week (at least)	une semaine (au moins)	ewn sermehn (oa mwang)
I don't know yet.	Je ne sais pas encore.	zher ner seh pah zahngkor

---

* Americans note: a type of sales tax in Belgium and France

NUMBERS, see page 147

Decision *Décision*

May I see the room?	**Puis-je voir la chambre?**	pweezh vwahr lah shahngbr
That's fine. I'll take it.	**D'accord. Je la prends.**	dahkor. zher lah prahng
No. I don't like it.	**Non, elle ne me plaît pas.**	nawng ehl ner mer pleh pah
It's too ...	**Elle est trop ...**	ehl eh troa
cold/hot	**froide/chaude**	frwahd/shoad
dark/small	**sombre/petite**	sawngbr/perteet
noisy	**bruyante**	brweeyahngt
I asked for a room with a bath.	**J'avais demandé une chambre avec salle de bains.**	zhahveh dermahngday ewn shahngbr ahvehk sahl der bang
Do you have anything ...?	**Avez-vous quelque chose ...?**	ahvay voo kehlker shoaz
better	**de mieux**	der myur
bigger	**de plus grand**	der plew grahng
cheaper	**de meilleur marché**	der mehyurr mahrshay
quieter	**de plus tranquille**	der plew trahngkeel
Do you have a room with a better view?	**Auriez-vous une chambre avec une meilleure vue?**	oaryay voo ewn shahngbr ahvehk ewn mehyurr vew

Registration *Enregistrement*

Upon arrival at a hotel or boarding house you'll be asked to fill in a registration form (*une fiche*—ewn feesh).

Nom/Prénom	Name/First name
Lieu de domicile/Rue/N°	Home address/Street/Number
Nationalité/Profession	Nationality/Profession
Date/Lieu de naissance	Date/Place of birth
Venant de .../Allant à ...	From .../To...
Numéro du passeport	Passport number
Lieu/Date	Place/Date
Signature	Signature

| What does this mean? | **Que signifie ceci?** | ker seeñeefee serssee |

Votre passeport, s'il vous plaît.	May I see your passport, please?
Voudriez-vous remplir cette fiche?	Would you mind filling in this registration form?
Signez ici, s'il vous plaît.	Please sign here.
Combien de temps resterez-vous?	How long will you be staying?

What's my room number?	**Quel est le numéro de ma chambre?**	kehl eh ler newmehroa der mah shahngbr
Will you have our luggage sent up?	**Pouvez-vous faire monter nos bagages?**	poovay voo fehr mawngtay noa bahgahzh
Where can I park my car?	**Où puis-je garer ma voiture?**	oo pweezh gahray mah vwahtewr
Does the hotel have a garage?	**L'hôtel a-t-il un garage?**	loatehl ahteel ang gahrahzh
I'd like to leave this in your safe.	**Je voudrais déposer ceci dans votre coffre-fort.**	zher voodreh daypoazay serssee dahng votr kofr for

Hotel staff *Personnel hôtelier*

hall porter	**le concierge**	ler kawngssyehrzh
maid	**la femme de chambre**	lah fahm der shahngbr
manager	**le directeur**	ler deerehkturr
page (bellboy)	**le chasseur**	ler shahssurr
porter	**le bagagiste**	ler bahgahzheest
receptionist	**le réceptionnaire**	ler rayssehpssyonnehr
switchboard operator	**la standardiste**	lah stahngdahrdeest
waiter	**le garçon**	ler gahrsawng
waitress	**la serveuse**	lah sehrvurz

Call the members of the staff *madame* (mahdahm), *mademoiselle* (mahdmwahzehl) or *monsieur* (mursyur). Address the waiter as *garçon* (gahrsawng) when calling for service.

TELLING THE TIME, see page 153

Hôtel

General requirements *Questions générales*

The key, please.	La clé, s'il vous plaît.	lah klay seel voo pleh
Will you please wake me at ...?	Pourriez-vous me réveiller à ...?	pooryay voo mer ray-vehyay ah
Is there a bath on this floor?	Y a-t-il une salle de bains à cet étage?	ee ahteel ewn sahl der bang ah seht aytahzh
What's the voltage here?	Quel est le voltage?	kehl eh ler voltahzh
Where's the socket (outlet) for the shaver?	Où est la prise pour le rasoir?	oo eh lah preez poor ler rahzwahr
Can you find me a ...?	Pouvez-vous me procurer ...?	poovay voo mer prokewray
babysitter	une garde d'enfants	ewn gahrd dahngfahng
secretary	une secrétaire	ewn serkraytehr
typewriter	une machine à écrire	ewn mahsheen ah aykreer
May I have a/an/some ...?	Puis-je avoir ...?	pweezh ahvwahr
ashtray	un cendrier	ang sahngdrjyay
bath towel	une serviette de bain	ewn sehrvyeht der bang
extra blanket	une couverture supplémentaire	ewn koovehrtewr sewplay-mahngtehr
envelopes	des enveloppes	day zahngverlop
(more) hangers	(d'autres) cintres	(doatr) sangtr
hot-water bottle	une bouillotte	ewn booyot
ice cubes	des glaçons	day glahssawng
extra pillow	encore un oreiller	ahngkor ang norehyay
needle and thread	une aiguille et du fil	ewn aygweey ay dew feel
reading-lamp	une lampe de chevet	ewn lahngp der sherveh
soap	du savon	dew sahvawng
writing-paper	du papier à lettres	dew pahpyay ah lehtr
Where's the ...?	Où est ...?	oo eh
bathroom	la salle de bains	lah sahl der bang
dining-room	la salle à manger	lah sahl ah mahngzhay
emergency exit	la sortie de secours	lah sortee der serkoor
hairdresser's	le salon de coiffure	ler sahlawng der kwahfewr
lift (elevator)	l'ascenseur	lahssahngssurr
Where are the toilets?	Où sont les toilettes?	oo sawng lay twahleht

BREAKFAST, see page 38

Hôtel

Telephone—Post (mail) *Téléphone – Courrier*

Can you get me Paris 123-45-67?	**Passez-moi le 123-45-67 à Paris, s'il vous plaît.**	pahssay mwah ler 123-45-67 ah pahree seel voo pleh
Do you have stamps?	**Avez-vous des timbres?**	ahvay voo day tangbr
Would you please mail this for me?	**Pourriez-vous mettre ceci à la poste?**	pooryay voo mehtr ser-ssee ah lah post
Is there any mail for me?	**Y a-t-il du courrier pour moi?**	ee ahteel dew kooryay poor mwah
Are there any messages for me?	**Y a-t-il des messages pour moi?**	ee ahteel day mehssahzh poor mwah
How much are my telephone charges?	**A combien se monte ma note de téléphone?**	ah kawngbyang ser mawngt mah not der taylayfon

Difficulties *Difficultés*

The ... doesn't work.	**... ne fonctionne pas.**	ner fawngksyon pah
air conditioner	**le climatiseur**	ler kleemahteezurr
bidet	**le bidet**	ler beedeh
fan	**le ventilateur**	ler vahngteelahturr
heating	**le chauffage**	ler shoafahzh
light	**la lumière**	lah lewmyehr
radio	**la radio**	lah rahdyoa
television	**la télévision**	lah taylayveezyawng
The tap (faucet) is dripping.	**Le robinet fuit.**	ler robeeneh fwee
There's no hot water.	**Il n'y a pas d'eau chaude.**	eel nee ah pah doa shoad
The wash-basin is blocked.	**Le lavabo est bouché.**	ler lahvahboa eh booshay
The window is jammed.	**La fenêtre est coincée.**	lah fernehtr eh kwangssay
The curtains are stuck.	**Les rideaux sont coincés.**	lay reedoa sawng kwangssay
The bulb is burned out.	**L'ampoule a sauté.**	lahngpool ah soatay
My room has not been made up.	**Ma chambre n'a pas été faite.**	mah shahngbr nah pah aytay feht

POST OFFICE AND TELEPHONE, see page 132

The ... is broken.	... est cassé(e).	eh kahssay
blind	le store	ler stor
lamp	la lampe	lah lahngp
plug	la fiche	lah feesh
shutter	le volet	ler voleh
switch	l'interrupteur	langtehrewpturr
Can you get it repaired?	Pouvez-vous le faire réparer?	poovay voo ler fehr raypahray

Laundry — Dry cleaner's   *Blanchisserie – Teinturerie*

I want these clothes ...	Je voudrais faire ... ces vêtements.	zher voodreh fehr ... say vehtermahng
cleaned	nettoyer	nehtwahyay
ironed	repasser	rerpahssay
pressed	repasser à la vapeur	rerpahssay ah lah vahpurr
washed	laver	lahvay
When will they be ready?	Quand seront-ils prêts?	kahng serrawng teel preh
I need them ...	Il me les faut ...	eel mer lay foa
today	aujourd'hui	oazhoordwee
tonight	ce soir	ser swahr
tomorrow	demain	dermang
before Friday	avant vendredi	ahvahng vahngdrerdee
Can you ... this?	Pouvez-vous ... ceci?	poovay voo ... serssee
mend	raccommoder	rahkommoday
patch	rapiécer	rahpyayssay
stitch	recoudre	rerkoodr
Can you sew on this button?	Pouvez-vous coudre ce bouton?	poovay voo koodr ser bootawng
Can you get this stain out?	Pouvez-vous faire partir cette tache?	poovay voo fehr pahrteer seht tahsh
Is my laundry ready?	Mon linge est-il prêt?	mawng langzh ehtel preh
This isn't mine.	Ce n'est pas à moi.	ser neh pah zah mwah
There's something missing.	Il me manque quelque chose.	eel mer mahngk kehlker shoaz
There's a hole in this.	Ce vêtement a un trou.	ser vehtermahng ah ang troo

Hairdresser—Barber   *Coiffeur*

Is there a hairdresser/ beauty salon in the hotel?	Y a-t-il un coiffeur/ salon de beauté à l'hôtel?	ee ahteel ang kwahfurr/ salawng der boatay ah loatehl
Can I make an appointment for sometime on Thursday?	Puis-je prendre rendez-vous pour jeudi?	pweezh prahngdr rahngday voo poor zhurdee
I'd like it cut and shaped.	Je voudrais une coupe et une mise en plis.	zher voodreh ewn koop eh ewn meez ahng plee
I want a haircut, please.	Une coupe de cheveux, s'il vous plaît.	ewn koop der shervur seel voo pleh
bleach	une décoloration	ewn daykolorahssyawng
blow-dry	un brushing	ang ''brushing''
colour rinse	une coloration	ewn kolorahssyawng
dye	une teinture	ewn tangtewr
face-pack	un masque de beauté	ang mahsk der boatay
manicure	une manucure	ewn mahnewkewr
permanent wave	une permanente	ewn pehrmahnahngt
setting lotion	un fixatif	ang feeksahteef
shampoo and set	un shampooing et une mise en plis	ang shahngpwang eh ewn meez ahng plee
with a fringe (bangs)	avec une frange	ahvehk ewn frahngzh
I'd like a shampoo for … hair.	Je voudrais un shampooing pour …	zher voodreh ang shahngpwang poor
normal/dry/ greasy (oily)	cheveux normaux/ secs/gras	shervur normoa/ sehk/grah
Do you have a colour chart?	Avez-vous un nuancier?	ahvay voo ang newahngssyay
Don't cut it too short.	Pas trop court, s'il vous plaît.	pah troa koor seel voo pleh
A little more off the …	Dégagez un peu plus …	daygahzhay ang pur plewss
back	derrière	dehryehr
neck	la nuque	lah newk
sides	les côtés	lay koatay
top	le haut de la tête	ler oa der lah teht
I don't want any hairspray.	Je ne veux pas de laque.	zher ner vur pah der lahk

DAYS OF THE WEEK, see page 151

I'd like a shave.	**Je voudrais me faire raser.**	zher voodreh mer fehr rahzay
Would you please trim my ...?	**Pourriez-vous me rafraîchir ...?**	pooryay voo mer rahfrehsheer
beard	**la barbe**	lah bahrb
moustache	**la moustache**	lah moostash
sideboards (sideburns)	**les favoris**	lay fahvohree

Checking out *Départ*

May I please have my bill?	**Puis-je avoir ma note, s'il vous plaît?**	pweezh ahvwahr mah not seel voo pleh
I'm leaving early in the morning. Please have my bill ready.	**Je pars demain de bonne heure. Veuillez préparer ma note.**	zher pahr dermang der bonurr. vuryay praypahray mah not
We'll be checking out around noon.	**Nous partirons vers midi.**	noo pahrteerawng vehr meedee
I must leave at once.	**Je dois partir immédiatement.**	zher dwah pahrteer eemaydyahtermahng
Is everything included?	**Tout est compris?**	too teh kawngpree
Can I pay by credit card?	**Puis-je payer avec une carte de crédit?**	pweezh pehyay ahvehk ewn kahrt der kraydee
You've made a mistake in this bill, I think.	**Je crois qu'il y a une erreur dans la note.**	zher krwah keel ee ah ewn ehrurr dahng lah not
Can you get us a taxi?	**Pouvez-vous nous appeler un taxi?**	poovay voo noo zahperlay ang tahksee
Would you send someone to bring down our luggage?	**Pourriez-vous faire descendre nos bagages?**	pooryay voo fehr dehssahngdr noa bahgahzh
Here's the forwarding address.	**Faites suivre mon courrier à cette adresse.**	feht sweevr mawng kooryay ah seht ahdrehss
You have my home address.	**Vous avez mon adresse habituelle.**	voo zahvay mawng nahdrehss ahbeetewehl
It's been a very enjoyable stay.	**Le séjour a été très agréable.**	ler sayzhoor ah aytay troh zahgrayahbl

TIPPING, see inside back-cover

Camping *Camping*

Camping is extremely popular and very well organized in France. The sites are classified from one to four stars depending on their amenities. In the summer season, it's important to book in advance. If you camp on private property, ask the landowner for permission. A *camping interdit* notice means the site is forbidden to campers.

Is there a camp site near here?	**Y a-t-il un camping près d'ici?**	ee ahteel ang kahngpeeng preh deessee
Can we camp here?	**Pouvons-nous camper ici?**	poovawng noo kahngpay eessee
Have you room for a tent/caravan (trailer)?	**Avez-vous de la place pour une tente/une caravane?**	ahvay voo der lah plahss poor ewn tahngt/ewn kahrahvahn
What's the charge ...?	**Quel est le tarif ...?**	kehl eh ler tahreef
per day	**par jour**	pahr zhoor
per person	**par personne**	pahr pehrson
for a car	**par voiture**	pahr vwahtewr
for a tent	**par tente**	pahr tahngt
for a caravan (trailer)	**par caravane**	pahr kahrahvahn
Is the tourist tax included?	**La taxe de séjour est-elle comprise?**	lah tahks der sayzhoor ehtehl kawngpreez
Is there/Are there (a) ...?	**Y a-t-il ...?**	ee ahteel
drinking water	**l'eau potable**	loa potahbl
electricity	**l'électricité**	laylehktreesseetay
playground	**un terrain de jeu**	ang tehrrang der zhur
restaurant	**un restaurant**	ang rehstoarahng
shopping facilities	**des commerces**	day kommehrs
swimming pool	**une piscine**	ewn peesseen
Where are the showers/toilets?	**Où sont les douches/ toilettes?**	oo sawng lay doosh/twahleht
Where can I get butane gas?	**Où puis-je trouver du butane?**	oo pweezh troovay dew bewtahn
Is there a youth hostel near here?	**Y a-t-il une auberge de jeunesse dans les environs?**	ee ahteel ewn oabehrzh der zhurnehss dahng lay zahngveerawng

CAMPING EQUIPMENT, see page 106

Eating out

There are many types of places where you can eat and drink.

Auberge
(oabehrzh)

An inn, often in the country; serves full meals and drink.

Bar
(bahr)

Bar; can be found on virtually every street corner; coffee and drinks served, sometimes light meals, too.

Bar à café
(bahr ah kahfay)

Coffee shop; alcoholic beverages aren't served, but light meals are (Switzerland).

Bistrot
(beestroa)

The nearest equivalent to an English pub or an American tavern though the atmosphere may be very different; usually only serves a few "dishes of the day", sometimes the choice is bigger.

Brasserie
(brahsserree)

A large café serving food and drink.

Buffet
(bewfeh)

A restaurant found in principal train stations; food is generally quite good.

Cabaret
(kahbahreh)

Features supper and show including song and dance acts, vaudeville patter and political satire.

Café
(kahfay)

Nowadays, a lot of cafés serve snacks and complete meals. At least you'll be able to get a crescent roll with your morning coffee. Cafés always serve beer, wine and liquor but don't ask for any fancy cocktails or highballs.

Carnotzet
(kahrnotzeh)

A cozy cellar restaurant found in French-speaking Switzerland; cheese specialities like *fondue* (fawngdew) and *raclette* (rahkleht) are the principal fare as well as locally produced cured, dried beef, sausages and the region's wine.

Hostellerie
(ostehlerree)

A handsome country restaurant furnished in a traditional style; the cuisine will usually please a gourmet's palate but the prices may be a bit steep.

Relais (de campagne) (rerleh [der kahngpahñ])	A country inn; menus range from a snack to a banquet; food can be superb.
Restaurant (rehstoarahng)	These are rated by scores of professional and amateur gourmets. You'll encounter restaurants classified by stars, forks and knives and endorsed by everyone including travel agencies, automobile associations and gastronomic guilds. Bear in mind that any form of classification is relative.
Restoroute (rehstoaroot)	A large restaurant just off a motorway (expressway); table and/or cafeteria service is available.
Rôtisserie (roateesserree)	Originally, such restaurants specialized in grilled meats and chicken. Today the word is frequently used synonymously with *restaurant*. You can usually count on a *rôtisserie* being smart and a bit on the expensive side.
Routier (rootyay)	Roughly equivalent to a roadside diner; the food is simple but can be surprisingly good if you happen to hit upon the right place.
Salon de thé (sahlawng der tay)	(*Tea-Room*, in Switzerland). Serves ice-cream and pastries in addition to nonalcoholic beverages. Some even serve snacks and full meals.
Snack bar	The French have taken over the word though you may see *buffet-express* (bewfeh ehxprehss) which is the same type of place.

Meal times *Heures de repas*

Breakfast (*le petit déjeuner*—ler pertee dayzhurnay): from 7 to 10 a.m.

Lunch (*le déjeuner*—ler dayzhurnay) is generally served from noon until 2 p.m.

Dinner (*le dîner*—ler deenay) is usually served later than at home, seldom beginning before 8 p.m. and until around 10.

The French like to linger over a meal, so service may seem on the leisurely side.

French cuisine *Cuisine française*

In 1825, Brillat-Savarin, a well-known gastronomic writer, declared that "cookery is the oldest form of art"; this is truly illustrated by the French, who have developed their culinary skills with brio throughout the centuries. There are few countries in the world where you can spend more delightful hours just eating. For, apart from many regional specialities which do ample justice to the local produce, you can sample, among others, gastronomic *haute cuisine*—sophisticated dishes made according to time-honoured recipes—or *nouvelle cuisine,* where a more refined preparation enhances the delicate flavours of the food. But most restaurants offer homely cooking and well-balanced, tasty menus: *hors-d'œuvre,* main dish, cheese and/or dessert. As for the famous French wines—they certainly live up to their reputation!

Que prendrez-vous?	What would you like?
Je vous recommande ceci.	I recommend this.
Que boirez-vous?	What would you like to drink?
Nous n'avons pas ...	We haven't got ...
Voulez-vous ...?	Do you want ...?

Hungry? *Avez-vous faim?*

I'm hungry/I'm thirsty.	**J'ai faim/J'ai soif.**	zhay fang/zhay swahf
Can you recommend a good restaurant?	**Pouvez-vous m'indiquer un bon restaurant?**	poovay voo mangdeekay ang bawng rehstoarahng
Are there any inexpensive restaurants around here?	**Y a-t-il des restaurants bon marché dans les environs?**	ee ahteel day rehstoarahng hawng mahrshay dahng lay zahngveerawng

If you want to be sure of getting a table in well-known restaurants, it may be better to telephone in advance.

I'd like to reserve a table for 4.	**Je voudrais réserver une table pour 4 personnes.**	zher voodreh rayzehrvay ewn tahbl poor 4 pehrson
We'll come at 8.	**Nous viendrons à 8 heures.**	noo vyangdrawng ah 8 urr
Could we have a table ...?	**Pouvons-nous avoir une table ...?**	poovawng noo ahvwahr ewn tahbl
in the corner	**dans un angle**	dahng zang nahngl
by the window	**près de la fenêtre**	preh der lah fernehtr
outside	**dehors**	deror
on the terrace	**sur la terrasse**	sewr lah tehrahss
in a non-smoking area	**dans un endroit pour non-fumeurs**	dahng zang nahngdrwah poor nawng fewmurr

Asking and ordering *Demandes et commandes*

Waiter/Waitress!	**Garçon/ Mademoiselle!**	gahrsawng/ mahdmwahzehl
I'd like something to eat/drink.	**Je voudrais manger/ boire quelque chose.**	zher voodreh mahngzhay/ bwahr kehlker shoaz
May I have the menu, please?	**Puis-je avoir la carte?**	pweezh ahvwahr lah kahrt
Do you have a set menu/local dishes?	**Avez-vous un menu/ des spécialités locales?**	ahvay voo ang mernew/ day spayssyahleetay lokahl
What do you recommend?	**Que me recomman- dez-vous?**	ker mer rerkommahngday voo
I'd like ...	**Je voudrais ...**	zher voodreh
Could we have a/ an ..., please?	**Pourrions-nous avoir ...?**	pooryawng noo ahvwahr
ashtray	**un cendrier**	ang sahngdryay
cup	**une tasse**	ewn tahss
fork	**une fourchette**	ewn foorsheht
glass	**un verre**	ang vehr
knife	**un couteau**	ang kootoa
napkin (serviette)	**une serviette**	ewn sehrvyeht
plate	**une assiette**	ewn ahssyeht
spoon	**une cuillère**	ewn kweeyehr
May I have some ...?	**Pourrais-je avoir ...?**	poorehzh ahvwahr
bread	**du pain**	dew pang
butter	**du beurre**	dew burr

lemon	du citron	dew seetrawng
mustard	de la moutarde	der lah mootahrd
oil	de l'huile	der lweel
pepper	du poivre	dew pwahvr
salt	du sel	dew sehl
seasoning	des condiments	day kawngdeemahng
sugar	du sucre	dew sewkr
vinegar	du vinaigre	dew veenehgr

Some useful expressions for dieters and special requirements:

I have to live on a diet.	Je suis au régime.	zher swee oa rayzheem
I mustn't eat food containing ...	Je dois éviter les plats contenant ...	zher dwah ayveetay lay plah kawngternahng
flour/fat	de la farine/du gras	der lah fahreen/dew grah
salt/sugar	du sel/du sucre	dew sehl/dew sewkr
Do you have ... for diabetics?	Avez-vous ... pour diabétiques?	ahvay voo ... poor dyahbayteek
cakes	des gâteaux	day gahtoa
fruit juice	du jus de fruits	dew zhew der frwee
special menu	un menu spécial	ang mernew spayssyahl
Do you have vege-tarian dishes?	Avez-vous des plats végétariens?	ahvay voo day plah vayzhaytahryang
Could I have ... instead of the dessert?	Pourrais-je avoir ... à la place du dessert?	poorehzh avwahr ... ah lah plahss dew dehssehr
Can I have an artificial sweetener?	Puis-je avoir de l'édulcorant?	pweezh avwahr der laydewlkorahng

And ...

I'd like some more.	J'en voudrais encore.	zhahng voodreh ahngkor
Can I have more ..., please.	Puis-je avoir encore un peu de ...	pweezh avwahr ahngkor ang pur der
Just a small portion.	Juste une petite portion.	zhewst ewn perteet porsyawng
Nothing more, thanks.	Je suis servi(e), merci.	zher swee sehrvee mehrssee
Where are the toilets?	Où sont les toilettes?	oo sawng lay twahleht

Breakfast *Petit déjeuner*

The French breakfast consists of coffee, rolls (*petits pains* —pertee pang), *croissants* (krwahssahng—flaky pastry in the form of a crescent) and jam, seldom marmalade. Most of the larger hotels, however, are now used to providing an English or American breakfast.

I'd like breakfast, please.	**Je voudrais prendre mon petit déjeuner.**	zher voodreh prahngdr mawng pertee dayzhurnay
I'll have a/an/ some ...	**Je prendrai ...**	zher prahngdray
bacon and eggs	**des œufs au bacon**	day zur oa baykon
boiled egg	**un œuf à la coque**	ang nurf ah lah kok
soft/hard	**mollet/dur**	molleh/dewr
cereal	**des céréales**	day sayrayahl
eggs	**des œufs**	day zur
fried eggs	**des œufs au plat**	day zur oa plah
scrambled eggs	**des œufs brouillés**	day zur brooyay
fruit juice	**un jus de fruits**	ang zhew der frwee
grapefruit	**pamplemousse**	pahngplermooss
orange	**orange**	orahngzh
ham and eggs	**des œufs au jambon**	day zur oa zhahngbawng
jam	**de la confiture**	der lah kawngfeetewr
marmalade	**de la marmelade**	der lah mahrmerlahd
toast	**du pain grillé**	dew pang greeyay
yoghurt	**un yaourt/yoghourt**	ang yahoort/yogoort
May I have some ...?	**Pourrais-je avoir ...?**	poorehzh ahvwahr
bread	**du pain**	dew pang
butter	**du beurre**	dew burr
(hot) chocolate	**un chocolat (chaud)**	ang shokolah (shoa)
coffee	**un café**	ang kahfay
caffein-free	**décaféiné**	daykahfayeenay
black/with milk	**noir/au lait**	nwahr/oa leh
honey	**du miel**	dew myehl
milk	**du lait**	dew leh
cold/hot	**froid/chaud**	frwah/shoa
pepper	**du poivre**	dew pwahvr
rolls	**des petits pains**	day pertee pang
salt	**du sel**	dew sehl
tea	**du thé**	dew tay
with milk	**au lait**	oa leh
with lemon	**au citron**	oa seetrawng
(hot) water	**de l'eau (chaude)**	der loa (shoad)

What's on the menu?   *Qu'y a-t-il au menu?*

Most restaurants display a menu *(la carte)* outside. Besides ordering à la carte, you can order a fixed-price menu *(le menu)*. Cheaper meals often run to three courses, with or without wine, but service is always included. More expensive menus stretch to four or even five courses, but hardly ever include wine. Words like *maison* or *du chef* next to a dish listed on the menu are clues that the dish is a speciality of the restaurant.

Under the headings below you'll find alphabetical lists of dishes that might be offered on a French menu with their English equivalent. You can simply show the book to the waiter. If you want some fruit, for instance, let *him* point to what's available on the appropriate list. Use pages 36 and 37 for ordering in general.

	page	
Starters (Appetizers)	41	**Hors-d'œuvre**
Salads	42	**Salades**
Omelets	42	**Omelettes**
Soups	43	**Potages et soupes**
Fish and seafood	44	**Poissons et fruits de mer**
Meat	46	**Viandes**
Game and poultry	48	**Gibier et volailles**
Vegetables	49	**Légumes**
Potatoes, rice, noodles	51	**Pommes de terre, riz, pâtes**
Sauces	51	**Sauces**
Cheese	53	**Fromages**
Fruit	54	**Fruits**
Dessert	55	**Desserts**
Drinks	56	**Boissons**
Wine	57	**Vins**
Nonalcoholic drinks	60	**Boissons sans alcool**
Snacks—Picnic	63	**Casse-croûte – Pique-nique**

EATING OUT

Restaurant

Reading the menu *Pour lire la carte*

Menu à prix fixe	Set menu
Plat du jour	Dish of the day
Boisson comprise	Drink included
Le chef vous propose ...	The chef proposes ...
Spécialités locales	Local specialities
Garniture au choix	Choice of vegetable accompaniment
Toutes nos viandes sont servies avec une garniture	All our meat dishes are accompanied by vegetables
Supplément pour changement de garniture	Extra charge for alternative vegetable accompaniment
Sur commande	Made to order
Supplément/En sus	Extra charge
En saison	In season
Selon arrivage	When available
Attente: 15 min	Waiting time: 15 minutes
Pour deux personnes	For two

boissons	bwahssawng	drinks
crustacés	krewstahssay	shellfish
desserts	dehssehr	desserts
entrées	ahngtray	first course
fromages	fromahzh	cheese
fruits	frwee	fruit
fruits de mer	frwee der mehr	seafood
gibier	zheebyay	game
glaces	glahss	ice-cream
grillades	greeyahd	grilled meat
légumes	laygewm	vegetables
pâtes	paht	pasta
pâtisseries	pahteesserree	pastries
poissons	pwahssawng	fish
potages	potahzh	soups
riz	ree	rice
salades	sahlahd	salads
viandes	vyahngd	meat
vins	vang	wine
volailles	volahy	poultry

Starters (Appetizers)   *Hors-d'œuvre*

I'd like an appetizer.	**Je voudrais un hors-d'œuvre.**	zher voodreh ang ordurvr
What do you recommend?	**Que nous/me recommandez-vous?**	ker noo/mer rerkommahng-day voo
assiette anglaise	ahssyeht ahngglehz	assorted cold cuts
assiette de charcuterie	ahssyeht der shahrkewterree	assorted pork products
cervelas	sehrverlah	type of sausage
crudités	krewdeetay	mixed raw vegetable salad
hors-d'œuvre variés	ordurvr vahryay	assorted appetizers
jambon (de Bayonne)	zhahngbawng (der bahyon)	(Bayonne) ham
jambonneau	zhahngbonnoa	cured pig's knuckle
jus de tomate	zhew der tomaht	tomato juice
mortadelle	mortahdehl	Bologna sausage
œufs à la diable	ur ah lah dyahbl	devilled eggs
olives farcies/noires/ vertes	oleev fahrsee/nwahr/ vehrt	olives stuffed/black/ green
saucisson	soasseessawng	cold sausage
viande séchée	vyahngd sayshay	cured dried beef

andouille(tte)
(ahngdooy [eht])
seasoned, aromatic sausage made from tripe, served grilled or fried

bouchée à la reine
(booshay ah lah rehn)
pastry shell usually filled with creamed sweetbreads and mushrooms

crépinette
(kraypeeneht)
small, flat sausage, highly seasoned

pâté
(pahtay)
an exquisite liver purée which may be blended with other meat like a *pâté de campagne; pâté de fois gras* indicates a fine paste of duck or goose liver, often with truffles *(truffé); pâté en croûte* would be enveloped in a pastry crust.

quenelles
(kernehl)
light dumplings made of fish, fowl or meat, served with a velvety sauce. The best known are *quenelles de brochet,* made of pike.

quiche
(keesh)
a flan or open-faced tart with a rich, creamy filling of cheese, vegetables, meat or seafood; *quiche lorraine* (keesh lorehn), the best known of the *quiches,* is garnished with bacon.

rillettes de porc (reeyeht der por)	minced pork, cooked in its own fat and served chilled in earthenware pots	
soufflé (sooflay)	a puffy, brown dish made of egg whites delicately flavoured with cheese, vegetables or seafood	
terrine (tehreen)	the same as a *pâté* but sliced and served from its *terrine* (traditionally an earthenware pot). It may resemble a perfectly flavoured meat loaf and be made of any meat including game or fowl.	

Salads *Salades*

A green or mixed salad is usually eaten after the main course —never with it. Other salads may be very well ordered as a first course.

What salads do you have?	**Quelles salades servez-vous?**	kehl sahlahd sehrvay voo
salade mêlée	sahlahd mehlay	mixed salad
salade de museau de bœuf	sahlahd der mewzoa der berf	marinated brawn (beef headcheese)
salade russe	sahlahd rewss	diced vegetable salad
salade de thon	sahlahd der tawng	tunny (tuna) salad
salade verte	sahlahd vehrt	green salad
salade niçoise (sahlahd neeswahz)	a Riviera combination salad which includes tuna, anchovies, olives and vegetables.	

Omelets *Omelettes*

A classic French *omelette* isn't merely scrambled eggs but is shaped like a smooth, slightly swelling golden oval. It should be tender and creamy inside and served either plain or flavoured with one or more ingredients:

omelette (nature)	omerleht (nahtewr)	(plain) omelet
aux champignons	oa shahngpeeñawng	mushroom
aux fines herbes	oa feen zehrb	herb
au fromage	oa fromahzh	cheese
au jambon	oa zhahngbawng	ham

Soups *Potages et soupes*

You may see one of any number of words for a type of soup on the menu, some of which may be main-course fare.

aïgo bouïdo	aheegoa bweedoa	garlic soup (Provençal speciality)
bisque	beesk	seafood stew (chowder)
d'écrevisses	daykrerveess	crayfish
de homard	der omahr	lobster
bouillabaisse	booyahbehss	fish and seafood stew (Marseilles speciality)
bouillon	booyawng	bouillon
de poule	der pool	chicken
consommé	kawngssommay	consommé
à l'œuf	ah lurf	with a raw egg
au porto	oa portoa	with port wine
crème	krehm	cream of ...
d'asperges	dahspehrzh	asparagus
de bolets	der boleh	boletus mushrooms
de volaille	der volahy	chicken
garbure	gahrbewr	cabbage soup, often with salt pork or preserved goose
pot-au-feu	po toa fur	stew of meat and vegetables
potage	potahzh	soup
à l'ail	ah lahy	garlic
au cresson	oa krehssawng	watercress
bonne femme	bon fahm	potato, leek and sometimes bacon
Condé	kawngday	mashed red beans
julienne	zhewlyehn	shredded vegetables
Parmentier	pahrmahngtyay	potato
soupe	soop	soup
à l'ail	ah lahy	garlic
aux choux	oa shoo	cabbage
du jour	dew zhoor	day's soup
à l'oignon	ah lonyawng	French onion soup
au pistou	oa peestoo	Provençal vegetable soup
velouté	verlootay	cream of ...
de tomates	der tomaht	tomato
de volaille	der volahy	chicken

Fish and seafood *Poissons et fruits de mer*

Don't miss the opportunity to sample some of the wide variety of fresh fish and seafood in coastal areas. Fish is most commonly baked or poached until just done, then dressed with a delicate sauce. Trout are often made *au bleu* which means they're freshly poached in a simmering bouillon.

I'd like some fish.	**Je voudrais du poisson.**	zher voodreh dew pwahssawng
What kinds of seafood do you have?	**Quel genre de fruits de mer servez-vous?**	kehl zhahngr der frwee der mehr sehrvay voo
aiglefin (aigrefin)	ehglerfang	haddock
anchois	ahngshwah	anchovies
anguille	ahnggeey	eel
bar	bahr	bass
barbue	bahrbew	brill
baudroie	boadrwah	angler
blanchaille	blahngshahy	whitebait
brochet	brosheh	pike
cabillaud	kahbeeyoa	(fresh) cod
calmars	kahlmahr	squid
carpe	kahrp	carp
carrelet	kahrerleh	plaice
crabe	krahb	crab
crevettes	krerveht	shrimp
cuisses de grenouilles	kweess der grernooy	frog's legs
daurade	doarahd	sea bream
écrevisses	aykrerveess	crayfish
éperlans	aypehrlahng	smelt
escargots	ehskahrgoa	snails
féra	fayrah	lake salmon
goujons	goozhawng	gudgeon
grondin	grawngdang	gurnet
harengs	ahrahng	herring
homard	omahr	lobster
huîtres	weetr	oysters
lamproie	lahngprwah	lamprey
langouste	lahnggoost	spiny lobster
langoustines	lahnggoosteen	Dublin bay prawns, scampi
lotte	lot	burbot
lotte de mer	lot der mehr	angler

loup	loo	sea bass
maquereau	mahkerroa	mackerel
merlan	mehrlahng	whiting
morue	morew	cod
moules	mool	mussels
omble (chevalier)	awngbl (shervahlyay)	char
palourdes	pahloord	clams
perche	pehrsh	perch
plie	plee	plaice
poulpes	poolp	octopus
rascasse	rahskahss	fish used in *bouillabaisse*
rouget	roozheh	red mullet
sardines	sahrdeen	sardines
saumon	soamawng	salmon
scampi	skahngpee	prawns
sole	sol	sole
thon	tawng	tunny (tuna)
truite	trweet	trout
turbot	tewrboa	turbot

baked	**au four**	oa foor
fried	**frit**	free
grilled	**grillé**	greeyay
marinated	**mariné**	mahreenay
poached	**poché**	poshay
sautéed	**sauté**	soatay
smoked	**fumé**	fewmay
steamed	**cuit à la vapeur**	kwee ah lah vahpurr

bourride (boorreed)	fish stew (chowder) from Marseilles
brandade de morue (brahngdahd der morow)	creamed salt cod
coquilles St-Jacques (kokeey sang zhahk)	scallops served in a creamy sauce on the half shell
homard à l'américaine (omahr ah lahmayreekehn)	sautéed diced lobster, flamed in cognac and then simmered in wine, aromatic vegetables, herbs and tomatoes
matelote (mahterlot)	fish (especially eel) stew with wine

Meat *Viandes*

I'd like some ...	Je voudrais ...	zher voodreh
beef/lamb	**du bœuf/de l'agneau**	dew burf/der lahñoa
pork/veal	**du porc/du veau**	dew por/dew voa
boulettes	booleht	meatballs
carré d'agneau	kahray dahñoa	rack of lamb
cervelle	sehrvehl	brains
charcuterie	shahrkewterree	assorted pork products
cochon de lait	koshawng der leh	suck(l)ing pig
côte	koat	rib
côtelettes	koaterleht	chops
épaule	aypoal	shoulder
escalope	ehskahlop	cutlet, scallop
foie	fwah	liver
gigot	zheegoa	leg
jambon	zhahngbawng	ham
jambonneau	zhahngbonnoa	pig's knuckle
jarret	zhahreh	knuckle
langue	lahngg	tongue
lard	lahr	bacon
médaillon	maydahyawng	a tenderloin steak (lamb, pork or veal)
pieds	pyay	trotters (feet)
ris de veau	ree der voa	veal sweetbreads
rognons	roñawng	kidneys
rosbif	rosbeef	roast beef
saucisses	soasseess	sausages
selle	sehl	saddle
steak/steack	stehk	steak (always beef)

Meat is cut differently in France than at home. Here are the names of some commonly seen cuts of beef with their approximate English equivalents:

chateaubriand	shahtoabryahng	double fillet steak (tenderloin of porterhouse steak)
contre-filet	kawngtr feeleh	loin strip steak
côte de bœuf	koat der burf	T-bone steak
entrecôte	ahngtrerkoat	rib or rib-eye steak
filet	feeleh	fillet steak
tournedos	toornerdoa	tenderloin of T-bone steak

baked	**au four**	na foor
baked in grease-proof paper	**en chemise**	ahng shermeez
boiled	**bouilli**	booyee
braised	**braisé**	brehzay
fried	**frit**	free
grilled	**grillé**	greeyay
roast	**rôti**	roatee
sautéed	**sauté**	soatay
stewed	**à l'étouffée**	ah laytoofay
very rare	**bleu**	blur
underdone (rare)	**saignant**	sehñahng
medium	**à point**	ah pwang
well-done	**bien cuit**	byang kwee

Meat dishes *Plats de viande*

In many restaurants, meat is dressed with some sort of creamy sauce or gravy—sometimes prepared at your table. Some establishments customarily serve low-calorie *nouvelle cuisine* sauces to go with their dishes.

bœuf bourguignon (burf boorgeeñawng)	a rich beef stew with vegetables, braised in red Burgundy wine
carbon(n)ade flamande (kahrbonnahd flah-mahngd)	beef slices and onions braised in beer (a Belgian speciality)
cassoulet toulousain (kahssooleh tooloozang)	a casserole of white beans, mutton or salt pork, sausages and preserved goose
choucroute garnie (shookroot gahrnee)	a mound of sauerkraut served with sausages and cured pork
ragoût (rahgoo)	a meat stew, generally served in a delicate gravy with vegetables; *ragoût* will be followed by words like *de bœuf* which will tell you it's a beef stew
tripes à la mode de Caen (treep ah lah mod der kahng)	tripe baked with calf's trotters (calf's feet), vegetables, apple brandy or cider

Game and poultry   *Gibier et volailles*

Chicken, duck and turkey can be found at any time of the
year on a French menu. But the hunting season is a unique
period in which to sample wild boar, venison or pheasant.
Some game is roasted and braised with fruits and vegetables
while other game is jugged and stewed. *Civet*—as in *civet de
lièvre*—will tell you that the preparation has been jugged.
Terrines, pâtés and *galantines* are often made of game
or fowl. We've also listed below some other seasonal de-
licacies.

I'd like some game.   **Je voudrais du gibier.**   zher voodreh dew zheebyay

alouette	ahlooeht	lark
bécasse	baykahss	woodcock
bécassine	baykahsseen	snipe
cabri	kahbree	kid goat
caille	kahy	quail
canard (sauvage)	kahnahr (soavahzh)	(wild) duck
caneton	kahnertawng	duckling
cerf	sehr	venison (red deer)
chapon	shahpawng	capon
chevreuil	shervrury	venison (roe deer)
coq de bruyère	kok der brweeyehr	woodgrouse
dinde	dangd	turkey
dindonneau	dangdonnoa	young turkey (cock)
faisan	fehzahng	pheasant
grive	greev	thrush
lapin	lahpang	rabbit
lièvre	lyehvr	wild hare
marcassin	mahrkahssang	young wild boar
oie	wah	goose
ortolan	ortolahng	ortolan bunting
perdreau	pehrdroa	young partridge
perdrix	pehrdree	partridge
pigeon	peezhawng	pigeon
pigeonneau	peezhonnoa	squab
pintade	pangtahd	guinea fowl
pintadeau	pangtahdoa	young guinea cock
poularde	poolahrd	fattened pullet
poule	pool	stewing fowl
poulet	pooleh	chicken
poussin	poossang	spring chicken
sanglier	sahngglyay	wild boar

sarcelle	sahrsehl	teal
suprême de volaille	sewprehm der volahy	chicken breast
volaille	volahy	fowl

canard (or **caneton**) **à l'orange** (kahnahr [kahnertawng] ah lorahngzh)	the best known of the French duck recipes; it's braised with oranges and orange liqueur
coq au vin (kok oa vang)	chicken stewed in red wine. Sometimes the menu will tell exactly what kind of wine was used, for instance, *coq au Chambertin*.
poule au pot (pool oa poa)	stewed chicken with vegetables

Vegetables *Légumes*

artichaut	ahrteeshoa	artichoke
asperges	ahspehrzh	asparagus
aubergines	oabehrzheen	aubergines (eggplant)
betterave	behterrahv	beet(root)
bolets	boleh	boletus mushrooms
cardon	kahrdawng	cardoon
carottes	kahrot	carrots
céleri (-rave)	sehlerree (rahv)	celery root
cèpes	sehp	flap mushrooms
champignons (de Paris)	shahngpeeñawng (der pahree)	mushrooms
chicorée	sheekoray	endive (Am. chicory)
chou (rouge)	shoo (roozh)	(red) cabbage
choucroute	shookroot	sauerkraut
chou-fleur	shoo flurr	cauliflower
choux de Bruxelles	shoo der brewssehl	Brussels sprouts
concombre	kawngkawngbr	cucumber
cornichons	korneeshawng	gherkins (pickles)
courgette	koorzheht	courgette (zucchini)
cresson	krehssawng	watercress
endives	ahngdeev	chicory (Am. endive)
épinards	aypeenahr	spinach
fenouil	fernooy	fennel
fèves	fohv	broad beans
flageolets	flahzholeh	small kidney beans
haricots blancs	ahreekoa blahng	haricot beans, white kidney beans
haricots verts	ahreekoa vehr	French (green) beans

laitue	lehtew	lettuce
lentilles	lahngteey	lentils
maïs	maheess	sweet corn (corn)
morilles	moreey	morels
navets	nahveh	turnips
oignons	oñawng	onions
petits pois	pertee pwah	peas
poireaux	pwahroa	leeks
pois mange-tout	pwah mahngzh too	string-peas
poivrons	pwahvrawng	sweet peppers
pommes (de terre)	pom (der tehr)	potatoes
potiron	poteerawng	pumpkin
radis	rahdee	radishes
raifort	rayfor	horseradish
tomates	tomaht	tomatoes
truffes	trewf	truffles

One popular vegetable dish comes from Provence:

| ratatouille | a casserole of stewed eggplant, onions, green |
| (rahtahtooy) | peppers and vegetable marrow (zucchini) |

Spices and herbs *Epices et fines herbes*

ail	ahy	garlic
aneth	ahneht	dill
anis	ahneess	aniseed
basilic	bahzeeleek	basil
cannelle	kahnehl	cinnamon
câpres	kahpr	capers
cerfeuil	sehrfery	chervil
ciboulette	seebooleht	chives
clous de girofle	kloo der zheerofl	clove
cumin	kewmang	caraway
échalote	ayshahlot	shallot
estragon	ehstrahgawng	tarragon
fines herbes	feen zehrb	mixture of herbs
gingembre	zhangzhahngbr	ginger
laurier	loryay	bay leaf
marjolaine	mahrzholehn	marjoram
menthe	mahngt	mint
moutarde	mootahrd	mustard
noix (de) muscade	nwah (der) mewskahd	nutmeg
origan	oreegahng	oregano
persil	pehrsee	parsley
piment	peemahng	pimiento

poivre	pwahvr	pepper
romarin	roamahrang	rosemary
safran	sahfrahng	saffron
sauge	soazh	sage
thym	tang	thyme

Potatoes, rice and noodles *Pommes de terre, riz et pâtes*

pâtes	paht	pasta
nouilles	nooy	noodles
pommes (de terre)	pom (der tehr)	potatoes
allumettes	ahlewmeht	matchsticks
chips	''chips''	crisps (Am. potato chips)
dauphine	doafeen	mashed in butter and egg-yolks, mixed in seasoned flour and deep-fried
duchesse	dewshehss	mashed with butter and egg-yolks
en robe des champs	ahng roh day shahng	in their jackets
frites	freet	chips (french fries)
mousseline	moosserleen	mashed
nature	natewr	boiled, steamed
nouvelles	noovehl	new
vapeur	vahpurr	steamed, boiled
riz	ree	rice
pilaf	peelahf	rice boiled in a bouillon with onions

Sauces and preparations *Sauces et préparations*

What would French cuisine be without its infinite variety of sauces, dressings and gravies? Some of them are creamy and velvety with the delicate taste of herbs, wine and other flavourings. Others are tangy and spicy. Below are a few common names of sauces and garnishes with a hint as to what they're made of.

aïoli	garlic mayonnaise
américaine	white wine, brandy, garlic, shallots, tomatoes, shrimp or lobster flavouring
béarnaise	a creamy sauce flavoured with vinegar, egg yolks, white wine, shallots, tarragon

béchamel	white sauce
beurre blanc	butter, shallots, vinegar, white wine
beurre noir	browned butter, vinegar and/or lemon juice
bigarade	with oranges
bordelaise	boletus mushrooms, red wine, shallots, beef marrow
bourguignonne	red wine, herbs
café de Paris	a butter flavoured with cognac, herbs
chasseur	wine, mushrooms, onions, shallots, herbs
chaud-froid	dressing containing gelatine
diable	hot-pepper sauce
duxelles	with mushrooms
financière	Madeira wine, truffles, olives, mushrooms
fines herbes	with herbs
florentine	with spinach
forestière	with mushrooms
hollandaise	egg yolks, butter, vinegar
indienne	curry sauce
lyonnaise	with onions
madère	with Madeira wine
maître d'hôtel	butter, parsley, lemon juice
marchand de vin	red wine, shallots
marinière	white wine, mussel broth thickened with egg yolks
meunière	brown butter, parsley, lemon juice
Mornay	cheese sauce
mousseline	mayonnaise with cream
moutarde	mustard sauce
normande	mushrooms, eggs and cream
Parmentier	with potatoes
Périgueux	with a goose—or duck—liver purée and truffles
poivrade	pepper sauce
porto	with port wine
provençale	onions, tomatoes, garlic
rémoulade	sauce flavoured with mustard and herbs
Soubise	onion-cream sauce
suprême	thickened chicken broth
tartare	mayonnaise flavoured with mustard and herbs
velouté	thickened chicken or meat stock
verte	mayonnaise with spinach, watercress and/or herbs
vinaigrette	vinegar dressing

Cheese *Fromages*

Below are the names of just a few of the most popular cheeses of France and Switzerland.

mild	beaufort, beaumont, belle étoile, boursin, brie, cantal, comté, coulommiers, mimolette, reblochon, saint-paulin, tomme de Savoie
sharp, tangy	bleu de Bresse, camembert, livarot, fromage au marc, munster, pont-l'évêque, roquefort
goat's milk cheese	st-marcellin, valençay
Swiss cheeses	emmenthal (which we call Swiss cheese), gruyère, vacherin; Swiss cheeses are almost all mild

The following dishes in French-speaking Switzerland make a meal in themselves:

fondue
(fawngdew)
a hot, bubbly mixture of melted cheese, white wine, a drop of kirsch and a hint of garlic; each guest dips a bite-size piece of bread on a fork into the pot of cheese.

raclette
(rahkleht)
a half round of a firm cheese which is heated against a fire or grilled until the surface begins to melt; the melting cheese is then scraped off onto a warmed plate and eaten with boiled potatoes, gherkins and pickled pearl onions.

And here are some cheese snacks which are favourites among the French and Swiss:

croque-monsieur
(krok mersyur)
toasted ham and cheese sandwich

croûte au fromage
(kroot oa fromahzh)
hot, melted cheese served over a slice of toast, sometimes with ham and topped by a fried egg

ramequin
(rahmerkang)
cheese ramekin (small cheese tart)

tarte au fromage
(tahrt oa fromahzh)
cheese tart

Fruit *Fruits*

Fruit is generally served after the cheese.

Do you have fresh fruit?	**Avez-vous des fruits frais?**	ahvay voo day frwee freh
I'd like a (fresh) fruit cocktail.	**Je voudrais une salade de fruits (frais).**	zher voodreh ewn sahlahd der frwee (freh)

abricot	ahbreekoa	apricot
amandes	ahmahngd	almonds
ananas	ahnahnahss	pineapple
banane	bahnahn	banana
brugnon	brewñawng	nectarine
cassis	kahsseess	blackcurrants
cerises (noires)	serreez (nwahr)	(black) cherries
citron	seetrawng	lemon
cacahouètes	kahkahooeht	peanuts
dattes	daht	dates
figues	feeg	figs
fraises	frehz	strawberries
framboises	frahngbwahz	raspberries
fruits secs	frwee sehk	dried fruit
groseilles	grozehy	redcurrants
à maquereau	ah mahkerroa	gooseberries
mandarine	mahngdahreen	tangerine
marrons	mahrawng	chestnuts
melon	merlawng	melon
mûres	mewr	mulberries blackberries
myrtilles	meerteey	bilberries, blueberries
noisettes	nwahzeht	hazelnuts
noix	nwah	walnuts
noix de coco	nwah der kokoa	coconut
orange	orahngzh	orange
pamplemousse	pahngplermooss	grapefruit
pastèque	pahstehk	watermelon
pêche	pehsh	peach
poire	pwahr	pear
pomme	pom	apple
pruneaux	prewnoa	prunes
prunes	prewn	plums
raisin	rehzang	grapes
blanc/noir	blahng/nwahr	green/blue
raisins secs	rehzang sehk	raisins
rhubarbe	rewbahrb	rhubarb

Dessert *Desserts*

I'd like a dessert, please.	**Je prendrai un dessert, s'il vous plaît.**	zher prahngdray ang dehssehr seel voo pleh
What do you recommend?	**Que me/nous recommandez-vous?**	ker mer/noo rerkommahngday voo
Something light, please.	**Quelque chose de léger, s'il vous plaît.**	kehlker shoaz der layzhay seel voo pleh
Just a small portion.	**Une petite portion, s'il vous plaît.**	ewn perteet porsyawng seel voo pleh

barquette (bahrkeht)	small boat-shaped pastry shell garnished with fruit
crêpe suzette (krehp sewzeht)	large, thin pancakes simmered in orange juice and flambéd with orange liqueur
poire Belle Hélène (pwahr behl aylehn)	pear with vanilla ice-cream and chocolate sauce
profiterole (profeeterrol)	puff pastry filled with whipped cream or custard
sabayon (sahbahyawng)	creamy dessert of egg yolks, wine, sugar and flavouring

colonel	kolonehl	lemon (water ice) doused with vodka
coupe (glacée)	koop glahssay	often means a sundae
crème caramel	krehm kahrahmehl	caramel pudding
crème Chantilly	krehm shahngteeyee	whipped cream
flan	flahng	custard
gâteau au chocolat	gahtoa oa shokolah	chocolate cake
glace aux fraises/ à la vanille	glahss oa frehz/ah lah vahneey	strawberry/vanilla ice-cream
mousse au chocolat	mooss oa shokolah	chocolate pudding
omelette norvégienne	omerleht norvayzhyehn	baked Alaska
sorbet	sorbeh	water ice (Am. sherbet)
soufflé au Grand-Marnier	sooflay oa grahng mahrnyay	soufflé made of orange liqueur
tarte aux pommes	tahrt oa pom	apple tart (pie)
tartelette	tahrterleht	small tart
tourte	toort	layer cake
vacherin glacé	vahsherrang glahssay	Ice-cream cake

Aperitifs *Apéritifs*

For most Frenchmen, the aperitif is just as important as
our cocktail or highball. Often bittersweet, some aperitifs
have a wine and brandy base with herbs and bitters (like
Amer Picon, Byrrh, Dubonnet), others called *pastis* have
an aniseed base (like Pernod, Ricard) or a vegetable base
(like Cynar produced from artichoke). An aperitif may also
be simply vermouth (like Noilly Prat) or a liqueur drink like
blanc-cassis or *"kir"* (chilled white wine mixed with a black-
currant syrup). An aperitif is rarely drunk neat (straight) but
usually with ice or seltzer water.

I'd like a Cynar ...	**Je voudrais un Cynar ...**	zher voodreh ang seenahr
neat (straight)	**sec**	sehk
on the rocks	**avec des glaçons**	ahvehk day glahssawng
with (seltzer) water	**à l'eau (au siphon)**	ah loa (oa seefawng)

À VOTRE SANTÉ
(ah votr sahngtay)
YOUR HEALTH!/CHEERS!

Beer *Bières*

Beer is a popular drink in some French-speaking areas. You
may like to sample some of the local brews, for instance
Kronenbourg in France, *Stella Artois* in Belgium and *Cardinal* in Switzerland.

I'd like a beer, please.	**Je voudrais une bière, s'il vous plaît.**	zher voodreh ewn byehr seel voo pleh
Do you have ... beer?	**Avez-vous de la bière ...?**	ahvay voo der lah byehr
bottled	**en bouteilles**	ahng bootehy
draught	**pression**	prehssyawng
foreign	**étrangère**	aytrahngzhehr
light/dark	**blonde/brune**	blawngd/brewn

Wine *Vins*

France is the world's greatest producer of fine wine so naturally the matter is taken quite seriously. However, you needn't be frightened off by an impressive list of expensive wines. There are a few rules of thumb to bear in mind, and the rest is largely up to your personal taste.

French cuisine and wine are inseparable components. The one complements the other. The enjoyment of a delicately flavoured *pâte de foie gras,* for instance, can be all the more enhanced with the proper wine.

There are some dishes, however, with which no wine should be drunk. Don't drink wine with salads or other dishes with vinegar preparations. Combining the two could result in a strange taste. Wine doesn't necessarily accompany soup. But if wine is an ingredient in the soup, like *consommé au porto,* then you could have the same wine—port wine in that case—with your soup.

Otherwise, the time-honoured general guideline has it that white wine goes well with fish, fowl and light meats while dark meats call for a red wine. A good rosé or dry champagne goes well with almost anything and can accompany the whole meal.

Everyone's heard of *Bordeaux* (we call it claret) and *Bourgogne* (burgundy) wine. But France has hundreds of kinds of wine going all the way from its prestigious *premiers crus* to the more humble *vins ordinaires.* Don't miss the opportunity to sample local wine. Much of it doesn't travel well and is therefore never exported. The wine of each region is imbued with the character of that district.

The chart on the next page will help to identify some of the good regional wine. Fine provincial cooking is well accompanied by good local wine whereas exquisite cuisine calls for a noble wine.

Restaurant

Type of wine	Examples	Accompanies
sweet white wine	best known are those in the Sauternes family; the noblest is Château-Yquem	desserts, especially custard, pudding, cake, sweet soufflé, pâté — at one time popular with oysters
light, dry white wine	Alsatian, Muscadet, Riesling, Sancerre; some types of Pouilly fumé, Pouilly-Fuissé, Chablis; local white wine and Swiss wine often fall into this category	oysters, cold meat or shellfish, grilled fish, boiled meat, egg dishes, first courses, Swiss raclette and fondue
full-bodied, dry white wine	white Burgundy, dry Côtes-du-Rhône, Graves	fish, fowl, veal served in creamy sauces, foie gras
rosé	Rosé d'Anjou	goes with almost anything but especially cold dishes, pâtés, eggs, pork, lamb
light-bodied red wine	Bordeaux from Médoc or Graves districts; a Beaujolais, local or Swiss wine often fits into this selection	roast chicken, turkey, veal, lamb, beef fillet, ham, liver, quail, pheasant, foie gras, soft-textured cheeses, stews, steaks
full-bodied red wine	any of the fine Burgundies or Châteauneuf-du-Pape; certain Bordeaux	duck, goose, kidneys, most game, tangy cheese like bleu — in short, any strong-flavoured preparations
extra dry champagne	any of this category	goes with anything, may be drunk as an aperitif or as the climax to the dinner
dry champagne	any of this category	as an aperitif; shellfish, foie gras, nuts and dried fruit
sweet champagne	any of this category	dessert and pastry

I'd like ... of ...	Je voudrais ... de ...	zher voodreh ... der
a carafe	une carafe	ewn kahrahf
a half bottle	une demi-bouteille	ewn dermee bootehy
a glass	un verre	ang vehr
a litre	un litre	ang leetr
I want a bottle of white/red wine.	J'aimerais une bouteille de vin blanc/rouge.	zhehmerreh ewn bootehy der vang blahng/roozh
A bottle of champagne, please.	Une bouteille de champagne, s'il vous plaît.	ewn bootehy der shangpahñ seel voo pleh
Please bring me another ...	Apportez-m'en encore ...	ahportay mahng ahngkor
Where does this wine come from?	De quelle région vient ce vin?	der kehl rayzhyawng vyang ser vang

red	rouge	roozh
white	blanc	blahng
rosé	rosé	roazay
dry	sec	sehk
light	léger	layzhay
full-bodied	corsé	korsay
sparkling	mousseux	moossur
very dry	brut	brewt
sweet	doux	doo

Other alcoholic drinks *Autres boissons alcoolisées*

You'll certainly want to take the occasion to sip a fine cognac after a meal. We usually consider cognac and brandy as being synonymous. In the strict sense of the word, cognac is the famed wine-distilled brandy from the Charente-Maritime region. Try one of these: *Courvoisier, Hennessy, Rémy-Martin*. Other areas are noted for their fruit-distilled brandies like *quetsche* (plum), *marc* (grape), *calvados* (apple), *kirsch* (cherry), *poire Williams* (pear).

| Are there any local specialities? | Avez-vous des spécialités locales? | ahvay voo day spayssyahleetay lokahl |

I'd like to try a glass of …, please.	**Je voudrais goûter un verre de …**	zher voodreh gootay ang vehr der
A (double) whisky, please.	**Un whisky (double), s'il vous plaît.**	ang "whisky" (doobl) seel voo pleh
brandy	**un cognac**	ang koñyahk
gin and tonic	**un gin-tonic**	ang "gin-tonic"
liqueur	**une liqueur**	ewn leekurr
port	**un porto**	ang portoa
rum	**un rhum**	ang rom
sherry	**un sherry**	ang "sherry"
vermouth	**un vermouth**	ang vehrmoot
vodka	**une vodka**	ewn vodka
neat (straight)	**sec**	sehk
on the rocks	**avec des glaçons**	ahvehk day glahssawng

Nonalcoholic drinks   *Boissons sans alcool*

apple juice	**un jus de pomme**	ang zhew der pom
(hot) chocolate	**un chocolat (chaud)**	ang shokolah (shoa)
coffee	**un café**	ang kahfay
black	**noir**	nwahr
with cream	**crème**	krehm
with milk	**au lait**	oa leh
caffein-free	**décaféiné**	daykahfayeenay
espresso coffee	**un express**	ang nehxprehss
fruit juice	**un jus de fruits**	ang zhew der frwee
grapefruit juice	**un jus de pample-mousse**	ang zhew der pahngpler-mooss
herb tea	**une tisane**	ewn teezahn
lemon juice	**un citron pressé**	ang seetrawng prehssay
lemonade	**une limonade**	ewn leemonahd
milk	**un lait**	ang leh
milkshake	**un frappé**	ang frahpay
mineral water	**de l'eau minérale**	der loa meenayrahl
fizzy (carbonated)	**gazeuse**	gahzurz
still	**non gazeuse**	nawng gahzurz
orange juice	**un jus d'orange**	ang zhew dorahngzh
orangeade	**une orangeade**	ewn orahngzhahd
tea	**un thé**	ang tay
cup of tea	**une tasse de thé**	ewn tahss der tay
with milk/lemon	**crème/citron**	krehm/seetrawng
iced tea	**un thé glacé**	ang tay glahssay
tomato juice	**un jus de tomate**	ang zhew der tomaht
tonic water	**un Schweppes**	ang "Schweppes"

Complaints *Réclamations*

There is a plate/glass missing.	Il manque une assiette/un verre.	eel mahngk ewn ahssyeht/ ang vehr
I have no knive/fork/ spoon.	Je n'ai pas de couteau/fourchette/ cuillère.	zher nay pah der kootoa/ foorsheht/kweeyehr
That's not what I ordered.	Ce n'est pas ce que j'ai commandé.	ser neh pah ser ker zhay kommahngday
I asked for ...	J'ai demandé ...	zhay dermahngday
There must be some mistake.	Il doit y avoir une erreur.	eel dwah ee avwahr ewn ehrurr
May I change this?	Pourriez-vous me changer ceci?	pooray voo mer shahngzhay serssee
I asked for a small portion (for the child).	J'avais demandé une petite portion (pour cet enfant).	zhahveh dermahngday ewn perteet porsyawng (poor seht ahngfahng)
The meat is ...	La viande est ...	lah vyahngd eh
overdone	trop cuite	troa kweet
underdone	pas assez cuite	pah zahssay kweet
too rare	trop saignante	troa sehñahngt
too tough	trop dure	troa dewr
This is too ...	C'est trop ...	seh troa
bitter/salty/sweet	amer/salé/sucré	ahmehr/sahlay/sewkray
I don't like this.	Je n'aime pas ceci.	zher nehm pah serssee
The food is cold.	C'est tout froid.	seh too frwah
This isn't fresh.	Ce n'est pas frais.	ser neh pah freh
What's taking you so long?	Pourquoi y a-t-il autant d'attente?	poorkwah ee ahteel oatahng dahtahngt
Have you forgotten our drinks?	Avez-vous oublié nos boissons?	ahvay voo zoobleeyay noa bwahssawng
The wine tastes of cork.	Ce vin a un goût de bouchon.	ser vang ah ang goo der booshawng
This isn't clean.	Ce n'est pas propre.	ser neh pah propr
Would you ask the head waiter to come over?	Envoyez-moi donc le maître d'hôtel.	ahngvwahyay mwah dawngk ler mehtr doatehl

The bill (check) *L'addition*

A service charge is generally included automatically in restaurant bills. Anything extra for the waiter is optional. Credit cards may be used in an increasing number of restaurants. Signs are posted indicating which cards are accepted.

I'd like to pay.	**L'addition, s'il vous plaît.**	lahdeessyawng seel voo pleh
We'd like to pay separately.	**Nous voudrions payer chacun notre part.**	noo voodreeyawng pehyay shahkang notr pahr
I think you made a mistake in this bill.	**Je crois qu'il y a une erreur dans l'addition.**	zher krwah keel ee ah ewn ehrurr dahng lahdeessyawng
What is this amount for?	**Que représente ce montant?**	ker rerprayzahngt ser mawngtahng
Is service included?	**Est-ce que le service est compris?**	ehss ker ler sehrveess eh kawngpree
Is the cover charge included?	**Est-ce que le couvert est compris?**	ehss ker ler koovehr eh kawngpree
Is everything included?	**Est-ce que tout est compris?**	ehss ker too teh kawngpree
Do you accept traveller's cheques?	**Acceptez-vous les chèques de voyage?**	ahksehptay voo lay shehk der vwahyahzh
Can I pay with this credit card?	**Puis-je payer avec cette carte de crédit?**	pweezh pehyay ahvehk seht kahrt der kraydee
Thank you, this is for you.	**Merci. Voici pour vous.**	mehrsee. vwahssee poor voo
Keep the change.	**Gardez la monnaie.**	gahrday lah monneh
That was a delicious meal.	**Le repas était délicieux.**	ler rerpah ayteh dayleessyur
We enjoyed it, thank you.	**C'était très bon, merci.**	sayteh treh bawng mehrsee

---

SERVICE COMPRIS
SERVICE INCLUDED

TIPPING, see inside back-cover

Snacks—Picnic *Casse-croûte – Pique-nique*

Cafés serve hearty sandwiches of long hunks of French bread filled with ham, cheese, pâté, tomatoes, green salad or hardboiled eggs. Thin-sliced sandwich bread *(pain de mie)* is used for *croque-monsieur* (toasted ham-and-cheese sandwich). Omelettes are always reliable fare, and so are the excellent thin-crusted pizzas (all flavours). The delicious *crêpes,* paper-thin pancakes dusted with sugar or filled with jam, are sold at small street stands.

I'll have one of these, please.	**J'en voudrais un de ceux-ci, s'il vous plaît.**	zhahng voodreh ang der surssee seel voo pleh
Give me two of these and one of those.	**Donnez-moi deux de ceux-ci et un de ceux-là.**	donnay mwah dur der surssee ay ang der surlah
to the left/right above/below	**à gauche/à droite au-dessus/au-dessous**	ah goash/ah drwaht oa derssew/oa derssoo
It's to take away.	**C'est pour emporter.**	seh poor ahngportay
I'd like a/some ...	**Je voudrais ...**	zher voodreh
chicken	**un poulet**	ang pooleh
half a roasted chicken	**un demi-poulet grillé**	ang dermee pooleh greeyay
chips (french fries)	**des frites**	day freet
pancake	**une crêpe**	ewn krehp
with sugar	**au sucre**	oa sewkr
with jam	**à la confiture**	ah lah kawngfeetewr
sandwich	**un sandwich**	ang "sandwich"
cheese	**au fromage**	oa fromahzh
ham	**au jambon**	oa zhahngbawng
vegetable salad	**des crudités**	day krewdeetay

Here's a basic list of food and drink that might come in useful when shopping for a picnic.

Please give me a/an/ some ...	**Donnez-moi ..., s'il vous plaît.**	donnay mwah ... seel voo pleh
apples	**des pommes**	day pom
bananas	**des bananes**	day bahnahn
biscuits (Br.)	**des biscuits**	day beeskwee
beer	**de la bière**	der lah byehr

bread	**du pain**	dew pang
butter	**du beurre**	dew burr
cake	**un gâteau**	ang gahtoa
cheese	**du fromage**	dew fromahzh
chips (Am.)	**des chips**	day "chips"
chocolate bar	**une plaque de chocolat**	ewn plahk der shokolah
coffee	**du café**	dew kahfay
cold cuts	**de la charcuterie**	der lah shahrkewterree
cookies	**des biscuits**	day beeskwee
crackers	**des biscuits salés**	day beeskwee sahlay
crisps	**des chips**	day "chips"
eggs	**des œufs**	day zur
gherkins (pickles)	**des cornichons**	day korneeshawng
grapes	**du raisin**	dew rehzang
ham	**du jambon**	dew zhahngbawng
ice-cream	**de la glace**	der lah glahss
lemon	**un citron**	ang seetrawng
milk	**du lait**	dew leh
mustard	**de la moutarde**	der lah mootahrd
oranges	**des oranges**	day zorahngzh
pastries	**des pâtisseries**	day pahteesserree
pepper	**du poivre**	dew pwahvr
roll	**un petit pain**	ang pertee pang
salt	**du sel**	dew sehl
sausage	**une saucisse**	ewn soasseess
soft drink	**une boisson non alcoolisée**	ewn bwahssawng nawng nahlkoleezay
sugar	**du sucre**	dew sewkr
tea	**du thé**	dew tay
yoghurt	**un yoghourt (yaourt)**	ang yogoort (yahoort)

... plus a choice of French bread:

baguette	bahgeht	long thin loaf of French bread
ficelle	feessehl	same as *baguette*, but thinner
pain	pang	bread
blanc/bis	blahng/bee	white/brown
complet	kawngpleh	wholemeal (whole-wheat)
de seigle	der sehgl	rye
petit pain	pertee pang	roll
au cumin	oa kewmang	with caraway seeds
aux pavots	oa pahvoa	with poppy seeds

Travelling around

Plane *Avion*

Is there a flight to Paris?	**Y a-t-il un vol pour Paris?**	ee ahteel ang vol poor pahree
Is it a direct flight?	**Est-ce un vol direct?**	ehss ang vol deerehkt
When's the next plane to Lyons?	**Quand part le prochain avion pour Lyon?**	kahng pahr ler proshang nahvyawng poor lyawng
Do I have to change planes?	**Est-ce que je dois changer d'avion?**	ehss ker zher dwah shahngzhay dahvyawng
Can I make a connection to Geneva?	**Puis-je avoir une correspondance pour Genève?**	pweezh ahvwahr ewn korrehspawngdahngss poor zhernehv
I'd like a ticket to Brussels.	**Je voudrais un billet pour Bruxelles.**	zher voodreh ang beeyeh poor brewssehl
single (one-way)	**aller**	ahlay
return (roundtrip)	**aller-retour**	ahlay rertoor
What time does the plane take off?	**A quelle heure part l'avion?**	ah kehl urr pahr lahvyawng
What time do I have to check in?	**A quelle heure est l'enregistrement?**	ah kehl urr eh lahngrerzheestrermahng
Is there a bus to the airport?	**Y a-t-il un bus pour l'aéroport?**	ee ahteel ang bewss poor lahayropor
What's the flight number?	**Quel est le numéro du vol?**	kehl eh ler newmayroa dew vol
What time do we arrive?	**A quelle heure arrivons-nous?**	ah kehl urr ahreevawng noo
I'd like to ... my reservation on flight no ...	**Je voudrais ... ma réservation sur le vol ...**	zher voodreh ... mah rayzehrvahssyawng sewr ler vol
cancel	**annuler**	ahnnewlay
change	**changer**	shahngzhay
confirm	**confirmer**	kawngfeermay

ARRIVÉE ARRIVAL	**DÉPART** DEPARTURE

Train *Train*

Rail travel in France is usually fast on the main lines, and the trains (diesel and electric) run on time. Unless otherwise indicated, the terms below apply equally to France, Belgium and Switzerland.

TGV (tay zhay vay)	Extra-high-speed train *(Train à Grande Vitesse)* operating on some routes; reservation compulsory, surcharge sometimes payable
TEE (tay ay ay)	Trans Europ Express; a luxury international service with first class only; reservation compulsory, surcharge payable
Rapide (rahpeed)	Long-distance express stopping only at main stations; luxury coaches; additional fare sometimes required (France)
Intercity (angtehrseetee)	Inter-city express with very few stops
Express (ehxprehss)	Ordinary long-distance train, stopping at main stations (France)
Direct (deerehkt)	The equivalent of the French *express* (Switzerland and Belgium)
Omnibus (omneebewss)	Local train stopping at all stations (France and Belgium)
Train régional (trang rayzhyonahl)	Local train stopping at all stations (Switzerland)
Autorail (oatorahy)	Small diesel used on short runs

Here are a few more useful terms which you may need:

Wagon-restaurant* (vahgawng rehstoarahng)	Dining-car
Wagon-lit* (vahgawng lee)	Sleeping-car with individual compartments (single or double) and washing facilities
Couchette (koosheht)	Berth (converted from seats) with blankets and pillows. You may want a *couchette supérieure* (koosheht sewpayryurr—upper berth) or a *couchette inférieure* (koosheht angfayryurr—lower berth)

---

* The term *voiture* (vwahtewr) is often used instead of *wagon*.

To the railway station *Pour aller à la gare*

Where's the railway station?	**Où se trouve la gare?**	oo ser troov lah gahr
Taxi!	**Taxi!**	tahksee
Take me to the railway station.	**Conduisez-moi à la gare.**	kawngdweezay mwah ah lah gahr
What's the fare?	**C'est combien?**	say kawngbyang

ENTRÉE	ENTRANCE
SORTIE	EXIT
ACCÈS AUX QUAIS	TO THE PLATFORMS
RENSEIGNEMENTS	INFORMATION

Where's the ...? *Où est ...?*

Where is/are the ...?	**Où est ...?**	oo eh
bar	**le bar**	ler bahr
booking office	**le bureau de réservation**	ler bewroa der rayzehrvahssyawng
currency exchange office	**le bureau de change**	ler bewroa der shahngzh
left-luggage office (baggage check)	**la consigne**	lah kawngsseeñ
lost property (lost and found) office	**le bureau des objets trouvés**	ler bewroa day zobzheh troovay
luggage lockers	**la consigne automatique**	lah kawngsseeñ oatomahteek
newsstand	**le kiosque à journaux**	ler kyosk ah zhoornoa
platform 7	**le quai 7**	ler kay 7
reservations office	**le bureau de réservation**	ler bewroa der rayzehrvahssyawng
restaurant	**le restaurant**	ler rehstoarahng
snack bar	**le buffet-express**	ler bewfeh exprehss
ticket office	**le guichet**	ler geesheh
waiting-room	**la salle d'attente**	lah sahl dahtahngt
Where are the toilets?	**Où sont les toilettes?**	oo sawng lay twahleht

TAXI, see page 21

Inquiries *Renseignements*

In Belgium, France and Switzerland $\boxed{i}$ means information office.

When is the ... train to Nice?	Quand part le ... train pour Nice?	kahng pahr ler ... trang poor neess
first/last next	premier/dernier prochain	prermyay/dehrnyay proshang
What time does the train for Calais leave?	A quelle heure part le train pour Calais?	ah kell urr pahr ler trang poor kahleh
What's the fare to Avignon?	Quel est le prix du billet pour Avignon?	kehl eh ler pree dew beeyeh poor ahveeñawng
Is it a through train?	Est-ce un train direct?	ehss ang trang deerehkt
Is there a connection to ...?	Est-ce qu'il existe une correspondance pour ...?	ehss keel ehxeest ewn korrehspawngdahngss poor
Do I have to change trains?	Dois-je changer (de train)?	dwahzh shahngzhay (der trang)
Is there sufficient time to change?	A-t-on le temps de changer?	ahtawng ler tahng der shahngzhay
Will the train leave on time?	Est-ce que le train partira à l'heure?	ehss ker ler trang pahrteerah ah lurr
What time does the train arrive at Bordeaux?	A quelle heure le train arrive-t-il à Bordeaux?	ah kell urr ler trang ahreev teel ah bordoa
Is there a dining-car/ sleeping-car on the train?	Y a-t-il un wagon-restaurant/un wagon-lit?	ee ahteel ang vahgawng rehstoarahng/ang vahgawng lee
Does the train stop at Mâcon?	Est-ce que le train s'arrête à Mâcon?	ehss ker ler trang sahreht ah mahkawng
What platform does the train for Strasbourg leave from?	De quel quai part le train pour Strasbourg?	der kehl kay pahr ler trang poor strahsboor
What platform does the train from Geneva arrive at?	Sur quel quai arrive le train de Genève?	sewr kehl kay ahreev ler trang der zhernehv
I'd like to buy a time-table.	Je voudrais acheter un horaire.	zher voodreh ahshertay ang norrehr

C'est un train direct.	It's a through train.
Changez à ...	You have to change at ...
Changez à ... et prenez un omnibus.	Change at ... and get a local train.
Le quai 7 se trouve ...	Platform 7 is ...
là-bas/en haut	over there/upstairs
à gauche/à droite	on the left/on the right
Il y a un train pour ... à ...	There's a train to ... at ...
Votre train partira du quai 8.	Your train will leave from platform 8.
Le train a un retard de ... minutes.	There'll be a delay of ... minutes.
Première classe en tête/ au milieu/en queue.	First class at the front/in the middle/at the end.

Tickets *Billets*

I want a ticket to Nice.	**Je voudrais un billet pour Nice.**	zher voodreh ang beeyeh poor neess
single (one-way)	**aller**	ahlay
return (roundtrip)	**aller-retour**	ahlay rertoor
first/second class	**première/deuxième classe**	prermyehr/durzyehm klahss
half price	**demi-tarif**	dermee tahreef

Reservation *Réservation*

I want to book a ...	**Je voudrais réserver ...**	zher voodreh rayzehrvay
seat (by the window)	**une place (côté fenêtre)**	ewn plahss (koatay fernehtr)
berth	**une couchette**	ewn koosheht
upper	**supérieure**	sewpayryurr
middle	**au milieu**	oa meelyur
lower	**inférieure**	angfayryurr
berth in the sleeping car	**une place en wagon-lit**	ewn plahss ang vahgawng lee

All aboard *En voiture*

Is this the right platform for the train to Paris?	**Est-ce bien de ce quai que part le train pour Paris?**	ehss byang der ser kay ker pahr ler trang poor pahree
Is this the right train to Marseilles?	**C'est bien le train pour Marseille, n'est-ce pas?**	seh byang ler trang poor mahrsehy nehss pah
Excuse me. May I get by?	**Pardon. Puis-je passer?**	pahrdawng pweezh pahssay
Is this seat taken?	**Cette place est-elle occupée?**	seht plahss ehtehl okkewpay

FUMEURS	**NON-FUMEURS**
SMOKER	NONSMOKER

I think that's my seat.	**Je crois que c'est ma place.**	zher krwah ker seh mah plahss
Would you let me know before we get to Liège?	**Pourriez-vous m'avertir quand nous arriverons à Liège?**	pooryay voo mahvehrteer kahng noo zahreeverrawng ah lyehzh
What station is this?	**A quelle gare sommes-nous?**	ah kehl gahr som noo
How long does the train stop here?	**Combien de temps le train s'arrête-t-il ici?**	kawngbyang der tahng ler trang sahreht teel eessee
When do we get to Orleans?	**Quand arriverons-nous à Orléans?**	kahng tahreevrawng noo ah orlayahng

Sleeping *En wagon-lit*

Are there any free compartments in the sleeping-car?	**Y a-t-il des compartiments libres dans le wagon-lit?**	ee ahteel day kawngpahrteemahng leebr dahng ler vahgawng lee
Where's the sleeping-car?	**Où se trouve le wagon-lit?**	oo ser troov ler vahgawng lee
Where's my berth?	**Où est ma couchette?**	oo eh mah koosheht

I'd like a lower berth.	**Je voudrais une couchette inférieure.**	zher voodreh ewn koosheht angfayryurr
Would you make up our berths?	**Pourriez-vous installer nos couchettes?**	pooryay voo angstahlay noa koosheht
Would you wake me at 7 o'clock?	**Pourriez vous me réveiller à 7 heures?**	pooryay voo mer rayvehyay ah 7 urr

Eating   *Au wagon-restaurant*

You can get snacks and drinks in the buffet-car and in the dining-car when it's not being used for main meals. On some trains an attendant comes around with snacks, coffee, tea, and soft drinks.

| Where's the dining-car? | **Où est le wagon-restaurant?** | oo eh ler vahgawng rehstoarahng |

Baggage and porters   *Bagages et porteurs*

Porter!	**Porteur?**	porturr
Can you help me with my luggage?	**Pouvez-vous m'aider à porter mes bagages?**	poovay voo mehday ah portay may bahgahzh
Where are the luggage trolleys (carts)?	**Où sont les chariots à bagages?**	oo sawng lay shahryoa ah bahgahzh
Where are the luggage lockers?	**Où est la consigne automatique?**	oo eh lah kawngseeñ oatomahteek
Where's the left-luggage office (baggage check)?	**Où est la consigne?**	oo eh lah kawngseeñ
I'd like to leave my luggage, please.	**Je voudrais déposer mes bagages, s'il vous plaît.**	zher voodreh daypoazay may bahgahzh seel voo pleh
I'd like to register (check) my luggage.	**Je voudrais faire enregistrer mes bagages.**	zher voodreh fehr ahngrergeestray may bahgahzh

---

ENREGISTREMENT DES BAGAGES
REGISTERING (CHECKING) BAGGAGE

PORTERS, see also page 18

Coach (long-distance bus)   *Car*

You'll find information on destinations and timetables at
the coach terminals, usually situated near railway stations.
Many companies offer coach tours, as do the French
National Railways.

When's the next coach to ...?	**A quelle heure est le prochain car pour ...?**	ah kehl urr eh ler proshang kahr poor
Does this coach stop at ...?	**Ce car s'arrête-t-il à ...?**	ser kahr sahreht teel ah
How long does the journey (trip) take?	**Combien de temps dure le trajet?**	kawngbyang der tahng dewr ler trahzheh

Note: Most of the phrases on the previous pages can be used
or adapted for travelling on local transport.

Bus—Tram (streetcar)   *Bus – Tram*

Many cities have introduced an automatic system of fare-
paying whereby you insert the exact change into a ticket dis-
penser at the bus or tram stop or have the machine validate
your prepaid ticket.

If you're planning to get around a lot in one city by bus,
tram, or *métro* (see next page), enquire about a booklet
of tickets or special runabout tickets, such as the *carte* or
abonnement d'un jour (one-day ticket), *carte orange* (valid
a week or a month, in Paris) or *billet touristique* (special
tourist ticket for two or more days).

I'd like a booklet of tickets.	**J'aimerais un carnet de tickets.**	zhehmerreh ang kahrneh der teekeh
Where can I get a bus to the opera?	**Où puis-je prendre le bus pour l'Opéra?**	oo pweezh prahngdr ler bewss poor lopayrah
What bus do I take for Montmartre?	**Quel bus dois-je prendre pour aller à Montmartre?**	kehl bewss dwahzh prahngdr poor ahlay ah mawngmahrtr
Where's the bus stop?	**Où se trouve l'arrêt de bus?**	oo ser troov lahreh der bewss

When is the ... bus to St. Germain?	Quand part le ... bus pour Saint-Germain?	kawng pahr ler ... bewss poor sang zhehrmang
first/last/next	premier/dernier/ prochain	prermyay/dehrnyay/ proshang
How much is the fare to ...?	Quel est le prix du trajet jusqu'à ...?	kehl eh ler pree dew trahzheh zhewskah
Do I have to change buses?	Dois-je changer de bus?	dwahzh shahngzhay der bewss
How many bus stops are there to ...?	Combien y a-t-il d'arrêts jusqu'à ...?	kawngbyang ee ahteel dahreh zhewskah
Will you tell me when to get off?	Pourriez-vous me dire quand je dois descendre?	pooryay voo mer deer kahng zher dwah dehssahngdr
I want to get off at Notre-Dame.	Je voudrais descendre à Notre-Dame.	zher voodreh dehssahngdr ah notrer dahm

| ARRÊT FIXE | REGULAR BUS STOP |
| ARRÊT SUR DEMANDE | STOPS ON REQUEST |

Underground (subway) *Métro*

The *métros* (maytroa) in Paris and Brussels correspond to the London underground or the New York subway. In both cities, the fare is always the same, irrespective of the distance you travel. There's first and second class. Big maps in every Métro station make the system easy to use.

Where's the nearest underground station?	Où se trouve la station de métro la plus proche?	oo ser troov lah stah-ssyawng der maytroa lah plew prosh
Does this train go to ...?	Est-ce que cette rame va à ...?	ehss ker seht rahm vah ah
Where do I change for ...?	Où faut-il changer pour aller à ...?	oo foateel shahngzhay poor ahlay ah
Is the next station ...?	La prochaine gare est-elle bien ...?	lah proshehn gahr ehtehl byang
Which line should I take for ...?	Quelle ligne dois-je prendre pour ...?	kehl leeñ dwahzh prahngdr poor

Boat service *Bateau*

When does the next boat for ... leave?	A quelle heure part le prochain bateau pour ...?	a kehl urr pahr ler proshang bahtoa poor
Where's the embarkation point?	Où s'effectue l'embarquement?	oo sehffehktew lahngbahrkermahng
How long does the crossing take?	Combien de temps dure la traversée?	kawngbyang der tahng dewr lah trahvehrsay
At which port(s) do we stop?	Quel(s) port(s) dessert ce bateau?	kehl por dehssehr ser bahtoa
I'd like to take a cruise.	Je voudrais faire une croisière.	zher voodreh fehr ewn krwahzyehr
boat	le bateau	ler bahtoa
cabin single/double	la cabine pour une personne/ deux personnes	lah kahbeen poor ewn pehrson/ dur pehrson
deck	le pont	ler pawng
ferry	le ferry	ler "ferry"
hovercraft	l'aéroglisseur	lahayrogleessurr
hydrofoil	l'hydroptère	leedroptehr
life belt/boat	la ceinture/le canot de sauvetage	la sangtewr/ler kahnoa der soavertahzh
ship	le navire	ler nahveer

Bicycle hire *Location de bicyclettes*

French National Railways operate a cycle-hire service at major stations. Bicycles may be hired at one station and returned at another.

I'd like to hire a bicycle.	Je voudrais louer une bicyclette.	zher voodreh looay ewn beesseekleht

Other means of transport *Autres moyens de transport*

cable car	la télécabine	lah taylaykahbeen
helicopter	l'hélicoptère	layleekoptehr
moped	le vélomoteur	ler vayloamoturr
motorbike/scooter	la moto/le scooter	lah moto/ler skootehr

Or perhaps you prefer:

to hitchhike	faire de l'auto-stop	fehr der loatostop
to walk	marcher	mahrshay

Car *Voiture*

In general roads are good in Belgium, France and Switzerland. Motorways (expressways) are subject to tolls *(le péage)* in France, they are free in Belgium. If you use the motorways in Switzerland you must purchase a sticker (valid for one year) to be displayed on the windscreen.

A red reflector warning triangle must be carried for use in case of a breakdown, and seat belts *(la ceinture de sécurité)* are obligatory.

Where's the nearest filling station?	Où est la station-service la plus proche?	oo eh lah stahssyawng sehrveess lah plew prosh
Full tank, please.	Le plein, s'il vous plaît.	ler plang seel voo pleh
Give me ... litres of petrol (gasoline).	Donnez-moi ... litres d'essence.	donnay mwah ... leetr dehssahngss
super (premium)/ regular/unleaded/ diesel	du super/de la normale/sans plomb/ gas-oil	dew sewpohr/der lah normahl/sahng plawng/ gahzoyl
Please check the ...	Veuillez contrôler ...	veryay kawngtroalay
battery	la batterie	lah bahterree
brake fluid	le liquide des freins	ler leekeed day frang
oil/water	l'huile/l'eau	lweel/loa
Would you check the tyre pressure?	Pourriez-vous contrôler la pression des pneus?	pooryay voo kawngtroalay lah prehssyawng day pnur
1.6 front, 1.8 rear.	1,6 à l'avant, 1,8 à l'arrière.	ang seess ah lahvahng ang weet ah lahryehr
Please check the spare tyre, too.	Vérifiez aussi la roue de secours.	vayreefyay oassee lah roo der serkoor
Can you mend this puncture (fix this flat)?	Pourriez-vous réparer ce pneu?	pooryay voo raypahray ser pnur
Would you please change the ...?	Pourriez-vous changer ...?	pooryay voo shahngzhay
bulb	l'ampoule	lahngpool
fan belt	la courroie du ventilateur	lah koorrwah dew vahngteelahturr

CAR HIRE, see page 20

spark(ing) plugs	les bougies	lay boozhee
tyre	le pneu	ler pnur
wipers	les essuie-glace	lay zehsswee glahss
Would you clean the windscreen (windshield)?	Pourriez-vous nettoyer le pare-brise?	pooryay voo nehtwahyay ler pahr breez

Asking the way—Street directions   *Pour demander son chemin*

Can you tell me the way to ...?	Pourriez-vous m'indiquer la route de ...?	pooryay voo mangdeekay lah root der
How do I get to ...?	Comment-puis-je aller à ...?	kommahng pweezh ahlay ah
Are we on the right road for ...?	Sommes-nous bien sur la route pour ...?	som noo byang sewr lah root poor
How far is the next village?	A quelle distance se trouve le prochain village?	ah kehl deestahngss ser troov ler proshang veelahzh
How far is it to ... from here?	A quelle distance sommes-nous de ...?	ah kehl deestahngss som noo der
Is there a motorway (expressway)?	Y a-t-il une autoroute?	ee ahteel ewn oatoroot
How long does it take by car/on foot?	Combien de temps est-ce que cela prend en voiture/à pied?	kawngbyang der tahng ehss ker serlah prahng ahng vwahtewr/ah pyay
Can I drive to the centre of town?	Puis-je gagner le centre-ville en voiture?	pweezh gahñay ler sahngtr veel ahng vwahtewr
Can you tell me, where ...is?	Pourriez-vous me dire où se trouve ...?	pooryay voo mer deer oo ser troov
How can I find this place?	Comment puis-je trouver cet endroit?	kommahng pweezh troovay seh tahngdrwah
Where can I find this address?	Où puis-je trouver cette adresse?	oo pweezh troovay seht ahdrehss
Where's this?	Où est-ce?	oo ehss
Can you show me on the map where I am?	Pouvez-vous me montrer sur la carte où je suis?	poovay voo mer mawngtray sewr lah kahrt oo zher swee

Vous êtes sur la mauvaise route.	You're on the wrong road.
Allez tout droit.	Go straight ahead.
C'est là-bas à ...	It's down there on the ...
gauche/droite	left/right
en face de/derrière ...	opposite/behind ...
à côté de/au-delà de ...	next to/after ...
nord/sud	north/south
est/ouest	east/west
Allez jusqu'au premier/ deuxième carrefour.	Go to the first/second crossroads (intersection).
Tournez à gauche après les feux.	Turn left at the traffic lights.
Tournez à droite au prochain coin de rue.	Turn right at the next corner.
Prenez la route de ...	Take the road for ...
Vous devez revenir jusqu'à ...	You have to go back to ...
Suivez la direction ''Nice''.	Follow signs for Nice.

Parking *Stationnement*

In town centres, most street parking is metered. The blue
zones require the *disque de stationnement* or parking disc
(obtainable from petrol stations), which you set to show
when you arrived and when you must leave.

Where can I park?	**Où puis-je me garer?**	oo pweezh mer gahray
Is there a car park nearby?	**Y a-t-il un parking à proximité?**	ee ahteel ang pahrkeeng ah proxeemeetay
May I park here?	**Puis-je me garer ici?**	pweezh mer gahray eessee
How long can I park here?	**Combien de temps puis-je rester ici?**	kawngbyang der tahng pweezh rehstay eessee
What's the charge per hour?	**Quel est le tarif horaire?**	kehl eh ler tahreef orehr
Do you have some change for the parking meter?	**Avez-vous de la monnaie pour le parcomètre?**	ahvay voo der lah monneh poor ler pahrkommehtr

Breakdown—Road assistance   *Pannes – Assistance routière*

Where's the nearest garage?	**Où se trouve le garage le plus proche?**	oo ser troov ler gahrahzh ler plew prosh
Excuse me. My car has broken down.	**Excusez-moi. Ma voiture est en panne.**	ehxkewzay mwah. mah vwahtewr eh tahng pahn
May I use your phone?	**Puis-je me servir de votre téléphone?**	pweezh mer sehrveer der votr taylayfon
I've had a breakdown at ...	**Je suis tombé en panne à ...**	zher swee tawngbay ahng pahn ah
Can you send a mechanic?	**Pouvez-vous envoyer un mécanicien?**	poovay voo ahngvwahyay ang maykahneessyang
My car won't start.	**Je n'arrive pas à démarrer.**	zher nahreev pah ah daymahray
The battery is dead.	**La batterie est à plat.**	lah bahterree eh ah plah
I've run out of petrol (gasoline).	**Je suis en panne d'essence.**	zher swee ahng pahn dehssahngss
I have a flat tyre.	**J'ai un pneu à plat.**	zhay ang pnur ah plah
The engine is overheating.	**Le moteur chauffe.**	ler moturr shoaf
There is something wrong with ...	**J'ai un problème avec ...**	zhay ang problehm ahvehk
brakes	**les freins**	lay frang
carburetor	**le carburateur**	ler kahrbewrahturr
exhaust pipe	**le pot d'échappement**	ler poa dayshahpmahng
radiator	**le radiateur**	ler rahdyahturr
wheel	**une roue**	ewn roo
Can you send a breakdown van (tow truck)?	**Pouvez-vous envoyer une dépanneuse?**	poovay voo ahngvwahyay ewn daypahnurz
How long will you be?	**Combien de temps faut-il compter?**	kawngbyang der tahng foateel kawngtay

Accident—Police   *Accident – Police*

Please call the police.	**Appelez la police, s'il vous plaît.**	ahperlay lah poleess seel voo pleh
There's been an accident. It's about 2 km. from ...	**Il y a eu un accident à environ 2 km de ...**	eel ee ah ew ang nahksseedahng ah ahngveerawng 2 keelomehtr der

Where is there a telephone?	Où y a-t-il un téléphone?	oo ee ahteel ang taylayfon
Call a doctor/an ambulance quickly.	Appelez d'urgence un médecin/une ambulance.	ahperlay dewrzhahngss ang maydsang/ewn ahngbewlahngss
There are people injured.	Il y a des blessés.	eel ee ah day blehssay
Here's my driving licence.	Voici mon permis de conduire.	vwahssee mawng pehrmee der kawngdweer
What's your name and address?	Quels sont vos nom et adresse?	kehl sawng voa nawng ay ahdrehss
What's your insurance company?	Auprès de quelle compagnie êtes-vous assuré?	oapreh der kehl kawngpahñee eht voo ahssewray

Road signs *Panneaux routiers*

ALLUMEZ VOS PHARES	Switch on headlights
ATTENTION	Caution
ATTENTION ÉCOLE	Caution, school
ATTENTION TRAVAUX	Road works ahead (men working)
CÉDER LE PASSAGE	Give way (Yield)
CIRCULATION DIFFICILE	Slow traffic
CHAUSSÉE DÉFORMÉE	Poor road surface
CHUTES DE PIERRES	Falling rocks
DÉVIATION	Diversion/detour
FIN DE L'INTERDICTION DE ...	End of no ... zone
FORTE DÉCLIVITÉ	Steep hill
INTERDICTION DE DOUBLER	No overtaking (no passing)
NIDS DE POULE	Potholes
PASSAGE À NIVEAU	Level (railroad) crossing
PÉAGE	Toll
PISTE RÉSERVÉE AUX TRANSPORTS PUBLICS	Lane reserved for public transport
POIDS LOURDS	Heavy vehicles
RALENTIR	Slow down
RÉSERVÉ AUX PIÉTONS	Pedestrians only
SERREZ À DROITE	Keep right
SORTIE DE CAMIONS	Lorry (truck) exit
STATIONNEMENT AUTORISÉ	Parking allowed
STATIONNEMENT INTERDIT	No parking
VERGLAS	Icy road
VIRAGES	Bends/curves

Sightseeing

Where's the tourist office?	Où se trouve le syndicat d'initiative (l'office du tourisme)?	oo ser troov ler sangdeekah deeneessyahteev (loffeess dew tooreezm)
What are the main points of interest?	Qu'y a-t-il de plus intéressant?	kee ahteel der plew zangtayrehssahng
We're here for ...	Nous sommes ici pour ...	noo som zeessee poor
only a few hours	quelques heures seulement	kehlker zurr surlermahng
a day	un jour	ang zhoor
a week	une semaine	ewn sermehn
Can you recommend a sightseeing tour/an excursion?	Pourriez-vous me conseiller une visite guidée/une excursion?	pooryay voo mer kawngssehyay ewn veezeet geeday/ewn ehxkewrsyawng
What's the point of departure?	D'où part-on?	doo pahrtawng
Will the bus pick us up at the hotel?	Le bus nous prendra-t-il à l'hôtel?	ler bewss noo prahngdrah teel ah loatehl
How much does the tour cost?	A combien revient l'excursion?	ah kawngbyang rervyang lehxkewrsyawng
What time does the tour start?	A quelle heure commence l'excursion?	ah kehl urr kommahngss lehxkewrsyawng
Is lunch included?	Le déjeuner est-il compris?	ler dayzhurnay ehteel kawngpree
What time do we get back?	A quelle heure serons-nous de retour?	ah kehl urr serrawng noo der rertoor
Do we have free time in ...?	Aurons-nous un peu de temps libre à ...?	oarawng noo ang pur der tahng leebr a
Is there an English-speaking guide?	Y a-t-il un guide qui parle anglais?	ee ahteel ang geed kee pahrl ahnggleh
I'd like to hire a private guide for ...	Je voudrais retenir un guide pour ...	zher voodreh rerterneer ang geed poor
half a day	une demi-journée	ewn dermee zhoornay
a full day	toute une journée	too tewn zhoornay

Where is/Where are the ...?	Où se trouve/ Où se trouvent ...?	oo ser troov/ oo ser troov
abbey	l'abbaye	lahbayee
art gallery	la galerie d'art	lah gahlerree dahr
artists' quarter	le quartier des artistes	ler kahrtyay day zahrteest
botanical gardens	le jardin botanique	ler zhahrdang bottahneek
building	le bâtiment	ler bahteemahng
business district	le quartier des affaires	ler kahrtyay day zahfehr
castle	le château	ler shahtoa
catacombs	les catacombes	lay kahtahkawngb
cathedral	la cathédrale	lah kahtaydrahl
cave	la grotte	lah grot
cemetery	le cimetière	ler seemertyehr
city centre	le centre (de la ville)	ler sahngtr (der lah veel)
chapel	la chapelle	lah shahpehl
church	l'église	laygleez
concert hall	la salle de concert	lah sahl der kawngssehr
convent	le couvent	ler koovahng
court house	le palais de justice	ler pahleh der zhewsteess
downtown area	le centre (de la ville)	ler sahngtr (der lah vèèl)
embankment	le quai	ler kay
exhibition	l'exposition	lehxpozeessyawng
factory	l'usine	lewzeen
fair	la foire	lah fwahr
flea market	le marché aux puces	ler mahrshay oa pewss
fortress	la forteresse	lah forterrehss
fountain	la fontaine	lah fawngtehn
gardens	le jardin public	ler zhahrdang pewbleek
harbour	le port	ler por
lake	le lac	ler lahk
library	la bibliothèque	lah beebleeyotehk
market	le marché	ler mahrshay
memorial	le monument	ler monewmahng
monastery	le monastère	ler monahstehr
monument	le monument	ler monewmahng
museum	le musée	ler mewzay
old town	la vieille ville	lah vyehy veel
opera house	l'opéra	lopayrah
palace	le palais	ler pahleh
park	le parc	ler pahrk
parliament building	le Parlement	ler pahrlermahng
planetarium	le planétarium	ler plahnaytahryom
royal palace	le palais royal	ler pahleh rwahyahl
ruins	les ruines	lay rween

82

shopping area	le quartier	ler kahrtyay
	commerçant	kommehrssahng
stadium	le stade	ler stahd
statue	la statue	lah stahtew
stock exchange	la bourse	lah boors
theatre	le théâtre	ler tayahtr
tomb	la tombe	lah tawngb
tower	la tour	lah toor
town hall	l'hôtel de ville	loatehl der veel
university	l'université	lewneevehrseetay
zoo	le jardin zoologique	ler zhahrdang zoalozheek

Admission   *A l'entrée*

Is ... open on Sundays?	Est-ce que ... est ouvert le dimanche?	ehss ker ... eh toovehr ler deemahngsh
When does it open?	A partir de quelle heure est-ce ouvert?	ah pahrteer der kehl urr ehss oovehr
When does it close?	Quelle est l'heure de fermeture?	kehl eh lurr der fermertewr
How much is the entrance fee?	Combien coûte l'entrée?	kawngbyang koot lahngtray
Is there any reduction for ...?	Y a-t-il une réduction pour ...?	ee ahteel ewn raydewksyawng poor
children	les enfants	lay zahngfahng
disabled	les handicapés	lay ahngdeekahpay
groups	les groupes	lay groop
pensioners	les retraités	lay rertrehtay
students	les étudiants	lay zaytewdyahng
Have you a guidebook (in English)?	Avez-vous un guide (en anglais)?	ahvay voo ang geed (ahng nahnggleh)
Can I buy a catalogue?	Puis-je acheter un catalogue?	pweezh ahshtay ang kahtahlog
Is it all right to take pictures?	Est-il permis de prendre des photos?	ehteel pehrmee der prahngdr day fotoa

| ENTRÉE LIBRE | ADMISSION FREE |
| INTERDICTION DE PHOTOGRAPHIER | NO CAMERAS ALLOWED |

Who — What — When? *Qui – Quoi – Quand?*

What's that building?	**Quel est ce bâtiment?**	kehl eh ser bahteemahng
Who was the ...?	**Qui était ...?**	kee ayteh
architect	**l'architecte**	lahrsheetehkt
artist	**l'artiste**	lahrteest
painter	**le peintre**	ler pangtr
sculptor	**le sculpteur**	ler skewlturr
Who built it?	**Qui l'a construit?**	kee lah kawngstrwee
Who painted that picture?	**Qui est l'auteur de ce tableau?**	kee eh loaturr der ser tahbloa
When did he live?	**A quelle époque vivait-il?**	ah kehl aypok veevehteel
When was it built?	**A quand remonte la construction?**	ah kahng rermawngt lah kawngstrewksyawng
Where's the house where ... lived?	**Où est la maison où vécut ...?**	oo eh lah mehzawng oo vaykew
We're interested in ...	**Nous nous intéressons ...**	noo noo zangtayrehssawng
antiques	**aux antiquités**	oa zahngteekeetay
archaeology	**à l'archéologie**	ah lahrkayolozhee
art	**à l'art**	ah lahr
botany	**à la botanique**	ah lah bottahneek
ceramics	**à la céramique**	ah lah sayrahmeek
coins	**aux monnaies**	oa monneh
fine arts	**aux beaux-arts**	oa boa zahr
furniture	**aux meubles**	oa murbl
geology	**à la géologie**	ah lah zhayolozhee
handicrafts	**à l'artisanat**	ah lahrteezahnah
history	**à l'histoire**	ah leestwahr
medicine	**à la médecine**	ah lah maydsseen
music	**à la musique**	ah lah mewzeek
natural history	**à l'histoire naturelle**	ah leestwahr nahtewrehl
ornithology	**à l'ornithologie**	ah lorneetolozhee
painting	**à la peinture**	ah lah pangtewr
pottery	**à la poterie**	ah lah potterree
religion	**à la religion**	ah lah rerleezhyawng
sculpture	**à la sculpture**	ah lah skewltewr
zoology	**à la zoologie**	ah lah zoalozhee
Where's the ... department?	**Où est le département de ...?**	oo eh ler daypahrtermahng der

It's ...	C'est ...	seh
amazing	étonnant	aytonnahng
awful	horrible	orreebl
beautiful	beau	boa
gloomy	sombre	sawngbr
impressive	impressionnant	angprehssyonnahng
interesting	intéressant	angtayrehssahng
magnificent	splendide	splahngdeed
overwhelming	imposant	angpoazahng
strange	étrange	aytrahngzh
superb	superbe	sewpehrb
terrifying	effrayant	ehfrayyahng
tremendous	formidable	formeedahbl
ugly	laid	leh

Religious services *Services religieux*

France is particularly rich in cathedrals and churches worth
visiting, while Geneva in Switzerland was the cradle of
Calvinism. Most places are open for the public to view,
except of course when a service is in progress.

If you're interested in taking photographs, you should
obtain permission first.

Is there a ... near here?	Y a-t-il près d'ici ...?	ee ahteel preh deessee
Catholic church	une église (catholique)	ewn aygleez (kahtoleek)
Protestant church	un temple (protestant)	ang tahngpl (protehstahng)
mosque	une mosquée	ewn moskay
synagogue	une synagogue	ewn seenahgog
At what time is ...?	A quelle heure commence ...?	ah kehl urr kommahngss
mass/the service	la messe/le culte	lah mehss/ler kewlt
Where can I find a ... who speaks English?	Où puis-je trouver un ... qui parle anglais?	oo pweezh troovay ang ... kee pahrl ahnggleh
priest/minister/rabbi	prêtre/pasteur/rabbin	prehtr/pahsturr/rahbang
I'd like to visit the church.	Je voudrais visiter l'église.	zher voodreh veezeetay laygleez

In the countryside *A la campagne*

Is there a scenic route to ...?	**Y a-t-il une route touristique pour ...?**	ee ahteel ewn root tooreesteek poor
How far is it to ...?	**A quelle distance est-on de ...?**	ah kehl deestahngss ehtawng der
Can we walk?	**Pouvons-nous y aller à pied?**	poovawng noo ee ahlay ah pyay
How high is that mountain?	**Quelle est l'altitude de cette montagne?**	kehl eh lahlteetewd der seht mawngtahñ
What's the name of that ...?	**Quel est le nom de ...?**	kehl eh ler nawng der
animal/bird	**cet animal/cet oiseau**	seht ahneemahl/seht wahzoa
flower/tree	**cette fleur/cet arbre**	seht flurr/seht ahrbr

Landmarks *Points de repère*

bridge	**le pont**	ler pawng
cliff	**la falaise**	lah fahlehz
farm	**la ferme**	lah fehrm
field	**le champ**	ler shahng
footpath	**le sentier**	ler sahngtyay
forest	**la forêt**	lah foreh
garden	**le jardin**	ler zhahrdang
hamlet	**le hameau**	ler ahmoa
hill	**la colline**	lah kolleen
house	**la maison**	lah mehzawng
lake	**le lac**	ler lahk
meadow	**le pré**	ler pray
mountain	**la montagne**	lah mawngtahñ
path	**le chemin**	ler shermang
peak	**le sommet**	ler sommeh
pond	**l'étang**	laytahng
river	**le fleuve/la rivière**	ler flurv/lah reevyehr
road	**la route**	lah root
sea	**la mer**	lah mehr
spring	**la source**	lah soorss
valley	**la vallée**	lah vahlay
village	**le village**	ler veelahzh
vineyard	**le vignoble**	ler veeñobl
wall	**le mur**	ler mewr
waterfall	**la chute d'eau**	lah shewt doa
wood	**le bois**	ler bwah

ASKING THE WAY, see page 76

Visites touristiques

Relaxing

Cinema (movies) — Theatre *Cinéma – Théâtre*

You can find out what's playing from newspapers and bill-boards. In Paris ask for the weekly entertainment guides *Pariscope* and *l'Officiel des Spectacles*. In Brussels ask for *Le Bulletin*. Most American and British films are dubbed. However, some cinemas in Paris and Geneva show original versions—usually with French subtitles.

What's showing at the cinema tonight?	**Qu'y a-t-il ce soir au cinéma?**	kee ahteel ser swahr oa seenaymah
What's playing at the ... Theatre?	**Que joue-t-on au théâtre ...?**	ker zhootawng oa tayahtr
What sort of play is it?	**De quel genre de pièce s'agit-il?**	der kehl zhahngr der pyehss sahzhee teel
Who's it by?	**Qui l'a écrite?**	kee lah aykreet
Can you recommend (a) ...?	**Pouvez-vous me conseiller ...?**	poovay voo mer kawngssehyay
good film	**un bon film**	ang bawng feelm
comedy	**une comédie**	ewn komaydee
musical	**une comédie musicale**	ewn komaydee mewseekahl
Where's that new film by ... being shown?	**Dans quel cinéma passe le nouveau film de ...?**	dahng kehl seenaymah pahss ler noovoa feelm der
Who's in it?	**Qui joue?**	kee zhoo
Who's playing the lead?	**Qui tient le rôle principal?**	kee tyang ler roal prangsseepahl
Who's the director?	**Qui en est le metteur en scène?**	kee ahng neh ler mehturr ahng sehn
At what theatre is that new play by ... being performed?	**Dans quel théâtre joue-t-on la nouvelle pièce de ...?**	dahng kehl tayahtr zhootawng lah noovehl pyehss der
Is there a sound-and-light show on some-where?	**Y a-t-il un spectacle son et lumière?**	ee ahteel ang spehktahkl sawng ay lewmyehr

What time does it begin?	A quelle heure le spectacle commence-t-il?	ah kehl urr ler spehktahkl kommahngss teel
Are there any seats for tonight?	Y a-t-il des places pour ce soir?	ee ahteel day plahss poor ser swahr
How much are the seats?	Combien coûtent les places?	kawngbyang koot lay plahss
I want to reserve 2 seats for the show on Friday evening.	Je voudrais réserver 2 places pour le spectacle de vendredi soir.	zher voodreh rayzehrvay 2 plahss poor ler spehktahkl der vahngdrerdee swahr
Can I have a ticket for the matinée on Tuesday?	Je voudrais un billet pour la matinée de mardi?	zher voodreh ang beeyeh poor lah mahteenay der mahrdee
I want a seat in the stalls (orchestra).	Je voudrais une place au parterre.	zher voodreh ewn plahss oa pahrtehr
Not too far back.	Pas trop loin.	pah troa lwang
Somewhere in the middle.	Vers le milieu.	vehr ler meelyur
How much are the seats in the circle (mezzanine)?	Combien coûtent les places au balcon?	kawngbyang koot lay plahss oa bahlkawng
May I please have a programme?	Le programme, s'il vous plaît.	ler programh seel voo pleh
Where's the cloakroom?	Où est le vestiaire?	oo eh ler vehstyehr

---

Je suis désolé(e), c'est complet.	I'm sorry, we're sold out.
Il ne reste que quelques places au balcon.	There are only a few seats left in the circle (mezzanine).
Votre billet, s'il vous plaît.	May I see your ticket?
Voici votre place.*	This is your seat.

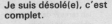

---

* It's customary to tip usherettes (l'ouvreuse) in most French and Belgian theatres.

DAYS OF THE WEEK, see page 151

Divertissements

Opera—Ballet—Concert *Opéra – Ballet – Concert*

Can you recommend a ...?	**Pouvez-vous me recommander ...?**	poovay voo mer rerkommahngday
ballet	**un ballet**	ang bahlleh
concert	**un concert**	ang kawngssehr
opera	**un opéra**	ang nopayrah
operetta	**une opérette**	ewn opayreht
Where's the opera house/the concert hall?	**Où se trouve l'Opéra/ la salle de concert?**	oo ser troov lopayrah/ lah sahl der kawngssehr
What's on at the opera tonight?	**Que joue-t-on ce soir à l'Opéra?**	ker zhootawng ser swahr ah lopayrah
Who's singing/ dancing?	**Qui chante/danse?**	kee shahngt/dahngss
What orchestra is playing?	**Quel est le nom de l'orchestre?**	kehl eh ler nawng der lorkehstr
What are they playing?	**Que jouera-t-on?**	ker zhoorah tawng
Who's the conductor/ soloist?	**Qui est le chef d'orchestre/le soliste?**	kee eh ler shehf dorkehstr/ ler soleest

Nightclubs *Boîtes de nuit*

Can you recommend a good nightclub?	**Pouvez-vous m'indiquer une bonne boîte de nuit?**	poovay voo mangdeekay ewn bon bwaht der nwee
Is there a floor show?	**Est-ce qu'il y a un spectacle de cabaret?**	ehss keel ee ah ang spehktahkl der kahbahreh
What time does the show start?	**A quelle heure commence le spectacle?**	ah kehl urr kommahngss ler spehktahkl
Is evening dress required?	**La tenue de soirée est-elle exigée?**	lah ternew der swahray ehtehl ehxeezhay

Discos *Discothèques*

Where can we go dancing?	**Où pouvons-nous danser?**	oo poovawng noo dahngssay
Is there a discotheque in town?	**Y a-t-il une discothèque en ville?**	ee ahteel ewn deeskotehk ahng veel
Would you like to dance?	**Voulez-vous danser?**	voolay voo dahngssay

Sports *Sports*

Football (soccer), tennis, boxing, wrestling and bicycle, car and horse racing are among popular spectator sports. If you like sailing, fishing, horseback riding, golf, tennis, hiking, cycling, swimming, golf or trap shooting, you'll find plenty of opportunity to satisfy your recreational bent.

Is there a football (soccer) match anywhere this Saturday?	Y a-t-il un match de football quelque part ce samedi?	ee ahteel ang "match" der "football" kehlker pahr ser sahmdee
Which teams are playing?	Quelles sont les équipes?	kehl sawng lay zaykeep
Can you get me a ticket?	Puis-je avoir un billet?	pwoozh ahvwahr ang beeyeh

basketball	le basket-ball	ler "basket-ball"
boxing	la boxe	lah box
car racing	les courses d'autos	lay koors doato
cycling	le cyclisme	ler seekleesm
football (soccer)	le football	ler "football"
horse racing	les courses (de chevaux)	lay koors (der shervoa)
skiing	le ski	ler skee
swimming	la natation	lah nahtahssyawng
tennis	le tennis	ler tehnees
volleyball	le volley-ball	ler vollehboal

I'd like to see a boxing match.	Je voudrais voir un match de boxe.	zher voodreh vwahr ang "match" der box
What's the admission charge?	Combien coûte l'entrée?	kawngbyang koot lahngtray
Where's the nearest golf course?	Où se trouve le terrain de golf le plus proche?	oo ser troov ler tehrang der golf ler plew prosh
Where are the tennis courts?	Où se trouvent les courts de tennis?	oo ser troov lay koor der tehneess
What's the charge per ...?	Quel est le tarif par ...?	kehl eh ler tahreef pahr
day/round/hour	jour/partie/heure	zhoor/pahrtee/urr

Can I hire (rent) rackets?	**Puis-je louer des raquettes?**	pweezh looay day rahkeht
Where's the race course (track)?	**Où est le champ de courses?**	oo eh ler shahng der koors
Is there any good fishing around here?	**Y a-t-il un bon endroit pour pêcher dans les environs?**	ee ahteel ang bawng nahngdrwah poor pehshay dahng lay zahngveerawng
Do I need a permit?	**Est-ce que j'ai besoin d'un permis?**	ehss ker zhay berzwang dang pehrmee
Where can I get one?	**Où puis-je m'en procurer un?**	oo pweezh mahng prokewray ang
Can one swim in the lake/river?	**Peut-on nager dans le lac/la rivière?**	purtawng nahzhay dahng ler lahk/lah reevyehr
Is there a swimming pool here?	**Y a-t-il une piscine?**	ee ahteel ewn peesseen
Is it open-air or indoor?	**Est-elle en plein air ou couverte?**	ehtehl ahng plehn ehr oo koovehrt
Is it heated?	**Est-elle chauffée?**	ehtehl shoafay
What's the temperature of the water?	**Quelle est la température de l'eau?**	kehl eh la tahngpay-rahtewr der loa
Is there a sandy beach?	**Y a-t-il une plage de sable?**	ee ahteel ewn plahzh der sahbl

On the beach   A la plage

Is it safe for swimming?	**Peut-on nager sans danger?**	purtawng nahzhay sahng dahngzhay
Is there a lifeguard?	**Y a-t-il un maître nageur?**	ee ahteel ang mehtr nahzhurr
Is it safe for children?	**Est-ce sans danger pour les enfants?**	ehss sahng dahngzhay poor lay zahngfahng
The sea is very calm.	**La mer est très calme.**	lah mehr eh treh kahlm
There are some big waves.	**Il y a de grosses vagues.**	eel ee ah der groass vahg
Are there any dangerous currents?	**Y a-t-il des courants dangereux?**	ee ahteel day koorahng dahngzherrur
What time is high tide/low tide?	**A quelle heure est la marée haute/basse?**	ah kehl urr eh lah mahray oat/bahss

I want to hire a/an/ some ...	Je voudrais louer ...	zher voodreh looay
bathing hut (cabana)	une cabine	ewn kahbeen
deck-chair	une chaise longue	ewn shehz lawngg
motorboat	un canot à moteur	ang kahnoa ah moturr
rowing-boat	une barque à rames	ewn bahrk ah rahm
sailboard	une planche à voile	ewn plahngsh ah vwahl
sailing-boat	un voilier	ang vwahlyay
skin-diving equipment	un équipement de plongée sous-marine	ang naykeepmahng der plawngzhay soomahreen
sunshade (umbrella)	un parasol	ang pahrahssol
surfboard	une planche de surf	ewn plahngsh der "surf"
water-skis	des skis nautiques	day skee noateek

PLAGE PRIVÉE   PRIVATE BEACH
BAIGNADE INTERDITE   NO SWIMMING

Winter sports   *Sports d'hiver*

Is there a skating rink near here?	Y a-t-il une patinoire près d'ici?	ee ahteel ewn pahteenwahr preh deessee
I'd like to ski.	Je voudrais faire du ski.	zher voodreh fehr dew skee
downhill/cross-country skiing	ski de piste/ski de fond	skee der peest/skee der fawng
Are there any ski runs for ...?	Y a-t-il des pistes pour ...?	ee ahteel day peest poor
beginners	débutants	daybewtahng
average skiers	skieurs moyens	skeeurr mwahyang
good skiers	bons skieurs	bawng skeeurr
Can I take skiing lessons?	Puis-je prendre des leçons de ski?	pweezh prahngdr day lerssawng der skee
Are there ski lifts?	Y a-t-il des téléskis?	ee ahteel day taylayskee
I want to hire ...	Je voudrais louer ...	zher voodreh looay
poles	des bâtons	day bahtawng
skates	des patins	day pahtang
ski boots	des chaussures de ski	day shoassewr der skee
skiing equipment	un équipement de ski	ang naykeepmahng der skee
skis	des skis	day skee

Making friends

Introductions *Présentations*

May I introduce ...?	**Puis-je vous présenter ...?**	pweezh voo prayzahngtay
John, this is ...	**Jean, voici ...**	zhahng vwahssee
My name is ...	**Je m'appelle ...**	zher mahpehl
Pleased to meet you.	**Enchanté(e).**	ahngshahngtay
What's your name?	**Comment vous appelez-vous?**	kommahng voo zahperlay voo
How are you?	**Comment allez-vous?**	kommahng tahlay voo
Fine, thanks. And you?	**Très bien, merci. Et vous?**	treh byang mehrsee. ay voo

Follow-up *Pour rompre la glace*

How long have you been here?	**Depuis combien de temps êtes-vous ici?**	derpwee kawngbyang der tahng eht voo zeessee
We've been here a week.	**Nous sommes ici depuis une semaine.**	noo som zeessee derpwee ewn sermehn
Is this your first visit?	**Est-ce la première fois que vous venez?**	ehss lah prermyehr fwah ker voo vernay
No, we came here last year.	**Non, nous sommes déjà venus l'an dernier.**	nawng noo som dayzhah vernew lahng dehrnyay
Are you enjoying your stay?	**Est-ce que vous vous plaisez ici?**	ehss ker voo voo plehzay eessee
Yes, I like it very much.	**Oui, je m'y plais beaucoup.**	wee zher mee pleh boakoo
I like the land-scape a lot.	**Ce paysage me plaît beaucoup.**	ser payeezahzh mer pleh boakoo
Do you travel a lot?	**Est-ce que vous voyagez beaucoup?**	ehss ker voo vwah-yahzhay boakoo
Where do you come from?	**D'où êtes-vous?**	doo eht voo
I'm from ...	**Je viens de ...**	zher vyang der
What nationality are you?	**Quelle est votre nationalité?**	kehl eh votr nahssyonahleetay

COUNTRIES, see page 146

I'm ...	Je suis de nationalité ...	zer swee der nahssyonahlootay
American	américaine	ahmayreekehn
British	britannique	breetahneek
Canadian	canadienne	kahnahdyehn
Irish	irlandaise	eerlahngdehz
Where are you staying?	Où logez-vous?	oo lozhay voo
Are you on your own?	Etes-vous seul(e)?	eht voo surl
I'm with my ...	Je suis avec ...	zher swee ahvehk
wife	ma femme	mah fahm
husband	mon mari	mawng mahree
family	ma famille	mah fahmeey
children	mes enfants	may zahngfahng
parents	mes parents	may pahrahng
boyfriend/girlfriend	mon ami/amie	mawng nahmee/nahmee

father/mother	le père/la mère	ler pehr/lah mehr
son/daughter	le fils/la fille	ler feess/lah feey
brother/sister	le frère/la sœur	ler frehr/lah surr
uncle/aunt	l'oncle/la tante	lawngkler/lah tahngt
nephew/niece	le neveu/la nièce	ler nurvur/lah nyehss
cousin	le cousin/la cousine	ler koozang/lah koozeen

Are you married/ single?	Etes-vous marié(e)/ célibataire?	eht voo mahryay/ sayleebahtehr
Do you have children?	Avez-vous des enfants?	ahvay voo day zahngfahng
What do you think of the country/people?	Comment trouvez-vous le pays/les gens?	kommahng troovay voo ler pehee/lay zhahng
What's your occupation?	Quelle est votre profession?	kehl eh votr profehssyawng
I'm a student.	Je suis étudiant(e).	zher swee zaytewdyahng(t)
What are you studying?	Qu'étudiez-vous?	kaytewdyay voo
I'm here on a business trip.	Je suis en voyage d'affaires.	zher swee zahng vwahyahzh dahfehr
Do you play cards/ chess?	Jouez-vous aux cartes/aux échecs?	zhooay voo oa kahrt/ oa zayshehk

The weather   *Le temps*

What a lovely day!	**Quelle belle journée!**	kehl behl zhoornay
What awful weather!	**Quel sale temps!**	kehl sahl tahng
Isn't it cold/ hot today?	**Qu'il fait froid/ Quelle chaleur!**	keel feh frwah/kehl shahlurr
Is it usually as warm as this?	**Fait-il toujours aussi chaud?**	fehteel toozhoor oassee shoa
Do you think it's going to ... tomorrow?	**Pensez-vous qu'il ... demain?**	pahngsay voo keel ... dermang
be a nice day	**fera beau**	ferrah boa
rain	**pleuvra**	plurvrah
snow	**neigera**	nehzherrah
What is the weather forecast?	**Quelles sont les prévisions météo?**	kehl sawng lay prayveezyawng maytayoa

cloud	**le nuage**	ler newahzh
fog	**le brouillard**	ler brooyahr
frost	**le gel**	ler zhehl
ice	**la glace**	lah glahss
lightning	**l'éclair**	layklehr
moon	**la lune**	lah lewn
rain	**la pluie**	lah plwee
sky	**le ciel**	ler syehl
snow	**la neige**	lah nehzh
star	**l'étoile**	laytwahl
sun	**le soleil**	ler solehy
thunder	**le tonnerre**	ler tonnehr
thunderstorm	**l'orage**	lorahzh
wind	**le vent**	ler vahng

Invitations   *Invitations*

Would you like to have dinner with us on ...?	**Voudriez-vous dîner avec nous ...?**	voodreeyay voo deenay ahvehk noo
May I invite you for lunch?	**Puis-je vous inviter à déjeuner?**	pweezh voo zangveetay ah dayzhurnay

DAYS OF THE WEEK, see page 151

Can you come over for a drink this evening?	**Pouvez-vous venir prendre un verre chez moi ce soir?**	poovay voo verneer prahngdr ang vehr shay mwah ser swahr
There's a party. Are you coming?	**Il y a une réception. Viendrez-vous?**	eel ee ah ewn rayssehp-syawng. vyangdray voo
That's very kind of you.	**C'est très aimable.**	seh treh zehmahbl
Great. I'd love to come.	**Je viendrai avec plaisir.**	zher vyangdray ahvehk plehzeer
What time shall we come?	**A quelle heure faut-il venir?**	ah kehl urr foateel verneer
May I bring a friend/ a girlfriend?	**Puis-je amener un ami/une amie?**	pweezh ahmernay ang nahmee/ewn ahmee
I'm afraid we've got to leave now.	**Nous devons partir maintenant.**	noo dervawng pahrteer mangternahng
Next time you must come to visit us.	**La prochaine fois, il faudra que vous veniez chez nous.**	lah proshehn fwah eel foadrah ker voo vernyay shay noo
Thanks for the evening. It was great.	**Merci pour la soirée. C'était formidable.**	mehrsee poor lah swahray. sayteh formeedahbl

Dating *Rendez-vous*

Do you mind if I smoke?	**Est-ce que ça vous dérange que je fume?**	ehss ker sah voo dayrahngzh ker zher fewm
Would you like a cigarette?	**Voulez-vous une cigarette?**	voolay voo ewn seegahreht
Do you have a light, please?	**Avez-vous du feu, s'il vous plaît?**	ahvay voo dew fur seel voo pleh
Why are you laughing?	**Pourquoi riez-vous?**	poorkwah reeyay voo
Is my French that bad?	**Mon français est-il si mauvais?**	mawng frahngsseh ehteel see moaveh
Do you mind if I sit down here?	**Me permettez-vous de m'asseoir ici?**	mer pehrmehtay voo der mahsswahr eessee
Can I get you a drink?	**Puis-je vous offrir un verre?**	pweezh voo zoffreer ang vehr
Are you waiting for someone?	**Attendez-vous quelqu'un?**	ahtahngday voo kehlkang

Are you free this evening?	**Etes-vous libre ce soir?**	eht voo leebr ser swahr
Would you like to go out with me tonight?	**Voulez-vous sortir avec moi ce soir?**	voolay voo sorteer ahvehk mwah ser swahr
Would you like to go dancing?	**Aimeriez-vous aller danser?**	ehmerryay voo ahlay dahngssay
I know a good discotheque.	**Je connais une bonne discothèque.**	zher konneh ewn bon deeskotehk
Shall we go to the cinema (movies)?	**Nous pourrions aller au cinéma.**	noo pooryawng ahlay oa seenaymah
Would you like to go for a drive?	**Aimeriez-vous faire un tour en voiture?**	ehmerryay voo fehr ang toor ahng vwahtewr
Where shall we meet?	**Où nous retrou-verons-nous?**	oo noo rertrooverrawng noo
I'll pick you up at your hotel.	**Je viendrai vous prendre à votre hôtel.**	zher vyangdray voo prahngdr ah votr oatehl
I'll call for you at 8.	**Je viendrai vous chercher à 8 heures.**	zher vyangdray voo shehrshay ah 8 urr
May I take you home?	**Puis-je vous raccompagner?**	pweezh voo rahkawngpahñay
Can I see you again tomorrow?	**Puis-je vous revoir demain?**	pweezh voo rervwahr dermang
What's your tele-phone number?	**Quel est votre nu-méro de téléphone?**	kehl eh votr newmayroa der taylayfon

... and you might answer:

I'd love to, thank you.	**Avec plaisir, merci.**	ahvehk plehzeer mehrsee
Thank you, but I'm busy.	**Merci, mais je suis pris(e).**	mehrsee meh zher swee pree(z)
No, I'm not inter-ested, thank you.	**Non, cela ne m'intéresse pas.**	nawng serlah ner mangtayrehss pah
Leave me alone, please!	**Laissez-moi tranquille!**	lehssay mwah trahngkeel
Thank you, it's been a wonderful evening.	**Merci, j'ai passé une merveilleuse soirée.**	mehrsee zhay pahssay ewn mehrvehyurz swahray
I've enjoyed myself.	**Je me suis bien amusé(e).**	zher mer swee byang nahmewzay

Shopping guide

This shopping guide is designed to help you find what you want with ease, accuracy and speed. It features:

1. a list of all major shops, stores and services (p. 98)

2. some general expressions required when shopping to allow you to be specific and selective (p. 100)

3. full details of the shops and services most likely to concern you. Here you'll find advice, alphabetical lists of items and conversion charts listed under the headings below.

		page
Bookshop/ Stationer's	books, magazines, newspapers, stationery	104
Camping equipment	all items required for camping	106
Chemist's (drugstore)	medicine, first-aid, cosmetics, toilet articles	108
Clothing	clothes and accessories, shoes	112
Electrical appliances	radios, cassette-recorders, shavers	119
Grocery	some general expressions, weights, measures and packaging	120
Jeweller's/ Watchmaker's	jewellery, watches, watch repairs	121
Optician	glasses, lenses, binoculars	123
Photography	cameras, films, developing, accessories	124
Tobacconist's	smoker's supplies	126
Miscellaneous	souvenirs, records, cassettes, toys	127

LAUNDRY, see page 29/HAIRDRESSER'S, see page 30

Shops, stores and services *Magasins et services*

Shops usually open at around 9 a.m. and close anytime between 5.30 and 7 p.m. (until 6 in Belgium and until 6.30 in Switzerland). Most businesses close for an hour or two at noon—except department stores. Some shops are open on Sundays and holidays in France. They generally close Saturdays at 5 p.m. in Switzerland. Shopkeepers take a day off during the week—usually Monday.

Where's the nearest ...?	Où est ... le/la plus proche?	oo eh ... ler/lah plew prosh
antique shop	l'antiquaire	lahngteekehr
art gallery	la galerie d'art	lah gahlerree dahr
baker's	la boulangerie	lah boolahngzherree
bank	la banque	lah bahngk
barber's	le coiffeur	ler kwahfurr
beauty salon	l'institut de beauté	langsteetew der boatay
bookshop	la librairie	lah leebrehree
butcher's	la boucherie	lah boosherree
cake shop	la pâtisserie	lah pahteesserree
camera shop	le magasin de photos	ler mahgahzang der fotoa
chemist's	la pharmacie	lah fahrmahsee
confectioner's	la confiserie	lah kawngfeezerree
dairy	la laiterie	lah lehterree
delicatessen	la charcuterie/ le traiteur	lah shahrkewterree/ ler trehturr
dentist	le dentiste	ler dahngteest
department store	le grand magasin	ler grahng mahgahzang
drugstore	la pharmacie	lah fahrmahsee
dry cleaner's	la teinturerie	lah tangtewrerree
electrician	l'électricien	laylehktreessyang
fishmonger's	la poissonnerie	lah pwahssonnerree
flower shop	le fleuriste	ler flurreest
furrier's	le fourreur	ler foorrurr
greengrocer's	le primeur	ler preemurr
grocery	l'épicerie/le magasin d'alimentation	laypeesserree/ler mahgahzang dahleemahngtah-ssyawng
hairdresser's (ladies/men)	le coiffeur (pour dames/messieurs)	ler kwahfurr (poor dahm/mehssyur)
hardware store	la quincaillerie	lah kangkahyerree
health food shop	le magasin de diététique	ler mahgahzang der dyaytayteek

hospital	l'hôpital	loapeetahl
ironmonger's	la quincaillerie	lah kangkahyorroo
jeweller's	la bijouterie	lah beezhooterree
launderette	la laverie automatique	lah lahverree oatomahteek
library	la bibliothèque	lah beebleeyotehk
laundry	la blanchisserie	lah blahngsheesserree
market	le marché	ler mahrshay
newsagent's	le marchand de journaux	ler mahrshahng der zhoornoa
newsstand	le kiosque à journaux	ler kyosk ah zhoornoa
optician	l'opticien	lopteessyang
pastry shop	la pâtisserie	lah pahteesserree
photographer	le photographe	ler fotograhf
police station	le poste de police	ler post der poleess
post office	le bureau de poste	ler bewroa der post
shoemaker's (repairs)	la cordonnerie	lah kordonnerree
shoe shop	le magasin de chaussures	ler mahgahzang der shoassewr
shopping centre	le centre commercial	ler sahngtr kommehrsyahl
souvenir shop	le magasin de souvenirs	ler mahgahzang der sooverneer
sporting goods shop	le magasin d'articles de sport	ler mahgahzang dahrteekl der spor
stationer's	la papeterie	lah pahpehterree
supermarket	le supermarché	ler sewpehrmahrshay
tailor's	le tailleur	ler tahyurr
telegraph office	le bureau du télégraphe	ler bewroa dew taylaygrahf
tobacconist's	le bureau de tabac	ler bewroa der tahbah
toy shop	le magasin de jouets	ler mahgahzang der zhooeh
travel agency	l'agence de voyages	lahzhahngss der vwahyahzh
vegetable store	le primeur	ler preemurr
veterinarian	le vétérinaire	ler vaytayreenehr
watchmaker's	l'horlogerie	lorlozherree
wine merchant	le marchand de vin	ler mahrshahng der vang

ENTRÉE	ENTRANCE
SORTIE	EXIT
SORTIE DE SECOURS	EMERGENCY EXIT

Guide des achats

General expressions *Expressions générales*

Where? *Où?*

Where's there a good ...?	**Où y a-t-il un bon/ une bonne ...?**	oo ee ahteel ang bawng/ ewn bon
Where can I find a ...?	**Où puis-je trouver ...?**	oo pweezh troovay
Where's the main shopping area?	**Où se trouve le quartier commerçant?**	oo ser troov ler kahrtyay kommehrssahng
Is it far from here?	**Est-ce loin d'ici?**	ehss lwang deessee
How do I get there?	**Comment puis-je m'y rendre?**	kommahng pweezh mee rahngdr

---

SOLDES	SALE

Service *Service*

Can you help me?	**Pourriez-vous m'aider?**	pooryay voo mehday
I'm just looking.	**Je ne fais que regarder.**	zher ner feh ker rergahrday
I want ...	**Je désire ...**	zher dayzeer
Can you show me some ...?	**Pourriez-vous me montrer ...?**	pooryay voo mer mawngtray
Do you have any ...?	**Avez-vous ...?**	ahvay voo
Where's the ... department?	**Où se trouve le rayon ...?**	oo ser troov ler rehyawng
Where is the lift (elevator)/escalator?	**Où est l'ascenseur/ l'escalier mécanique?**	oo eh lahssahngssurr/ lehskahlyay maykahneek
Where do I pay?	**Où est la caisse?**	oo eh lah kehss

That one *Celui-là*

Can you show me ...?	**Pouvez-vous me montrer ...?**	poovay voo mer mawngtray
this/that	**ceci/cela**	serssee/serlah
the one in the window/in the display case	**celui qui est en vitrine/ à l'étalage**	serlwee kee eh ahng veetreen/ah laytahlahzh

Defining the article *Description de l'article*

I'd like a ... one.	Je désire un ...	zher dayzeer ang
big	grand	grahng
cheap	bon marché	bawng mahrshay
dark	foncé	fawngssay
good	bon	bawng
heavy	lourd	loor
large	grand	grahng
light (weight)	léger	layzhay
light (colour)	clair	klehr
oval	ovale	ovahl
rectangular	rectangulaire	rehktahnggewlehr
round	rond	rawng
small	petit	pertee
square	carré	kahray
sturdy	solide	soleed

I don't want anything too expensive.	Je ne voudrais pas quelque chose de trop cher.	zher ner voodreh pah kehlker shoaz der troa shehr

Preference *Préférences*

Can you show me some more?	Pouvez-vous m'en montrer d'autres?	poovay voo mahng mawngtray doatr
Haven't you anything ...?	N'auriez-vous pas quelque chose de ...?	noaray voo pah kehlker shoaz der
cheaper/better	meilleur marché/ mieux	mehyurr mahrshay/myur
larger/smaller	plus grand/plus petit	plew grahng/plew pertee

How much? *Combien?*

How much is this?	Combien coûte ceci?	kawngbyang koot serssee
How much are they?	Combien coûtent-ils?	kawngbyang koot teel
I don't understand.	Je ne comprends pas.	zher ner kawngprahng pah
Please write it down.	Pourriez-vous l'écrire, s'il vous plaît?	pooryay voo laykreer seel voo pleh
I don't want to spend more than ... francs.	Je ne veux pas dépenser plus de ... francs.	zher ner vur pah daypahngssay plew der ... frahng

COLOURS, see page 113

Decision *Décision*

It's not quite what I want.	**Ce n'est pas exacte-ment ce que je veux.**	ser neh pah zehxahkter-mahng ser ker zher vur
No, I don't like it.	**Non, cela ne me plaît pas.**	nawng serlah ner mer pleh pah
I'll take it.	**Je le prends.**	zher ler prahng

Ordering *Commande*

| Can you order it for me? | **Pourriez-vous me le commander?** | pooryay voo mer ler kommahngday |
| How long will it take? | **Combien de temps cela prendra-t-il?** | kawngbyang der tahng serlah prahngdrah teel |

Delivery *Livraison*

I'll take it with me.	**Je l'emporte.**	zher lahngport
Deliver it to the ... Hotel.	**Veuillez le livrer à l'Hôtel ...**	vuryay ler leevray ah loatehl
Please send it to this address.	**Veuillez l'envoyer à cette adresse.**	vuryay lahngvwahyay ah seht ahdrehss
Will I have any difficulty with the customs?	**Aurai-je des diffi-cultés avec la douane?**	oarehzh day deefeekewltay ahvehk lah dwahn

Paying *Paiement*

How much is it?	**Combien vous dois-je?**	kawngbyang voo dwahzh
Can I pay by traveller's cheque?	**Puis-je payer en chèques de voyage?**	pweezh pehyay ahng shehk der vwahyahzh
Do you accept dollars/pounds?	**Acceptez-vous les dollars/livres?**	ahksehptay voo lay dollar/leevr
Do you accept credit cards?	**Acceptez-vous les cartes de crédit?**	ahksehptay voo lay kahrt der kraydee
Do I have to pay the VAT (sales tax)?	**Dois-je payer la T.V.A.?**	dwahzh pehyay lah tay vay ah
Haven't you made a mistake in the bill?	**N'y a-t-il pas une erreur dans la facture?**	nee ahteel pah zewn ehrurr dahng lah fahktewr

Anything else?   *Autre chose?*

No, thanks, that's all.	**Non merci, ce sera tout.**	nawng mehrsee ser serrah too
Yes, I want ...	**Oui, je voudrais ...**	wee zher voodreh
Show me ...	**Veuillez me montrer ...**	vuryay mer mawngtray
May I have a bag, please?	**Puis-je avoir un sac, s'il vous plaît?**	pweezh ahvwahr ang sahk seel voo pleh

Dissatisfied?   *Mécontent?*

Can you please exchange this?	**Pourriez-vous échanger ceci?**	pooryay voo ayshahngzhay serssee
I want to return this.	**Je voudrais vous rendre ceci.**	zher voodreh voo rahngdr serssee
I'd like a refund. Here's the receipt.	**Je voudrais me faire rembourser. Voici la quittance.**	zher voodreh mer fehr rahngboorsay. vwahssee lah keetahngss

---

Puis-je vous être utile?	Can I help you?
Que désirez-vous?	What would you like?
Quelle ... désirez-vous?	What ... would you like?
couleur/forme qualité/quantité	colour/shape quality/quantity
Je suis désolé(e), nous n'en avons pas.	I'm sorry, we haven't any.
Notre stock est épuisé.	We're out of stock.
Pouvons-nous le commander?	Shall we order it for you?
Désirez-vous l'emporter ou faut-il vous l'envoyer?	Will you take it with you or shall we send it?
Autre chose?	Anything else?
Cela fera ... francs, s'il vous plaît.	That's ... francs, please.
La caisse se trouve là-bas.	The cashier's over there.

Bookshop—Stationer's   *Librairie – Papeterie*

In France, bookshops and stationers' are usually separate shops, though the latter will often sell paperbacks. Newspapers and magazines are sold at newsstands.

Where's the nearest ...?	**Où est ... le/la plus proche?**	oo eh ... ler/lah plew prosh
bookshop	**la librairie**	lah leebrehree
stationer's	**la papeterie**	lah pahpehterree
newsstand	**le kiosque à journaux**	ler kyosk ah zhoornoa
Where can I buy an English-language newspaper?	**Où puis-je acheter un journal en anglais?**	oo pweezh ahshertay ang zhoornahl ahng nahnggleh
Where's the guide-book section?	**Où sont les guides de voyage?**	oo sawng lay geed der vwahyahzh
Where do you keep the English books?	**Où se trouvent les livres en anglais?**	oo ser troov lay leevr ahng nahnggleh
Have you any of ...'s books in English?	**Avez-vous des livres de ... en anglais?**	ahvay voo day leevr der ... ahng nahnggleh
Do you have second-hand books?	**Avez-vous des livres d'occasion?**	ahvay voo day leevr dokahzyawng
I want to buy a/an/ some ...	**Je voudrais acheter ...**	zher voodreh ahshertay
address book	**un carnet d'adresses**	ang kahrneh dahdrehss
ball-point pen	**un stylo à bille**	ang steeloa ah beey
book	**un livre**	ang leevr
calendar	**un calendrier**	ang kahlahngdreeyay
carbon paper	**du papier carbone**	dew pahpyay kahrbon
cellophane tape	**du ruban adhésif**	dew rewbahng ahdayzeef
crayons	**des crayons de couleur**	day krehyawng der koolurr
dictionary	**un dictionnaire**	ang deeksyonnehr
French-English	**français-anglais**	frahngsseh ahnggleh
pocket	**de poche**	der posh
drawing paper	**du papier à dessin**	dew pahpyay ah dehssang
drawing pins	**des punaises**	day pewnehz
envelopes	**des enveloppes**	day zahngverlop
eraser	**une gomme**	ewn gom
exercise book	**un cahier**	ang kahyay
felt-tip pen	**un crayon feutre**	ang krehyawng furtr

fountain pen	un stylo	ang steeloa
glue	de la colle	der lah kol
grammar book	une grammaire	ewn grahmehr
guidebook	un guide	ang geed
ink	de l'encre	der lahngkr
black/red/blue	noire/rouge/bleue	nwahr/roozh/blur
(adhesive) labels	des étiquettes (autocollantes)	day zayteekeht (oatokollahngt)
magazine	une revue	ewn rervew
map	une carte (géographique)	ewn kahrt (zhayoagrahfeek)
map of the town	un plan de ville	ang plahng der veel
road map of ...	une carte routière de ...	ewn kahrt rootyehr der
mechanical pencil	un porte-mine	ang port meen
newspaper	un journal	ang zhoornahl
American/English	américain/anglais	amayreekang/ahnggleh
notebook	un bloc-notes	ang blok not
note paper	du papier à lettres	dew pahpyay ah lehtr
paintbox	une boîte de couleurs	ewn bwaht der koolurr
paper	du papier	dew pahpyay
paperback	un livre de poche	ang leevr der posh
paperclips	des trombones	day trawngbon
paper napkins	des serviettes en papier	day sehrvyeht ahng pahpyay
paste	de la colle	der lah kol
pen	une plume	ewn plewm
pencil	un crayon	ang krehyawng
pencil sharpener	un taille-crayon	ang tahy krehyawng
playing cards	des cartes à jouer	day kahrt ah zhooay
pocket calculator	une calculatrice de poche	ewn kahlkewlahtreess der posh
postcard	une carte postale	ewn kahrt postahl
propelling pencil	un porte-mine	ang port meen
refill (for a pen)	une recharge (pour stylo)	ewn rershahrzh (poor steeloa)
rubber	une gomme	ewn gom
ruler	une règle	ewn rehgl
staples	des agrafes	day zahgrahf
string	de la ficelle	der lah feessehl
thumbtacks	des punaises	day pewnehz
tissue paper	du papier de soie	dew pahpyay der swah
typewriter ribbon	un ruban de machine à écrire	ang rewbahng der mahsheen ah aykreer
typing paper	du papier à machine	dew pahpyay ah mahsheen
writing pad	un bloc	ang blok

Camping equipment *Matériel de camping*

I'd like a/an/some ...	**Je voudrais ...**	zher voodreh
bottle-opener	**un ouvre-bouteilles**	ahng noovr bootehy
bucket	**un seau**	ahng soa
butane gas	**du butane**	dew bewtahn
campbed	**un lit de camp**	ang lee der kahng
can opener	**un ouvre-boîtes**	ang noovr bwaht
candles	**des bougies**	day boozhee
(folding) chair	**une chaise (pliante)**	ewn shehz (pleeyahngt)
charcoal	**du charbon de bois**	dew shahrbawng der bwah
clothes pegs	**des pinces à linge**	day pangss ah langzh
compass	**une boussole**	ewn boossol
cool box	**une glacière**	ewn glahssyehr
corkscrew	**un tire-bouchon**	ang teer booshawng
crockery	**de la vaisselle**	der lah vehssehl
cutlery	**des couverts**	day koovehr
deck-chair	**une chaise longue**	ewn shehz lawngg
dishwashing detergent	**du produit (à) vaisselle**	dew prodwee (ah) vehssehl
first-aid kit	**une trousse de premiers secours**	ewn trooss der prermyay serkoor
fishing tackle	**un attirail de pêche**	ang nahteerahy der pehsh
flashlight	**une lampe de poche**	ewn lahngp der posh
food box	**une boîte à conservation**	ewn bwaht ah kawng-ssehrvahssyawng
frying-pan	**une poêle**	ewn pwahl
groundsheet	**un tapis de sol**	ang tahpee der sol
hammer	**un marteau**	ang mahrtoa
hammock	**un hamac**	ang ahmahk
haversack	**une musette**	ewn mewzeht
ice pack	**une cartouche réfrigérante**	ewn kahrtoosh rayfree-zhayrahngt
kerosene	**du pétrole**	dew paytrol
knapsack	**un sac à dos**	ang sahk ah doa
lamp	**une lampe**	ewn lahngp
lantern	**une lanterne**	ewn lahngtehrn
matches	**des allumettes**	day zahlewmeht
mattress	**un matelas**	ang mahterlah
methylated spirits	**de l'alcool à brûler**	der lahlkol ah brewlay
mosquito net	**une moustiquaire**	ewn moosteekehr
pail	**un seau**	ang soa
paper napkins	**des serviettes en papier**	day sehrvyeht ahng pahpyay
paraffin	**du pétrole**	dew paytrol
penknife	**un canif**	ang kahneef

CAMPING, see page 32

picnic basket	un panier à pique-nique	ang pahnyay ah peekneek
plastic bag	un sac en plastique	ang sahk ahng plahsteek
rope	de la corde	der lah kord
rucksack	un sac de montagne	ang sahk der mawngtañ
saucepan	une casserole	ewn kahsserrol
scissors	des ciseaux	day seezoa
screwdriver	un tournevis	ang toornerveess
sleeping bag	une sac de couchage	ang sahk der kooshahzh
stew pot	une marmite	ewn mahrmeet
(folding) table	une table (pliante)	ewn tahbl (pleeyahngt)
tent	une tente	ewn tahngt
tent pegs	des piquets de tente	day peekeh der tahngt
tent pole	un montant de tente	ang mawngtahng der tahngt
tinfoil	du papier d'aluminium	dew pahpyay dahlewmeenyom
tin opener	un ouvre-boîtes	ang noovr bwaht
tongs	une pince	ewn pangss
torch	une lampe de poche	ewn lahngp der posh
vacuum flask	un thermos	ang tehrmoass
washing powder	de la lessive	der lah lehsseev
water flask	une gourde	ewn goord
wood alcohol	de l'alcool à brûler	der lahlkol ah brewlay

Crockery *Vaisselle*

cups	des tasses	day tahss
mugs	des grosses tasses	day gross tahss
plates	des assiettes	day zahssyeht
saucers	des soucoupes	day sookoop
tumblers	des gobelets	day goberleh

Cutlery *Couverts*

forks	des fourchettes	day foorsheht
knives	des couteaux	day kootoa
dessert knives	des couteaux à dessert	day kootoa ah dehssehr
spoons	des cuillères	day kweeyehr
teaspoons	des cuillères à café	day kweeyehr ah kahfay
(made of) plastic	(en) plastique	ahng plahsteek
(made of) stainless steel	(en) inox	(ahng) eenox

Chemist's (drugstore) *Pharmacie*

You will recognize a chemist's by the sign outside—a green cross, which is lit at night. In the window you'll see a notice telling you where the nearest all-night chemist's is. Go to a *parfumerie* (pahrfewmerree) for perfume and cosmetics. Otherwise, other toilet and household articles can be bought from a *droguerie* (drogerree).

This section is divided into two parts:

1. Pharmaceutical—medicine, first-aid, etc.
2. Toiletry—toilet articles, cosmetics

General *Généralités*

Where's the nearest (all-night) chemist's?	**Où se trouve la pharmacie (de nuit) la plus proche?**	oo ser troov lah fahrmahssee der nwee lah plew prosh
What time does the chemist's open/ close?	**A quelle heure ouvre/ ferme la pharmacie?**	ah kehl urr oovr/fehrm lah fahrmahssee

1—Pharmaceutical *Médicaments, premiers soins, etc.*

I want something for ...	**Je voudrais quelque chose contre ...**	zher voodreh kehlker shoaz kawngtr
a cold/a cough	**le rhume/la toux**	ler rewm/lah too
hay fever	**le rhume des foins**	ler rewm day fwang
insect bites	**les piqûres d'insectes**	lay peekewr dangsehkt
a hangover	**la gueule de bois**	lah gurl der bwah
sunburn	**les coups de soleil**	lay koo der solehy
travel sickness	**le mal du voyage**	ler mahl dew vwahyahzh
an upset stomach	**les indigestions**	lay zangdeezhehstyawng
Can you make up this prescription for me?	**Pourriez-vous me préparer cette ordonnance?**	pooryay voo mer praypahray seht ordonnahngss
Can I get it without a prescription?	**Puis-je l'obtenir sans ordonnance?**	pweezh lobterneer sahng zordonnahngss
Shall I wait?	**Dois-je attendre?**	dwahzh ahtahngdr

DOCTOR, see page 137

Can I have a/an/como ...?	**Puis-je avoir ...?**	pweezh ahvwahr
analgesic	**un analgésique**	ang nahnahlzhayzeek
antiseptic cream	**de la pommade antiseptique**	der lah pommahd ahngteessehpteek
aspirin	**de l'aspirine**	der lahspeereen
bandage	**un bandage**	ang bahngdahzh
elastic bandage	**bandage élastique**	bahngdahzh aylahsteek
Band-Aids	**du sparadrap**	dew spahrahdrah
contraceptives	**des contraceptifs**	day kawngtrahssehpteef
corn plasters	**des emplâtres pour les cors**	day zahngplahtr poor lay kor
cotton wool (absorbent cotton)	**du coton hydrophile**	dew kotawng eedrofeel
cough drops	**des pastilles contre la toux**	day pahsteey kawngtr lah too
disinfectant	**un désinfectant**	ang dayzangfehktahng
ear drops	**des gouttes pour les oreilles**	day goot poor lay zorehy
Elastoplast	**du sparadrap**	dew spahrahdrah
eye drops	**des gouttes oculaires**	day goot okewlehr
gauze	**de la gaze**	der lah gahz
insect repellent/spray	**de la crème anti-insecte/une bombe insecticide**	der lah krehm ahngtee-angssehkt/ewn bawngb angssehkteesseed
iodine	**de la teinture d'iode**	der lah tangtewr dyod
laxative	**un laxatif**	ang lahxahteef
mouthwash	**un gargarisme**	ang gahrgahreezm
nose drops	**des gouttes nasales**	day goot nahzahl
sanitary towels (napkins)	**des serviettes hygiéniques**	day sehrvyeht eezhyayneek
sleeping pills	**un somnifère**	ang somneefehr
suppositories	**des suppositoires**	day sewpoazeetwahr
... tablets	**des comprimés ...**	day kawngpreemay
tampons	**des tampons hygiéniques**	day tahngpawng eezhyayneek
thermometer	**un thermomètre**	ang tehrmomehtr
throat lozenges	**des pastilles pour la gorge**	day pahsteey poor lah gorzh
tranquillizers	**un tranquillisant**	ang trahngkeeleezahng
vitamin pills	**des vitamines**	day veetahmeen

POISON	POISON
POUR USAGE EXTERNE	FOR EXTERNAL USE ONLY

2—Toiletry   *Articles de toilette*

I'd like a/an/some ...	Je voudrais ...	zher voodreh
after-shave lotion	de la lotion après rasage	der lah lossyawng ahpreh rahzahzh
astringent	un astringent	ang nahstrangzahzh
bath essence	du bain de mousse	dew bang der mooss
bath salts	des sels de bain	day sehl der bang
cream	une crème	ewn krehm
cleansing cream	une crème démaquillante	ewn krehm daymahkeeyahngt
foundation cream	du fond de teint	dew fawng der tang
moisturizing cream	une crème hydratante	ewn krehm eedrahtahngt
night cream	une crème de nuit	ewn krehm der nwee
cuticle remover	un produit pour enlever les cuticules	ahng prodwee poor ahnglervay lay kewteekewl
deodorant	un déodorant	ang dayodorahng
emery board	une lime à ongles	ewn leem ah awnggl
eye liner	un eye-liner	ang "eye liner"
eye pencil	un crayon pour les yeux	ang krehyawng poor lay zyur
eye shadow	du fard à paupières	dew fahr ah poapyehr
face powder	de la poudre	der lah poodr
foot cream	de la crème pour les pieds	der lah krehm poor lay pyay
hand cream	de la crème pour les mains	der lah krehm poor lay mang
lipsalve	du beurre de cacao	dew burr der kahkahoa
lipstick	du rouge à lèvres	dew roozh ah lehvr
make-up remover pads	des disques démaquillants	day deesk daymahkeeyahng
nail brush	une brosse à ongles	ewn bross ah awnggl
nail clippers	un coupe-ongles	ang koop awnggl
nail file	une lime à ongles	ewn leem ah awnggl
nail polish	du vernis à ongles	dew vehrnee ah awnggl
nail polish remover	du dissolvant	dew deessolvahng
nail scissors	des ciseaux à ongles	day seezoa ah awnggl
perfume	du parfum	dew pahrfang
powder	de la poudre	der lah poodr
powder puff	une houppette	ewn oopeht
razor	un rasoir	ang rahzwahr
razor blades	des lames de rasoir	day lahm der rahzwahr
rouge	du fard à joues	dew fahr ah zhoo
safety pins	des épingles de sûreté	day zaypanggl der sewrtay

shaving brush	un blaireau	ang blehroa
shaving cream	de la crème à raser	der lah krehm ah rahzay
soap	du savon	dew sahvawng
sponge	une éponge	ewn aypawngzh
sun-tan cream	de la crème solaire	der lah krehm solehr
sun-tan oil	de l'huile solaire	der lweel solehr
talcum powder	du talc	dew tahlk
tissues	des mouchoirs en papier	day mooshwahr ahng pahpyay
toilet paper	du papier hygiénique	dew pahpyay eezhyayneek
toilet water	de l'eau de toilette	der loa der twahleht
toothbrush	une brosse à dents	ewn bross ah dahng
toothpaste	du dentifrice	dew dahngteefreess
towel	une serviette	ewn sehrvyeht
tweezers	une pince à épiler	ewn pangss ah aypeelay

For your hair *Pour vos cheveux*

bobby pins	des pinces à cheveux	day pangss ah shervur
colour shampoo	un shampooing colorant	ang shahngpwang kolorahng
comb	un peigne	ang pehñ
curlers	des bigoudis	day beegoodee
dry shampoo	un shampooing sec	ang shahngpwang sehk
dye	une teinture	ewn tangtewr
hairbrush	une brosse à cheveux	ewn bross ah shervur
hairgrips	des pinces à cheveux	day pangss ah shervur
hair lotion	une lotion capillaire	ewn lossyawng kahpeelehr
hairpins	des épingles à cheveux	day zaypanggl ah shervur
hair spray	de la laque	der lah lahk
setting lotion	un fixatif	ang feexahteef
shampoo	du shampooing	dew shahngpwang
for dry/greasy (oily) hair	pour cheveux secs/gras	poor shervur sehk/grah
tint	une coloration	ewn kolorahssyawng
wig	une perruque	ewn pehrewk

For the baby *Pour votre bébé*

baby food	des aliments pour bébés	day zahleemahng poor baybay
dummy (pacifier)	une tétine	own taytoon
feeding bottle	un biberon	ang beeberrawng
nappies (diapers)	des couches	day koosh

Clothing   *Habillement*

If you want to buy something specific, prepare yourself in advance. Look at the list of clothing on page 116. Get some idea of the colour, material and size you want. They're all listed on the next few pages.

General   *Généralités*

I'd like ...	**Je voudrais ...**	zher voodreh
I want ... for a 10-year-old boy/girl.	**Je voudrais ... pour un garçon/une fillette de 10 ans.**	zher voodreh ... poor ang gahrsawng/ewn feeyeht der 10 ahng
I want something like this.	**Je voudrais quelque chose dans ce genre.**	zher voodreh kehlker shoaz dahng ser zhahngr
I like the one in the window.	**Celui qui est en vitrine me plaît.**	serlwee kee eh tahng veetreen mer pleh
How much is that per metre?	**Combien coûte le mètre?**	kawngbyang koot ler mehtr

1 centimetre (cm.)	= 0.39 in.	1 inch = 2.54 cm.
1 metre (m.)	= 39.37 in.	1 foot = 30.5 cm.
10 metres	= 32.81 ft.	1 yard = 0.91 m.

Colour   *Couleur*

I want something in ...	**Je voudrais quelque chose en ...**	zher voodreh kehlker shoaz ahng
I want a darker/lighter shade.	**Je voudrais un ton plus foncé/plus clair.**	zher voodreh ang tawng plew fawngssay/plew klehr
I want something to match this.	**Je voudrais quelque chose d'assorti à cela.**	zher voodreh kehlker shoaz dahssortee ah serlah
I don't like the colour.	**Je n'aime pas cette couleur.**	zher nehm pah seht koolurr

beige	**beige**	behzh
black	**noir**	nwahr
blue	**bleu**	blur
brown	**brun**	brang
fawn	**fauve**	foav
golden	**doré**	doray
green	**vert**	vehr
grey	**gris**	gree
mauve	**mauve**	moav
orange	**orange**	orahngzh
pink	**rose**	roaz
purple	**violet**	vyoleh
red	**rouge**	roozh
scarlet	**écarlate**	aykahrlaht
silver	**argenté**	ahrzhahngtay
turquoise	**turquoise**	tewrkwahz
white	**blanc**	blahng
yellow	**jaune**	zhoan
light ...	... **clair**	... klehr
dark ...	... **foncé**	... fawngssay

uni
(ewnee)

à rayures
(ah rehyewr)

à pois
(ah pwah)

à carreaux
(ah kahroa)

fantaisie
(fahngtayzee)

Material *Tissus*

Do you have anything in ...?	**Avez-vous quelque chose en ...?**	ahvay voo kehlker shoaz ahng
Is that ...?	**Est-ce ...?**	ehss
handmade	**fait à la main**	feh ah lah mang
imported	**importé**	angportay
made here	**de fabrication locale**	der fahbreekahssyawng lokahl
I want something thinner.	**Je voudrais quelque chose de plus mince.**	zher voodreh kehlker shoaz der plew mangss
Do you have any better quality?	**N'auriez-vous pas une meilleure qualité?**	noaryay voo pah zewn mehyurr kahleetay

What's it made of? | **En quoi est-ce?** | ahng kwah ehss

cambric	**batiste**	bahteest
camel-hair	**poil de chameau**	pwahl der shahmoa
chiffon	**mousseline**	moosserleen
corduroy	**velours côtelé**	verloor koaterlay
cotton	**coton**	kotawng
crepe	**crêpe**	krehp
denim	**toile de coton**	twahl der kotawng
felt	**feutre**	furtr
flannel	**flanelle**	flahnehl
gabardine	**gabardine**	gahbahrdeen
lace	**dentelle**	dahngtehl
leather	**cuir**	kweer
linen	**lin**	lang
poplin	**popeline**	popperleen
satin	**satin**	sahtang
silk	**soie**	swah
suede	**daim**	dang
terrycloth	**tissu-éponge**	teessew aypawngzh
velvet	**velours**	verloor
velveteen	**velours de coton**	verloor der kotawng
wool	**laine**	lehn
worsted	**peigné**	pehñay

Is it ...? | **Est-ce ...?** | ehss

pure cotton/wool | **pur coton/pure laine** | pewr kotawng/pewr lehn
synthetic | **synthétique** | sangtayteek
colour fast | **grand teint** | grahng tang
wrinkle resistant | **infroissable** | angfrwahssahbl

Is it hand washable/ | **Peut-on le laver** | purtawng ler lahvay
machine washable? | **à la main/** | ah lah mang/
  | **à la machine?** | ah lah mahsheen

Will it shrink? | **Est-ce que cela** | ehss ker serlah raytraysee
  | **rétrécit au lavage?** | oa lahvahzh

Size Taille

I take size 38. | **Je porte du 38.** | zher port dew 38
Could you | **Pouvez-vous prendre** | poovay voo prahngdr
measure me? | **mes mesures?** | may merzewr
I don't know the | **Je ne connais pas** | zher ner konneh pah lay
French sizes. | **les tailles françaises.** | tahy frahngssehz

Sizes can vary somewhat from one manufacturer to another, so be sure to try on shoes and clothing before you buy.

Women *Dames*

Dresses/Suits					
American	8	10	12	14	16	18
British	10	12	14	16	18	20
Continental	36	38	40	42	44	46

Stockings							Shoes			
American	8	8½	9	9½	10	10½	6	7	8	9
British							4½	5½	6½	7½
Continental	0	1	2	3	4	5	37	38	40	41

Men *Messieurs*

Suits/Overcoats							Shirts			
American										
British	36	38	40	42	44	46	15	16	17	18
Continental	46	48	50	52	54	56	38	41	43	45

Shoes									
American									
British	5	6	7	8	8½	9	9½	10	11
Continental	38	39	41	42	43	43	44	44	45

A good fit? *Un essayage?*

Can I try it on?	**Puis-je l'essayer?**	pweezh lehssehyay
Where's the fitting room?	**Où est la cabine d'essayage?**	oo eh lah kahbeen dehssehyahzh
Is there a mirror?	**Y a-t-il un miroir?**	ee ahteel ang meerwahr
It fits very well.	**Cela va très bien.**	serlah vah treh byang
It doesn't fit.	**Cela ne me va pas.**	serlah ner mer vah pah

NUMBERS, see page 147

It's too ...	C'est trop ...	seh troa
short/long	court/long	koor/lawng
tight/loose	étroit/large	aytrwah/lahrzh
How long will it take to alter?	Combien de temps faut-il compter pour la retouche?	kawngbyang der tahng foa-teel kawngtay poor lah rertoosh

Clothes and accessories   Vêtements et accessoires

I would like a/an some ...	Je voudrais ...	zher voodreh
anorak	un anorak	ang nahnorahk
bathing cap	un bonnet de bain	ang bonneh der bang
bathing suit	un costume de bain	ang kostewm der bang
bathrobe	un peignoir (de bain)	ang pehnwahr (der bang)
blouse	un chemisier	ang shermeezyay
bow tie	un nœud papillon	ang nur pahpeeyawng
bra	un soutien-gorge	ang sootyang gorzh
braces	des bretelles	day brertehl
briefs	un slip	ang sleep
cap	une casquette	ewn kahskeht
cardigan	un cardigan	ang kahrdeegahng
coat	un manteau	ang mahngtoa
dress	une robe	ewn rob
dressing gown	un peignoir	ang pehnwahr
evening dress (woman's)	une robe du soir	ewn rob dew swahr
girdle	une gaine	ewn gehn
gloves	des gants	day gahng
handbag	un sac à main	ang sahk ah mang
handkerchief	un mouchoir	ang mooshwahr
hat	un chapeau	ang shahpoa
jacket (man's)	un veston	ang vehstawng
jacket (woman's)	une jaquette	ewn zhahkeht
jeans	des jeans	day "jeans"
jersey	un tricot	ang treekoa
jumper (Br.)	un chandail	ang shahngdahy
nightdress	une chemise de nuit	ewn shermeez der nwee
overalls	une salopette	ewn sahlopeht
pair of ...	une paire de ...	ewn pehr der
panties	un slip	ang sleep
pants (Am.)	un pantalon	ang pahngtahlawng
panty girdle	une gaine-culotte	ewn gehn kewlot
panty hose	un collant	ang kollahng

pullover	un pull(over)	ang pewl(ovehr)
roll-neck (turtle-neck)	à col roulé	ah kol roolay
round-neck	à col rond	ah kol rawng
V-neck	à col en V	ah kol ahng vay
with long/short sleeves	avec manches longues/courtes	ahvehk mahngsh lawngg/koort
without sleeves	sans manches	sahng mahngsh
pyjamas	un pyjama	ang peezhahmah
raincoat	un imperméable	ang nangpehrmayahbl
scarf	un foulard	ang foolahr
shirt	une chemise	ewn shermeez
shorts	un short	ang short
skirt	une jupe	ewn zhewp
slip	un jupon	ang zhewpawng
socks	des chaussettes	day shoasseht
sports jacket	une veste de sport	ewn vehst der spor
stockings	des bas	day bah
suit (man's)	un complet	ang kawngpleh
suit (woman's)	un tailleur	ang tahyurr
suspenders (Am.)	des bretelles	day brertehl
sweater	un chandail	ang shahngdahy
sweatshirt	un sweatshirt	ang "sweatshirt"
swimming trunks	un maillot de bain	ang mahyoa der bang
swimsuit	un costume de bain	ang kostewm der bang
T-shirt	un teeshirt	ang teeshirt
tie	une cravate	ewn krahvaht
tights	un collant	ang kollahng
top coat	un pardessus	ang pahrderssew
tracksuit	un survêtement	ang sewrvehtermahng
trousers	un pantalon	ang pahngtahlawng
umbrella	un parapluie	ang pahrahplwee
underpants	un caleçon/slip	ang kahlssawng/sleep
undershirt	un maillot de corps	ang mahyoa der kor
vest (Am.)	un gilet	ang zheeleh
vest (Br.)	un maillot de corps	ang mahyoa der kor
waistcoat	un gilet	ang zheeleh

belt	une ceinture	ewn sangtewr
buckle	une boucle	ewn bookl
button	un bouton	ang bootawng
pocket	une poche	ewn posh
press stud (snap fastener)	un bouton-pression	ang bootawng prehssyawng
zip (zipper)	une fermeture-éclair	ewn fehrmertewr ayklehr

Shoes *Chaussures*

I'd like a pair of …	**Je voudrais une paire de …**	zher voodreh ewn pehr der
boots	**bottes**	bot
moccasins	**mocassins**	mokahssang
plimsolls (sneakers)	**tennis**	tehneess
sandals	**sandales**	sahngdahl
shoes	**chaussures**	shoassewr
flat	**à talons plats**	ah tahlawng plah
with a heel	**à talons hauts**	ah tahlawng oa
slippers	**pantoufles**	pahngtoofl
These are too …	**Ceux-ci sont trop …**	sursee sawng troa
narrow/wide	**étroits/larges**	aytrwah/lahrzh
large/small	**grands/petits**	grahng/pertee
Do you have a larger/smaller size?	**Avez-vous une pointure plus grande/ plus petite?**	ahvay voo zewn pwangtewr plew grahngd/plew perteet
Do you have the same in black?	**Avez-vous les mêmes en noir?**	ahvay voo lay mehm ang nwahr
cloth	**en toile**	ang twahl
leather	**en cuir**	ang kweer
rubber	**en caoutchouc**	ang kahootshoo
suede	**en daim**	ang dang
Is it genuine leather?	**Est-ce du cuir véritable?**	ehss dew kweer vayreetahbl
I need some shoe polish/shoelaces.	**Je voudrais du cirage/des lacets.**	zher voodreh dew seerahzh/day lahsseh

Shoes worn out? Here's the key to getting them fixed again:

Can you repair these shoes?	**Pouvez-vous réparer ces chaussures?**	poovay voo raypahray say shoassewr
Can you stitch this?	**Pouvez-vous coudre ceci?**	poovay voo koodr serssee
I want new soles and heels.	**Je voudrais un res-semelage complet.**	zher voodreh ang rersser-merlahzh kawngpleh
When will they be ready?	**Quand seront-elles prêtes?**	kahng serrawng tehl preht

COLOURS, see page 113

Electrical appliances   *Appareils électriques*

220-volt, 50-cycle A.C. is used almost everywhere in France, Switzerland and Belgium.

What's the voltage?	**Quel est le voltage?**	kehl eh ler voltahzh
Do you have a battery for this?	**Avez-vous une pile pour ceci?**	ahvay voo ewn peel poor serssee
This is broken. Can you repair it?	**Ceci est cassé. Pouvez-vous le réparer?**	serssee eh kahssay. poovay voo ler raypahray
Can you show me how it works?	**Pourriez-vous me montrer comment cela fonctionne?**	pooryay voo mer mawngtray kommahng serlah fawngksyon
I'd like (to hire) a video cassette.	**Je voudrais (louer) une vidéocassette.**	zher voodreh (looay) ewn veedayoakahsseht
I'd like a/an/some ...	**Je voudrais ...**	zher voodreh
adaptor	**une prise de raccordement**	ewn preez der rahkordermang
amplifier	**un amplificateur**	ang nahngpleefeekahturr
bulb	**une ampoule**	ewn ahngpool
clock-radio	**un radio-réveil**	ang rahdyoa rayvehy
electric toothbrush	**une brosse à dents électrique**	ewn bross ah dahng aylehktreek
extension lead (cord)	**un prolongateur**	ang prolawnggahturr
hair dryer	**un sèche-cheveux**	ang sehsh shervur
headphones	**un casque à écouteurs**	ang kahsk ah aykooturr
(travelling) iron	**un fer à repasser (de voyage)**	ang fehr ah rerpahssay (der vwahyahzh)
lamp	**une lampe**	ewn lahngp
plug	**une fiche**	ewn feesh
portable ...	**... portatif**	... portahteef
radio	**un poste de radio**	ang post der rahdyoa
car radio	**un autoradio**	ang noatorahdyoa
record player	**un tourne-disque**	ang toorner deesk
shaver	**un rasoir électrique**	ang rahzwahr aylehktreek
speakers	**des haut-parleurs**	day oa pahrlurr
(cassette) tape recorder	**un magnétophone (à cassettes)**	ang mahñaytofon (ah kahsseht)
(colour) television	**un téléviseur (en couleur)**	ang taylayveezurr (ang koolurr)
transformer	**un transformateur**	ang trahngsformahturr
video-recorder	**un magnétoscope**	ang mahñaytoskop

Grocery *Magasin d'alimentation*

I'd like some bread, please.	**Je voudrais du pain, s'il vous plaît.**	zher voodreh dew pang seel voo pleh
What sort of cheese do you have?	**Quelle sorte de fromage avez-vous?**	kehl sort der fromahzh ahvay voo
A piece of ...	**Un morceau de ...**	ang morsoa der
that one	**celui-là**	serlwee lah
the one on the shelf	**celui sur l'étagère**	serlwee sewr laytahzhehr
I'll have one of those, please.	**Je prendrai un de ceux-là, s'il vous plaît.**	zher prahngdray ang der sur lah seel voo pleh
May I help myself?	**Puis-je me servir?**	pweezh mer sehrveer
I'd like ...	**Je voudrais ...**	zher voodreh
a kilo of apples	**un kilo de pommes**	ang keeloa der pom
half a kilo of tomatoes	**un demi-kilo/une livre de tomates**	ang dermee keeloa/ewn leevr der tomaht
100 grams of butter	**100 grammes de beurre**	sahng grahm der burr
a litre of milk	**un litre de lait**	ang leetr der leh
half a dozen eggs	**une demi-douzaine d'œufs**	ewn dermee doozehn dur
4 slices of ham	**4 tranches de jambon**	4 trahngsh der zhahngbawng
a packet of tea	**un paquet de thé**	ang pahkeh der tay
a jar of jam	**un pot de confiture**	ang poa der kawngfeetewr
a tin (can) of peaches	**une boîte de pêches**	ewn bwaht der pehsh
a tube of mustard	**un tube de moutarde**	ang tewb der mootahrd
a box of chocolates	**une boîte de chocolats**	ewn bwaht der shokolah

---

1 kilogram or kilo (kg.) = 1000 grams (g.)

100 g. = 3.5 oz.   ½ kg. = 1.1 lb.
200 g. = 7.0 oz.   1 kg. = 2.2 lb.

1 oz. =   28.35 g.
1 lb. = 453.60 g.

---

1 litre (l.) = 0.88 imp. qt. or 1.06 U.S. qt.

1 imp. qt. = 1.14 l.   1 U.S. qt. = 0.95 l.
1 imp. gal. = 4.55 l.   1 U.S. gal.= 3.8   l.

FOOD, see also page 63

Jeweller's—Watchmaker's *Bijouterie – Horlogerie*

Could I please see that?	**Pourrais-je voir ceci, s'il vous plaît?**	poorehzh vwahr serssee seel voo pleh
Do you have anything in gold?	**Avez-vous quelque chose en or?**	ahvay voo kehlker shoaz ahng nor
How many carats is this?	**Combien de carats y a-t-il?**	kawngbyang der kahrah ee ahteel
Is this real silver?	**Est-ce de l'argent véritable?**	ehss der lahrzhahng vayreetahbl
Can you repair this watch?	**Pouvez-vous réparer cette montre?**	poovay voo raypahray seht mawngtr
I'd like a/an/some ...	**Je voudrais ...**	zher voodreh
alarm clock	**un réveil**	ang rayvehy
bangle	**un bracelet**	ang brahsserleh
battery	**une pile**	ewn peel
bracelet	**un bracelet**	ang brahsserleh
chain bracelet	**une gourmette**	ewn goormeht
charm bracelet	**un bracelet à breloques**	ang brahsserleh ah brerlok
brooch	**une broche**	ewn brosh
chain	**une chaînette**	ewn shehneht
charm	**une breloque**	ewn brerlok
cigarette case	**un étui à cigarettes**	ang naytwee ah seegahrreht
cigarette lighter	**un briquet**	ang breekeh
clip	**un clip**	ang kleep
clock	**une pendule**	ewn pahngdewl
cross	**une croix**	ewn krwah
cuckoo clock	**un coucou**	ang kookoo
cuff links	**des boutons de manchettes**	day bootawng der mahngsheht
cutlery	**des couverts**	day koovehr
earrings	**des boucles d'oreilles**	day bookl dorehy
gem	**une pierre précieuse**	ewn pyehr prayssyurz
jewel box	**un coffret à bijoux**	ang kofreh ah beezhoo
mechanical pencil	**un porte-mine**	ang port meen
music box	**une boîte à musique**	ewn bwaht ah mewzeek
necklace	**un collier**	ang kollyay
pendant	**un pendentif**	ang pahngdahngteef
pin	**une épingle**	ewn aypanggl
pocket watch	**une montre de gousset**	ewn mawngtr der goosseh

powder compact	**un poudrier**	ang poodreeyay
propelling pencil	**un porte-mine**	ang port meen
ring	**une bague**	ewn bahg
engagement ring	**une bague de fiançailles**	ewn bahg der fyahngssahy
signet ring	**une chevalière**	ewn shervahlyehr
wedding ring	**une alliance**	ewn ahlyahngss
rosary	**un chapelet**	ang shaperleh
silverware	**de l'argenterie**	der lahrzhahngterree
tie clip	**une pince à cravate**	ewn pangss ah krahvaht
tie pin	**une épingle à cravate**	ewn aypanggl ah krahvaht
watch	**une montre**	ewn mawngtr
automatic	**automatique**	oatomahteek
digital	**digitale**	deezheetahl
quartz	**à quartz**	ah kwahrtss
with a second hand	**avec trotteuse**	ahvehk trotturz
watchstrap	**un bracelet de montre**	ang brahsserleh der mawngtr
wristwatch	**une montre-bracelet**	ewn mawngtr brahsserleh

amber	**ambre**	ahngbr
amethyst	**améthyste**	ahmayteest
chromium	**chrome**	kroam
copper	**cuivre**	kweevr
coral	**corail**	korahy
crystal	**cristal**	kreestahl
cut glass	**cristal taillé**	kreestahl tahyay
diamond	**diamant**	dyahmahng
emerald	**émeraude**	aymerroad
enamel	**émail**	aymahy
gold	**or**	or
gold plate	**plaqué or**	plahkay or
ivory	**ivoire**	eevwahr
jade	**jade**	zhahd
onyx	**onyx**	oneeks
pearl	**perle**	pehrl
pewter	**étain**	aytang
platinum	**platine**	plahteen
ruby	**rubis**	rewbee
sapphire	**saphir**	sahfeer
silver	**argent**	ahrzhahng
silver plate	**plaqué argent**	plahkay ahrzhahng
stainless steel	**inox**	eenox
topaz	**topaze**	topahz
turquoise	**turquoise**	tewrkwahz

Optician   *Opticien*

I've broken my glasses.	**J'ai cassé mes lunettes.**	zhay kahssay may lewneht
Can you repair them for me?	**Pouvez-vous me les réparer?**	poovay voo mer lay raypahray
When will they be ready?	**Quand seront-elles prêtes?**	kahng serrawng tehl preht
Can you change the lenses?	**Pouvez-vous changer les verres?**	poovay voo shahngzhay lay vehr
I want tinted lenses.	**Je voudrais des verres teintés.**	zher voodreh day vehr tangtay
The frame is broken.	**La monture est cassée.**	lah mawngtewr eh kahssay
I'd like a spectacle case.	**Je voudrais un étui à lunettes.**	zher voodreh ang naytwee ah lewneht
I'd like to have my eyesight checked.	**Je voudrais faire contrôler ma vue.**	zher voodreh fehr kawngtroalay mah vew
I'm short-sighted/ long-sighted.	**Je suis myope/ presbyte.**	zher swee myop/prehsbeet
I want some contact lenses.	**Je voudrais des verres de contact.**	zher voodreh day vehr der kawngtahkt
I've lost one of my contact lenses.	**J'ai perdu un verre de contact.**	zhay pehrdew ang vehr der kawngtahkt
Could you give me another one?	**Pouvez-vous m'en donner un autre?**	poovay voo mahng donnay ang noatr
I have hard/soft lenses.	**J'ai des verres de contact durs/ souples.**	zhay day vehr der kawngtahkt dewr/soopl
Have you any contact-lens liquid?	**Avez-vous un liquide pour verres de contact?**	ahvay voo ang leekeed poor vehr der kawngtahkt
I'd like to buy a pair of sunglasses.	**Je voudrais acheter une paire de lunettes de soleil.**	zher voodreh ahshtay ewn pehr der lewneht der solehy
May I look in a mirror?	**Puis-je me voir dans un miroir?**	pweezh mer vwahr dahng zang meerwahr
I'd like to buy a pair of binoculars.	**Je voudrais acheter des jumelles.**	zher voodreh ahshtay day zhewmehl

Photography *Photographie*

I want a(n) ... camera.	Je voudrais un appareil de photo ...	zher voodreh ang nahpahrehy der fotoa
automatic	automatique	oatomahteek
inexpensive	bon marché	bawng mahrshay
simple	simple	sangpl
Show me some cine (movie) cameras, please.	Veuillez me montrer des caméras, s'il vous plaît.	vuryay mer mawngtray day kahmayrah seel voo pleh
I'd like to have some passport photos taken.	Je voudrais me faire faire des photos d'identité.	zher voodreh mer fehr fehr day fotoa deetahngteetay

Film *Film*

I'd like a film for this camera.	Je voudrais un film pour cet appareil.	zher voodreh ang feelm poor seht ahpahrehy
black and white	en noir et blanc	ang nwahr ay blahng
colour	en couleurs	ang koolurr
colour negative	pour négatifs couleurs	poor naygahteef koolurr
colour slide	pour diapositives	poor dyahpoazeeteev
cartridge	un chargeur	ang shahrzhurr
roll film	une bobine	ewn bobeen
video cassette	une vidéocassette	ewn veedayoakahsseht
24/36 exposures	vingt-quatre/trente-six poses	vangt kahtr/trahngt see poaz
this size	ce format	ser formah
this ASA/DIN number	ce chiffre ASA/DIN	ser sheefr ahzah/deen
artificial light type	pour lumière artificielle	poor lewmyehr ahrteefeessyehl
daylight type	pour lumière du jour	poor lewmyehr dew zhoor
fast (high-speed)	ultrarapide	ewltrahrahpeed
fine grain	à grain fin	ah grang fang

Processing *Développement*

| How much do you charge for developing? | Combien coûte le développement? | kawngbyang koot ler dayvlopmahng |

I want ... prints of each negative	Je voudrais ... copies de chaque négatif.	zher voodreh ... koppee der shahk naygahteef
with a mat finish	sur papier mat	sewr pahpyay maht
with a glossy finish	sur papier brillant	sewr pahpyay breeyahng
Will you please enlarge this?	Veuillez agrandir ceci, s'il vous plaît.	vuryay ahgrahngdeer serssee seel voo pleh
When will the photos be ready?	Quand les photos seront-elles prêtes?	kahng lay fotoa serrawng tehl preht

Accessories and repairs *Accessoires et réparations*

I want a/an/some ...	Je voudrais ...	zher voodreh
battery	une pile	ewn peel
cable release	un déclencheur	ang dayklahngshurr
camera case	un étui (à appareil photo)	ang naytwee (ah ahpahrehy fotoa)
(electronic) flash	un flash (électronique)	ang "flash" (aylehktroneek)
filter	un filtre	ang feeltr
for black and white	pour noir et blanc	poor nwahr ay blahng
for colour	pour la couleur	poor lah koolurr
lens	un objectif	ang nobzhehkteef
telephoto lens	un téléobjectif	ang taylayobzhehkteef
wide-angle lens	un grand-angulaire	ang grahng tahngewlehr
lens cap	un capuchon (d'objectif)	ang kahpewshawng (dobzhehkteef)
Can you repair this camera?	Pouvez-vous réparer cet appareil?	poovay voo raypahray seht ahpahrehy
The film is jammed.	Le film est bloqué.	ler feelm eh blokay
There's something wrong with the ...	Il y a quelque chose qui ne va pas avec ...	eel ee ah kehlker shoaz kee ner vah pah ahvehk
exposure counter	le compte-poses	ler kawngt poaz
film winder	le levier d'avancement	ler lervyay dahvahngssmahng
flash attachment	la glissière du flash	lah gleessyehr dew "flash"
lens	l'objectif	lobzhehkteef
light meter	la cellule photo-électrique	lah sehllewl foto-aylehktrook
rangefinder	le télémètre	ler taylaymehtr
shutter	l'obturateur	lobtewrahturr

NUMBERS, see page 147

Tobacconist's *Bureau de tabac*

Tobacco is a state monopoly in France. You recognize licensed tobacconist's—cafés, bars and many newsstands—by the conspicuous red cone. In Belgium and Switzerland you can also buy cigarettes in restaurants, supermarkets, etc.

A packet of cigarettes, please.	**Un paquet de cigarettes, s'il vous plaît.**	ang pahkeh der seegahreht seel voo pleh
Do you have any American/English cigarettes?	**Avez-vous des cigarettes américaines/anglaises?**	ahvay voo day seegahreht ahmayreekehn/ahngglehz
I'd like a carton.	**J'en voudrais une cartouche.**	zhahng voodreh ewn kahrtoosh
Give me a/some ..., please.	**Donnez-moi ..., s'il vous plaît.**	donnay mwah ... seel voo pleh
candy	**des bonbons**	day bawngbawng
chewing gum	**du chewing-gum**	dew "chewing gum"
chewing tobacco	**du tabac à chiquer**	dew tahbah ah sheekay
chocolate	**du chocolat**	dew shokolah
cigarette case	**un étui à cigarettes**	ang naytwee ah seegahreht
cigarette holder	**un fume-cigarette**	ang fewm seegahreht
cigarettes	**des cigarettes**	day seegahreht
filter-tipped/	**avec filtre/**	ahvehk feeltr/
without filter	**sans filtre**	sahng feeltr
light/dark tobacco	**du tabac blond/brun**	dew tahbah blawng/brang
mild/strong	**légères/fortes**	layzhehr/fort
menthol	**mentholées**	mahngtolay
king-size	**long format**	lawng formah
cigars	**des cigares**	day seegahr
lighter	**un briquet**	ang breekeh
lighter fluid/gas	**de l'essence/du gaz à briquet**	der lehssahngss/dew gahz ah breekeh
matches	**des allumettes**	day zahlewmeht
pipe	**une pipe**	ewn peep
pipe cleaners	**des nettoie-pipes**	day nehtwah peep
pipe tobacco	**du tabac pour pipe**	dew tahbah poor peep
pipe tool	**un cure-pipe**	ang kewr peep
postcard	**une carte postale**	ewn kahrt postahl
snuff	**du tabac à priser**	dew tahbah ah preezay
stamps	**des timbres**	day tangbr
sweets	**des bonbons**	day bawngbawng
wick	**une mèche**	ewn mehsh

SHOPPING GUIDE

127

Miscellaneous *Divers*

Souvenirs *Souvenirs*

Here are some suggestions for articles which you might like
to bring back as a souvenir or a gift. Some regions of France
produce articles which you may be specially interested in,
e.g., lace in Brittany, Normandy and Auvergne, porcelain
in Limoges and Sèvres, pottery in Brittany, Alsace and
Provence.

crystal	**le cristal**	ler kreestahl
cutlery	**la coutellerie**	lah kootehlerree
lace	**les dentelles**	lay dahngtehl
perfume	**le parfum**	ler pahrfang
porcelain	**la porcelaine**	lah porserlehn
pottery	**la poterie**	lah poterree
women's top fashion	**la haute couture**	lah oat kootewr

Lace, crystal and porcelain are also good buys in Belgium.
In addition, you might consider buying there:

copperware	**les objets en cuivre**	lay zobzheh ahng kweevr
diamonds	**les diamants**	lay dyahmahng
tapestry	**la tapisserie**	lah tahpeesserree

Some typical products of Switzerland are:

chocolate	**le chocolat**	ler shokolah
cuckoo clock	**le coucou**	ler kookoo
fondue forks	**les fourchettes à fondue**	lay foorsheht ah fawngdew
fondue pot	**le caquelon**	ler kahkerlawng
watch	**la montre**	lah mawngtr

Records—Cassettes *Disques – Cassettes*

Do you have any records by ...?	**Avez-vous des disques de ...?**	ahvay voo day deesk der
I'd like a ...	**Je voudrais ...**	zher voodreh
cassette	**une cassette**	ewn kahsseht
video cassette	**une vidéocassette**	ewn veedayoakahsseht
compact disc	**un disque compact**	ang deesk kawngpahkt

Guide des achats

L.P. (33 rpm)	33 T. (Tours)	trahngt trwah (toor)
E.P. (45 rpm)	Super 45 T.	sewpehr kahrahngt sangk
		toor
single	45 T. Simple	kahrahngt sangk toor
		sangpl

Have you any songs by ...?	Avez-vous des chansons de ...?	ahvay voo day shahng-ssawng der
Can I listen to this record?	Puis-je écouter ce disque?	pweezh aykootay ser deesk
chamber music	la musique de chambre	lah mewzeek der shahngbr
classical music	la musique classique	lah mewzeek klahsseek
folk music	la musique folklorique	lah mewzeek folkloreek
instrumental music	la musique instrumentale	lah mewzeek angstrewmahngtahl
jazz	le jazz	ler jazz
light music	la musique légère	lah mewzeek layzhehr
orchestral music	la musique symphonique	lah mewzeek sangfoneek
pop music	la musique pop	lah mewzeek pop

Toys *Jouets*

I'd like a toy/game ...	Je voudrais un jouet/jeu ...	zher voodreh ang zhooeh/zhur
for a boy	pour un garçon	poor ang gahrssawng
for a 5-year-old girl	pour une fillette de 5 ans	poor ewn feeyeht der 5 ahng
(beach) ball	un ballon (de plage)	ang bahlawng (der plahzh)
bucket and spade (pail and shovel)	un seau et une pelle	ang soa ay ewn pehl
building blocks (bricks)	un jeu de construction	ang zhur der kawngstrewksyawng
card game	un jeu de cartes	ang zhur der kahrt
chess set	un jeu d'échecs	ang zhur dayshehk
doll	une poupée	ewn poopay
electronic game	un jeu électronique	ang zhur aylehktroneek
flippers	des palmes	day pahlm
roller skates	des patins à roulettes	day pahtang ah rooleht
snorkel	un tuba	ang tewbah

Your money: banks—currency

In all European French-speaking countries, the basic unit of currency is the *franc* (frahng), divided into 100 *centimes* (sahngteem). However, these various francs have different value. *Franc* is abbreviated to *Fr* or *F*.

In France, there are coins of 5, 10, 20 and 50 centimes and of 1, 2, 5 and 10 francs. Banknotes come in denominations of 20, 50, 100, 200 and 500 francs.

In Switzerland there are coins of 5, 10, 20 and 50 centimes and of 1, 2 and 5 francs. There are banknotes of 10, 20, 50, 100, 500 and 1,000 francs.

Belgium has coins of 50 centimes and of 1, 5, 20 and 50 francs; there are banknotes of 50, 100, 500, 1,000 and 5,000 francs.

Though hours can vary, banks are generally open from 8.30 or 9 a.m. to noon and from 1.30 or 2 to 4.30 or 5 p.m., Monday to Friday. Main branches often remain open during the lunch hours. In all three countries, you will find currency exchange offices *(bureaux de change)* which are often open outside regular banking hours.

Credit cards may be used in an increasing number of hotels, restaurants, shops, etc. Signs are posted indicating which cards are accepted.

Traveller's cheques are accepted by hotels, travel agents and many shops, although the exchange rate is invariably better at a bank. Don't forget to take your passport when going to cash a traveller's cheque. Eurocheques are also accepted.

| Where's the nearest bank? | Où est la banque la plus proche? | oo eh lah bahngk lah plew prosh |
| Where's the nearest currency exchange office? | Où est le bureau de change le plus proche? | oo eh ler bewroa der shahngzh ler plew prosh |

At the bank   *A la banque*

I want to change some dollars/pounds.	**Je voudrais changer des dollars/livres.**	zher voodreh shahngzhay day dollahr/leevr
I want to cash a traveller's cheque.	**Je désire toucher ce chèque de voyage.**	zher dayzeer tooshay ser shehk der vwahyahzh
What's the exchange rate?	**Quel est le cours du change?**	kehl eh ler koor dew shahngzh
How much commission do you charge?	**Quelle commission prenez-vous?**	kehl kommeessyawng prernay voo
Can you cash a personal cheque?	**Puis-je toucher un chèque à ordre?**	pweezh tooshay ang shehk ah ordr
Can you telex my bank in London?	**Pouvez-vous envoyer un télex à ma banque à Londres?**	poovay voo ahngvwahyay ang taylehx ah mah bahngk ah lawngdr
I have a/an/some ...	**Je possède ...**	zher possehd
bank card	**une carte d'identité bancaire**	ewn kahrt deedahngteetay bahngkehr
credit card	**une carte de crédit**	ewn kahrt der kraydee
Eurocheques	**des eurocheques**	day zurroshehk
introduction from ...	**une introduction de ...**	ewn angtrodewksyawng der
letter of credit	**une lettre de crédit**	ewn lehtr der kraydee
I'm expecting some money from New York. Has it arrived?	**J'attends de l'argent de New York. Est-il déjà arrivé?**	zhahtahng der lahrzhahng der New York. ehteel dayzhah ahreevay
Please give me ... notes (bills) and some small change.	**Donnez-moi ... billets et de la monnaie, s'il vous plait.**	donnay mwah ... beeyeh ay der lah monneh seel voo pleh
Give me ... large notes and the rest in small notes.	**Donnez-moi ... grosses coupures, et le reste en petites coupures.**	donnay mwah ... groass koopewr ay ler rehst ahng perteet koopewr

Deposit—Withdrawal   *Dépôts – Retraits*

I want to credit this to my account.	**Je voudrais déposer ceci sur mon compte.**	zher voodreh daypoazay serssee sewr mawng kawngt
I want to ...	**Je désire ...**	zher dayzeer
open an account	**ouvrir un compte**	oovreer ang kawngt
withdraw ... francs	**retirer ... francs**	rerteeray ... frahng

NUMBERS, see page 147

| I want to credit this to Mr , , ,'s account. | **Je voudrais créditer de cette somme le compte de M. ...** | zher voodreh kraydeetay der seht som ler kawngt der mersyur |
| Where should I sign? | **Où dois-je signer?** | oo dwahzh seeñay |

Business terms   *Termes d'affaires*

My name is ...	**Je m'appelle ...**	zher mahpehl
Here's my card.	**Voici ma carte.**	vwahssee mah kahrt
I have an appointment with ...	**J'ai rendez-vous avec ...**	zhay rahngday voo ahvehk
Can you give me an estimate of the cost?	**Pouvez-vous me donner une estimation du coût?**	poovay voo mer donnay ewn ehsteemahssyawng dew koo
What's the rate of inflation?	**Quel est le taux d'inflation?**	kehl eh ler toa dangflahssyawng
Can you provide me with an interpreter/ a secretary?	**Pourriez-vous me procurer un interprète/une secrétaire?**	pooryay voo mer prokewray ang nangtehrpreht/ewn serkraytehr
Where can I make photocopies?	**Où puis-je faire des photocopies?**	oo pweezh fehr day fotokopee

amount	**la somme**	lah som
balance	**la position**	lah poazeessyawng
capital	**le capital**	ler kahpeetahl
cheque book	**le carnet de chèques**	ler kahrneh der shehk
contract	**le contrat**	ler kawngtrah
expenses	**les frais**	lay freh
interest	**l'intérêt**	langtayreh
investment	**l'investissement**	langvehsteessmahng
invoice	**la facture**	lah fahktewr
loss	**la perte**	lah pehrt
mortgage	**l'hypothèque**	leepotehk
payment	**le paiement**	ler pehmahng
percentage	**le pourcentage**	ler poorssahngtahzh
profit	**le bénéfice**	ler baynayfeess
purchase	**l'achat**	lahshah
sale	**la vente**	lah vahngt
share	**l'action**	lahksyawng
transfer	**le transfert**	lor trohngsfehr
value	**la valeur**	lah vahlurr

At the post office

Post offices in France bear the sign *Postes et Télécommunications* or *P&T,* and are generally open from 8 a.m. to noon and from 2 to 6.30 p.m. Swiss post offices are recognized by a *PTT* sign and are open from 7.30 a.m. to noon and from 1.45 to 6.30 p.m. In Belgium, post offices are marked *Postes/Posterijen.* Main ones are open from 9 a.m. to 6 p.m. Note that telephone and telegraph services in Belgium are separated from the post office. In all three countries, post offices are open only in the morning on Saturdays.

In France you can buy stamps either at the post office or a tobacco shop. Letter boxes (mailboxes) are painted yellow in France and Switzerland and red in Belgium.

Where's the nearest post office?	**Où se trouve le bureau de poste le plus proche?**	oo ser troov ler bewroa der post ler plew prosh
What time does the post office open/close?	**A quelle heure ouvre/ferme la poste?**	ah kehl urr oovr/fehrm lah post
A stamp for this letter/postcard, please.	**Un timbre pour cette lettre/carte postale, s'il vous plaît.**	ang tangbr poor seht lehtr/kahrt postahl seel voo pleh
I want ... ...-centime stamps.	**Je voudrais ... timbres à ... centimes.**	zher voodreh ... tangbr ah ... sahngteem
What's the postage for a letter to London?	**Quel est le tarif d'une lettre pour Londres?**	kehl eh ler tahreef dewn lehtr poor lawngdr
What's the postage for a postcard to Los Angeles?	**Quel est le tarif d'une carte postale pour Los Angeles?**	kehl eh ler tahreef dewn kahrt postahl poor Los Angeles
Where's the letter box (mailbox)?	**Où se trouve la boîte aux lettres?**	oo ser troov lah bwaht oa lehtr
I want to send this parcel.	**Je voudrais expédier ce colis.**	zher voodreh ehxpaydyay ser kolee

I want to send this by ...	**Je voudrais envoyer ceci ...**	zher voodreh ahngvwahyay serssee
airmail	**par avion**	pahr ahvyawng
express (special delivery)	**par exprès**	pahr ehxprehss
registered mail	**recommandé**	rerkommahngday
At which counter can I cash an international money order?	**A quel guichet puis-je toucher un mandat international?**	ah kehl geesheh pweez tooshay ang mahngdah angtehrnahssyonahl
Where's the poste restante (general delivery)?	**Où se trouve la poste restante?**	oo ser troov lah post rehstahngt
Is there any mail for me? My name is ...	**Y a-t-il du courrier pour moi? Je m'appelle ...**	ee ahteel dew kooryay poor mwah. zher mahpehl

TIMBRES	STAMPS
COLIS	PARCELS
MANDATS	MONEY ORDERS

Telegrams *Télégrammes*

In France and Switzerland cables and telegrams are dispatched by the post office. In Belgium you must got to a separate *Téléphone/Télégraphe* office.

I want to send a telegram/telex.	**Je voudrais envoyer un télégramme/télex.**	zher voodreh ahngvwahyay ang taylaygrahm/taylehx
May I please have a form?	**Puis-je avoir une formule, s'il vous plaît?**	pweezh ahvwahr ewn formewl seel voo pleh
How much is it per word?	**Quel est le tarif par mot?**	kehl eh ler tahreef pahr moa
How long will a cable to Boston take?	**Combien de temps met un télégramme pour arriver à Boston?**	kawngbyang der tahng meh ang taylaygrahm poor ahreevay ah Boston
How much will this telex cost?	**Combien coûtera ce télex?**	kawngbyang kooterrah ser taylehx

Telephoning *Pour téléphoner*

The telephone system in France, Belgium and Switzerland is virtually entirely automatic. International or long-distance calls can be made from phone boxes, but if you need assistance in placing the call, go to the post office (in Belgium, to the *Téléphone/Télégraphe* office) or ask at your hotel. Local calls in France can also be made from cafés, where you might have to buy a *jeton* (token) to put into the phone.

Telephone numbers are given in pairs in French so that 12 34 56 would be expressed in French, twelve, thirty-four, fifty-six.

Where's the telephone?	**Où se trouve le téléphone?**	oo ser troov ler taylayfon
I would like a telephone token.	**Je voudrais un jeton (de téléphone).**	zher voodreh ang zhertawng (der taylayfon)
Where's the nearest telephone booth?	**Où se trouve la cabine téléphonique la plus proche?**	oo ser troov lah kahbeen taylayfoneek lah plew prosh
May I use your phone?	**Puis-je utiliser votre téléphone?**	pweezh ewteeleezay votr taylayfon
Do you have a telephone directory for Lyons?	**Avez-vous un annuaire télé-phonique de Lyon?**	ahvay voo ang nahnewehr taylayfoneek der lyawng
What's the dialling (area) code for ...?	**Quel est l'indicatif de ...?**	kehl eh langdeekahteef der
How do I get the international operator?	**Comment obtient-on le service inter-national?**	kommahng obtyang tawng ler sehrveess angtehr-nahssyonahl

Operator *Opératrice*

Good morning, I want Geneva 23 45 67.	**Bonjour, je vou-drais le 23 45 67 à Genève.**	bawngzhoor zher voodreh ler 23 45 67 ah zhernehv
Can you help me get this number?	**Pouvez-vous m'aider à obtenir ce numéro?**	poovay voo mehday ah obterneer ser newmayroa

NUMBERS, see page 147

| I want to place a personal (person-to-person) call. | **Je voudrais une communication avec préavis.** | zher voodreh ewn kommewneekahssyawng ahvehk prayahvee |
| I want to reverse the charges. | **Je voudrais téléphoner en P.C.V.** | zher voodreh taylayfonay ahng pay say vay |

Speaking *Au téléphone*

Hello. This is ... speaking.	**Allô. C'est ... à l'appareil.**	ahloa. seh ... ah lahpahrehy
I want to speak to ...	**Je désire parler à ...**	zher dayzeer pahrlay ah
I want extension ...	**Je voudrais l'interne ...**	zher voodreh langtehrn
Speak louder/more slowly, please.	**Veuillez parler plus fort/lentement.**	vuryay pahrlay plew for/lahngtmahng

Bad luck *Pas de chance*

Would you please try again later?	**Pourriez-vous rappeler un peu plus tard, s'il vous plaît?**	pooryay voo rahperlay ang pur plew tahr seel voo pleh
Operator, you gave me the wrong number.	**Mademoiselle, vous m'avez donné un faux numéro.**	mahdmwahzehl voo mahvay donnay ang foa newmayroa
Operator, we were cut off.	**Mademoiselle, nous avons été coupés.**	mahdmwahzehl noo zahvawng zaytay koopay

---

Telephone alphabet *Code d'épellation*

A	**Anatole**	ahnahtol	N	**Nicolas**	neekolah
B	**Berthe**	behrt	O	**Oscar**	oskahr
C	**Célestin**	saylehstang	P	**Pierre**	pyehr
D	**Désiré**	dayzeeray	Q	**Quintal**	kangtahl
E	**Eugène**	urzhehn	R	**Raoul**	rahool
F	**François**	frahngsswah	S	**Suzanne**	sewzahn
G	**Gaston**	gahstawng	T	**Thérèse**	tayrehz
H	**Henri**	ahngree	U	**Ursule**	ewrsewl
I	**Irma**	eermah	V	**Victor**	veektor
J	**Joseph**	zhozohf	W	**William**	veelyahm
K	**Kléber**	klaybehr	X	**Xavier**	ksahvyay
L	**Louis**	looee	Y	**Yvonne**	eevon
M	**Marcel**	mahrssehl	Z	**Zoé**	zoay

Not there *La personne n'est pas là ...*

When will he/she be back?	**Quand sera-t-il/elle de retour?**	kahng serrah teel/tehl der rertoor
Will you tell him/her I called? My name is ...	**Veuillez lui dire que j'ai appelé. Je m'appelle ...**	vuryay lwee deer ker zhay ahperlay. zher mahpehl
Would you ask him/her to call me?	**Pourriez-vous lui demander de me rappeler?**	pooryay voo lwee dermahngday der mer rahperlay
Would you please take a message?	**Pourriez-vous prendre un message, s'il vous plaît?**	pooryay voo prahngdr ang mehssahzh seel voo pleh

Charges *Taxes*

What was the cost of that call?	**Quel est le prix de la communication?**	kehl eh ler pree der lah kommewneekahssyawng
I want to pay for the call.	**Je voudrais payer la communication.**	zher voodreh pehyay lah kommewneekahssyawng

---

☞	🖐
Il y a un appel (téléphonique) pour vous.	There's a telephone call for you.
Quel numéro demandez-vous?	What number are you calling?
Ce n'est pas libre.	The line's engaged.
Il n'y a personne.	There's no answer.
Vous vous êtes trompé(e) de numéro.	You've got the wrong number.
Le téléphone est en dérangement.	The phone is out of order.
Un moment!	Just a moment.
Ne quittez pas!	Hold on, please.
Il/Elle est absent(e) pour le moment.	He's/She's out at the moment.

Doctor

To be at ease, make sure your health insurance policy covers any illness or accident while on holiday. If not, ask your insurance representative, automobile association or travel agent for details of special health insurance.

General *Généralités*

Can you get me a doctor?	**Pouvez-vous m'appeler un médecin?**	poovay voo mahperlay ang maydssang
Is there a doctor here?	**Y a-t-il un médecin ici?**	ee ahteel ang maydssang eessee
I need a doctor, quickly.	**J'ai besoin d'un médecin, vite.**	zhay berzwang dang maydssang veet
Where can I find a doctor who speaks English?	**Où puis-je trouver un médecin qui parle anglais?**	oo pweezh troovay ang maydssang kee pahrl ahnggleh
Where's the surgery (doctor's office)?	**Où est le cabinet de consultation?**	oo eh ler kahbeeneh der kawngssewltahssyawng
What are the surgery (office) hours?	**Quelles sont les heures de consultation?**	kehl sawng lay zurr der kawngssewltahssyawng
Could the doctor come to see me here?	**Le médecin pourrait-il venir me voir?**	ler maydssang pooreh teel verneer mer vwahr
What time can the doctor come?	**A quelle heure peut-il venir?**	ah kehl urr purteel verneer
Can you recommend a/an ...?	**Pouvez-vous m'indiquer ...?**	poovay voo mangdeekay
general practitioner	**un généraliste**	ang zhaynayrahleest
children's doctor	**un pédiatre**	ang paydyahtr
eye specialist	**un oculiste**	ang nokewleest
gynaecologist	**un gynécologue**	ang zheenaykolog
Can I have an appointment ...?	**Puis-je avoir un rendez-vous ...?**	pweezh ahwahr ang rahngday voo
tomorrow	**pour demain**	poor dermang
as soon as possible	**dès que possible**	deh ker posseebl

CHEMIST'S, see page 108

Parts of the body   *Parties du corps*

appendix	l'appendice	lahpangdeess
arm	le bras	ler brah
artery	l'artère	lahrtehr
back	le dos	ler doa
bladder	la vessie	lah vehssee
bone	l'os	loss
bowels	les intestins	lay zangtehstang
breast	le sein	ler sang
chest	la poitrine	lah pwahtreen
ear	l'oreille	lorehy
eye(s)	l'œil (les yeux)	lery (lay zyur)
face	le visage	ler veezahzh
finger	le doigt	ler dwah
foot	le pied	ler pyay
gland	la glande	lah glahngd
hand	la main	lah mang
head	la tête	lah teht
heart	le cœur	ler kurr
jaw	la mâchoire	lah mahshwahr
joint	l'articulation	lahrteekewlahssyawng
kidney	le rein	ler rang
knee	le genou	ler zhernoo
leg	la jambe	lah zhahngb
lip	la lèvre	lah lehvr
liver	le foie	ler fwah
lung	le poumon	ler poomawng
mouth	la bouche	lah boosh
muscle	le muscle	ler mewskl
neck	le cou	ler koo
nerve	le nerf	ler nehr
nervous system	le système nerveux	ler seestehm nehrvur
nose	le nez	ler nay
rib	la côte	lah koat
shoulder	l'épaule	laypoal
skin	la peau	lah poa
spine	la colonne vertébrale	lah kolon vehrtaybrahl
stomach	l'estomac	lehstomah
tendon	le tendon	ler tahngdawng
thigh	la cuisse	lah kweess
throat	la gorge	lah gorzh
thumb	le pouce	ler pooss
toe	l'orteil	lortehy
tongue	la langue	lah lahngg
tonsils	les amygdales	lay zahmeedahl
vein	la veine	lah vehn

Accident—Injury   *Accidents – Blessures*

There has been an accident.	**Il est arrivé un accident.**	eel eh tahreevay ang nahkseedahng
My child has had a fall.	**Mon enfant a fait une chute.**	mawng nahngfahng ah feh ewn shewt
He/She has hurt his/her head.	**Il/Elle s'est blessé(e) à la tête.**	eel/ehl seh blehssay ah lah teht
He's/She's unconscious.	**Il/Elle s'est évanoui(e).**	eel/ehl seh tayvahnooee
He's/She's bleeding (heavily).	**Il/Elle saigne (abondamment).**	eel/ehl sehñ (ahbawngdahmmahng)
He's/She's (seriously) injured.	**Il/Elle s'est (grièvement) blessé(e).**	eel/ehl seh (gryehvmahng) blehssay
His/Her arm is broken.	**Il/Elle s'est cassé le bras.**	eel/ehl seh kahssay ler brah
His/Her ankle is swollen.	**Sa cheville est enflée.**	sah sherveey eh tahngflay
I've been stung.	**Quelque chose m'a piqué.**	kehlker shoaz mah peekay
I've got something in my eye.	**J'ai reçu quelque chose dans l'œil.**	zhay rerssew kehlker shoaz dahng lery
I've got a/an ...	**J'ai ...**	zhay
blister	**une ampoule**	ewn ahngpool
boil	**un furoncle**	ang fewrawngkl
bruise	**une contusion**	ewn kawngtewzyawng
burn	**une brûlure**	ewn brewlewr
cut	**une coupure**	ewn koopewr
graze	**une éraflure**	ewn ayraflewr
insect bite	**une piqûre d'insecte**	ewn peekewr dangssehkt
lump	**une bosse**	ewn boss
rash	**une éruption**	ewn ayrewpsyawng
sting	**une piqûre**	ewn peekewr
swelling	**une enflure**	ewn ahngflewr
wound	**une blessure**	ewn blehssewr
Could you have a look at it?	**Pourriez-vous l'examiner?**	pooryay voo lehxahmeenay
I can't move my ...	**Je ne peux pas bouger le/la/les ...**	zher ner pur pah boozhay ler/lah/lay ...
It hurts.	**Cela me fait mal.**	serlah mer feh mahl

Où avez-vous mal?	Where does it hurt?
Quel genre de douleur éprouvez-vous?	What kind of pain is it?
sourde/aiguë/lancinante persistante/intermittente	dull/sharp/throbbing constant/on and off
C'est ...	It's ...
cassé/foulé déboîté/déchiré	broken/sprained dislocated/torn
Il faut vous faire une radio.	I want you to have an X-ray taken.
Il faudra vous mettre un plâtre.	You'll get a plaster.
C'est infecté.	It's infected.
Etes-vous vacciné(e) contre le tétanos?	Have you been vaccinated against tetanus?
Je vais vous donner un antiseptique/calmant.	I'll give you an antiseptic/ a painkiller.

Illness *Maladies*

I'm not feeling well.	Je ne me sens pas bien.	zher ner mer sahng pah byang
I'm ill.	Je suis malade.	zher swee mahlahd
I feel ...	J'ai ...	zhay
dizzy	des vertiges	day vehrteezh
nauseous	des nausées	day noazay
shivery	des frissons	day freessawng
I've got a fever.	J'ai de la fièvre.	zhay der lah fyehvr
My temperature is 38 degrees.	J'ai 38 de fièvre.	zhay 38 de fyehvr
I've been vomiting.	J'ai eu des vomissements.	zhay ew day voameessmahng
I'm constipated/ I've got diarrhoea.	Je suis constipé(e)/ J'ai la diarrhée.	zher swee kawngsteepay/ zhay la dyahray
My ... hurt(s).	J'ai mal à ...	zhay mahl ah

I've got (a/an) ...	J'ai ...	zhay
asthma	de l'asthme	der lahsm
backache	mal aux reins	mahl oa rang
cold	un rhume	ang rewm
cough	la toux	lah too
cramps	des crampes	day krahngp
earache	mal aux oreilles	mahl oa zorehy
hay fever	le rhume des foins	ler rewm day fwang
headache	mal à la tête	zhay mahl ah lah teht
indigestion	une indigestion	ewn angdeezhehstyawng
nosebleed	des saignements de nez	day sehñmahng der nay
palpitations	des palpitations	day pahlpeetahssyawng
rheumatism	des rhumatismes	day rewmahteezm
sore throat	mal à la gorge	mahl ah lah gorzh
stiff neck	un torticolis	ang torteekolee
stomach ache	mal à l'estomac	mahl ah lehstomah
sunstroke	une insolation	ewn angsolahssyawng

I have difficulties breathing.	J'ai de la peine à respirer.	zhay der lah pehn ah rehspeeray
I have a pain in my chest.	Je ressens une douleur dans la poitrine.	zher rersahng ewn doolurr dahng lah pwahtreen
I had a heart attack ... years ago.	J'ai eu une crise cardiaque il y a ... ans.	zhay ew ewn kreez kahrdyahk eel ee ah ... ahng
My blood pressure is too high/too low.	Ma tension est trop élevée/basse.	mah tahngssyawng eh troa paylervay/bahss
I'm allergic to ...	Je suis allergique à ...	zher swee zahlehrzheek ah
I'm a diabetic.	Je suis diabétique.	zher swee dyahbayteek

Women's section   *Typiquement féminin ...*

I have period pains.	J'ai des règles douloureuses.	zhay day rehgl dooloorurz
I have a vaginal infection.	J'ai une infection vaginale.	zhay ewn angfehksyawng vahzheenahl
I'm on the pill.	Je prends la pilule.	zher prahng lah peelewl
I haven't had my period for 2 months.	Je n'ai pas eu mes règles depuis 2 mois.	zher nay pah ew may rehgl derpwee 2 mwah
I'm (3 months) pregnant.	Je suis enceinte (de 3 mois).	zher swee zahngssangt (der 3 mwah)

DOCTOR

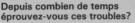

Depuis combien de temps éprouvez-vous ces troubles?	How long have you been feeling like this?
Est-ce la première fois que vous en souffrez?	Is this the first time you've had this?
Je vais prendre votre température/tension.	I'll take your temperature/ blood pressure.
Relevez votre manche.	Roll up your sleeve, please.
Déshabillez-vous (jusqu'à la ceinture), s'il vous plaît.	Please undress (down to the waist).
Etendez-vous là, s'il vous plaît.	Please lie down over here.
Ouvrez la bouche.	Open your mouth.
Respirez à fond.	Breathe deeply.
Toussez, s'il vous plaît.	Cough, please.
Où avez-vous mal?	Where do you feel the pain?
Vous avez . . .	You've got (a/an) . . .
l'appendicite	appendicitis
une cystite	cystitis
une gastrite	gastritis
la grippe	flu
une inflammation de . . .	inflammation of . . .
une intoxication alimentaire	food poisoning
la jaunisse	jaundice
une maladie vénérienne	venereal disease
une pneumonie	pneumonia
la rougeole	measles
Je vais vous faire une piqûre.	I'll give you an injection.
Je voudrais un prélèvement de votre sang/de vos selles/ de votre urine.	I want a specimen of your blood/stools/urine.
Vous devrez garder le lit . . . jours.	You must stay in bed for . . . days.
Vous devriez consulter un spécialiste.	I want you to see a specialist.
Je désire que vous alliez à l'hôpital vous faire faire un bilan (de santé).	I want you to go to the hospital for a general check-up.

Médecin

Prescription — Treatment   *Ordonnance – Traitement*

This is my usual medicine.	**Voici mon médicament habituel.**	vwahssee mawng maydee-kahmahng ahbeetewehl
Can you give me a prescription for this?	**Pouvez-vous me donner une ordonnance pour cela?**	poovay voo mer donnay ewn ordonnahngss poor serlah
Can you prescribe a/an/some ...?	**Pourriez-vous me prescrire ...?**	pooryay voo mer prehskreer
antidepressant	**un remontant**	ang rermawngtahng
sleeping pills	**un somnifère**	ang somneefehr
tranquillizer	**un tranquillisant**	ang trahngkeeleezahng
I'm allergic to antibiotics/penicilline.	**Je suis allergique aux antibiotiques/à la pénicilline.**	zher swee zahlehrzheek oa zahngteebyoteek/ah lah payneesseeleen
I don't want anything too strong.	**Je ne veux pas quelque chose de trop fort.**	zher ner vur pah kehlker shoaz der troa for
How many times a day should I take it?	**Combien de fois par jour faut-il le prendre?**	kawngbyang dor fwah pahr zhoor foateel ler prahngdr
Must I swallow them whole?	**Dois-je les avaler?**	dwahzh lay zahvahlay

---

Quel traitement suivez-vous?	What treatment are you having?
Quel médicament prenez-vous?	What medicine are you taking?
En injection ou par voie orale?	Injection or oral?
Prenez ... cuillères à café de ce médicament ...	Take ... teaspoons of this medicine ...
Prenez une pilule avec un verre d'eau ...	Take one pill with a glass of water ...
toutes les ... heures	every ... hours
... fois par jour	... times a day
avant/après les repas	before/after each meal
le matin/le soir	in the morning/at night
en cas de douleurs	in case of pain
pendant ... jours	for ... days

CHEMISTS'S, see p. 108

Fee *Honoraires*

How much do I owe you?	**Combien vous dois-je?**	kawngbyang voo dwahzh
May I have a receipt for my health insurance?	**Puis-je avoir une quittance pour mon assurance maladie?**	pweezh ahvwahr ewn keettahngss poor mawng nahssewrahngss mahlahdee
Can I have a medical certificate?	**Puis-je avoir un certificat médical?**	pweezh ahvwahr ang sehrteefeekah maydeekahl
Would you fill in this health insurance form, please?	**Ayez l'obligeance de remplir cette feuille maladie.**	ehyay lobleezhahngss der rahngpleer seht fury mahlahdee

Hospital *Hôpital*

What are the visiting hours?	**Quelles sont les heures de visite?**	kehl sawng lay zurr der veezeet
When can I get up?	**Quand pourrai-je me lever?**	kahng poorehzh mer lervay
When will the doctor come?	**Quand le médecin doit-il passer?**	kahng ler maydssang dwahteel pahssay
I'm in pain.	**J'ai mal.**	zhay mahl
I can't eat/sleep.	**Je ne peux pas manger/dormir.**	zher ner pur pah mahngzhay/dormeer
Can I have a pain-killer/some sleeping pills?	**Puis-je avoir un calmant/somnifère?**	pweezh ahwahr ang kahlmahng/somneefehr
Where is the bell?	**Où est la sonnette?**	oo eh lah sonneht

nurse	**l'infirmière**	langfeermyehr
patient	**le patient/la patiente**	ler pahssyahng/ lah pahssyahngt
anaesthetic	**l'anesthésique**	lahnehstayzeek
blood transfusion	**la transfusion (sanguine)**	lah trahngsfewzyawng (sahnggeen)
injection	**la piqûre**	lah peekewr
operation	**l'opération**	lopayrahssyawng
bed	**le lit**	ler lee
bedpan	**le bassin**	ler bahssang
thermometer	**le thermomètre**	ler tehrmomehtr

Dentist *Dentiste*

Can you recommend a good dentist?	**Pouvez-vous m'indiquer un bon dentiste?**	poovay voo mangdeekay ang bawng dahngteest
Can I make an (urgent) appointment to see Dr...?	**Puis-je prendre un rendez-vous (urgent) avec le docteur ...?**	pweezh prahngdr ang rahngday voo (ewrzhahng) ahvehk ler dokturr
Can't you possibly make it earlier than that?	**Ne pourriez-vous pas me prendre plus tôt?**	ner pooryay voo pah mer prahngdr plew toa
I have a broken tooth.	**Je me suis cassé une dent.**	zher mer swee kahssay ewn dahng
I have a toothache.	**J'ai mal aux dents.**	zhay mahl oa dahng
I have an abscess.	**J'ai un abcès.**	zhay ang nahbsee
This tooth hurts.	**Cette dent me fait mal.**	seht dahng mer feh mahl
at the top	**en haut**	ahng oa
at the bottom	**en bas**	ahng bah
in the front	**devant**	dervahng
at the back	**au fond**	oa fawng
Can you fix it temporarily?	**Pouvez-vous faire un traitement provIsoire?**	poovay voo fehr ang trehtmahng proveezwahr
I don't want it extracted.	**Je ne voudrais pas me la faire arracher.**	zher ner voodreh pah mer lah fehr ahrahshay
Could you give me an anaesthetic?	**Pouvez-vous faire une anesthésie locale?**	poovay voo fehr ewn ahnehstayzee lokahl
I've lost a filling.	**J'ai perdu un plombage.**	zhay pehrdew ang plawngbahzh
The gum ...	**La gencive ...**	lah zhahngsseev
is very sore	**est très douloureuse**	eh treh dooloorurz
is bleeding	**saigne**	sehñ
I've broken this denture.	**J'ai cassé mon dentier.**	zhay kahssay mawng dahngtyay
Can you repair this denture?	**Pouvez-vous réparer ce dentier?**	poovay voo raypahray ser dahngtyay
When will it be ready?	**Quand sera-t-il prêt?**	kahng serrah teel preh

Reference section

Where do you come from? *D'où venez-vous?*

Africa	l'Afrique	lahfreek
Asia	l'Asie	lahzee
Australia	l'Australie	loastrahlee
Europe	l'Europe	lurrop
North America	l'Amérique du Nord	lahmayreek dew nor
South America	l'Amérique du Sud	lahmayreek dew sewd
Algeria	l'Algérie	lahlzhayree
Austria	l'Autriche	loatreesh
Belgium	la Belgique	lah behlzheek
Canada	le Canada	ler kahnahdah
China	la Chine	lah sheen
Denmark	le Danemark	ler dahnmahrk
England	l'Angleterre	lahngglertehr
Finland	la Finlande	lah fanglahngd
France	la France	lah frahngss
Germany	l'Allemagne	lahlmahñ
Great Britain	la Grande-Bretagne	lah grahngd brertañ
Greece	la Grèce	lah grehss
India	l'Inde	langd
Ireland	l'Irlande	leerlahngd
Israel	Israël	eesrahehl
Italy	l'Italie	leetahlee
Japan	le Japon	ler zhahpawng
Luxembourg	le Luxembourg	ler lewxahngboor
Morocco	le Maroc	ler mahrok
Netherlands	les Pays-Bas	lay peheebah
New Zealand	la Nouvelle-Zélande	lah noovehl zaylahngd
Norway	la Norvège	lah norvehzh
Portugal	le Portugal	ler portewgahl
Scotland	l'Ecosse	laykoss
South Africa	l'Afrique du Sud	lahfreek dew sewd
Soviet Union	l'Union soviétique	lewnyawng sovyayteek
Spain	l'Espagne	lehspañ
Sweden	la Suède	lah swehd
Switzerland	la Suisse	lah sweess
Tunisia	la Tunisie	lah tewneezee
Turkey	la Turquie	lah tewrkee
United States	les Etats-Unis	lay zaytah zewnee
Wales	le Pays de Galles	ler pehee der gahl
Yugoslavia	la Yougoslavie	lah yoogoslahvee

Numbers *Nombres*

0	**zéro**	zayroa
1	**un, une**	ang ewn
2	**deux**	dur
3	**trois**	trwah
4	**quatre**	kahtr
5	**cinq**	sangk
6	**six**	seess
7	**sept**	seht
8	**huit**	weet
9	**neuf**	nurf
10	**dix**	deess
11	**onze**	awngz
12	**douze**	dooz
13	**treize**	trehz
14	**quatorze**	kahtorz
15	**quinze**	kangz
16	**seize**	sehz
17	**dix-sept**	deess seht
18	**dix-huit**	deez weet
19	**dix-neuf**	deez nurf
20	**vingt**	vang
21	**vingt et un**	vang tay ang
22	**vingt-deux**	vangt dur
23	**vingt-trois**	vangt trwah
24	**vingt-quatre**	vangt kahtr
25	**vingt-cinq**	vangt sangk
26	**vingt-six**	vangt seess
27	**vingt-sept**	vangt seht
28	**vingt-huit**	vangt weet
29	**vingt-neuf**	vangt nurf
30	**trente**	trahngt
31	**trente et un**	trahngt ay ang
32	**trente-deux**	trahngt dur
33	**trente-trois**	trahngt trwah
40	**quarante**	kahrahngt
41	**quarante et un**	kahrahngt ay ang
42	**quarante-deux**	kahrahngt dur
43	**quarante-trois**	kahrahngt trwah
50	**cinquante**	sangkahngt
51	**cinquante et un**	sangkahngt ay ang
52	**cinquante-deux**	sangkahngt dur
53	**cinquante-trois**	sangkahngt trwah
60	**soixante**	swahssahngt
61	**soixante et un**	swahssahngt ay ang
62	**soixante-deux**	swahssahngt dur

63	**soixante-trois**	swahssahngt trwah
70*	**soixante-dix**	swahssahngt deess
71	**soixante et onze**	swahssahngt ay awngz
72	**soixante-douze**	swahssahngt dooz
73	**soixante-treize**	swahssahngt trehz
80*	**quatre-vingts**	kahtrer vang
81	**quatre-vingt-un**	kahtrer vang ang
82	**quatre-vingt-deux**	kahtrer vang dur
83	**quatre-vingt-trois**	kahtrer vang trwah
90*	**quatre-vingt-dix**	kahtrer vang deess
91	**quatre-vingt-onze**	kahtrer vang awngz
92	**quatre-vingt-douze**	kahtrer vang dooz
93	**quatre-vingt-treize**	kahtrer vang trehz
100	**cent**	sahng
101	**cent un**	sahng ang
102	**cent deux**	sahng dur
110	**cent dix**	sahng deess
120	**cent vingt**	sahng vang
130	**cent trente**	sahng trahngt
140	**cent quarante**	sahng kahrahngt
150	**cent cinquante**	sahng sangkahngt
160	**cent soixante**	sahng swahssahngt
170	**cent soixante-dix**	sahng swahssahngt deess
180	**cent quatre-vingts**	sahng kahtrer vang
190	**cent quatre-vingt-dix**	sahng kahtrer vang deess
200	**deux cents**	dur sahng
300	**trois cents**	trwah sahng
400	**quatre cents**	kahtrer sahng
500	**cinq cents**	sang sahng
600	**six cents**	seess sahng
700	**sept cents**	seht sahng
800	**huit cents**	wee sahng
900	**neuf cents**	nurf sahng
1000	**mille**	meel
1100	**mille cent**	meel sahng
1200	**mille deux cents**	meel dur sahng
2000	**deux mille**	dur meel
5000	**cinq mille**	sang meel
10,000	**dix mille**	dee meel
50,000	**cinquante mille**	sangkahngt meel
100,000	**cent mille**	sahng meel
1,000,000	**un million**	ang meelyawng
1,000,000,000	**un milliard**	ang meelyahr

---

* In certain areas, particularly in Belgium and Switzerland, older forms are still in use:
70 = **septante** (sehptahngt), 80 = **huitante** (weetahngt), 90 = **nonante** (nonahngt).

first	**premier (1er)**	prermyay
second	**deuxième (2e)**	durzyehm
third	**troisième (3e)**	trwahzyehm
fourth	**quatrième**	kahtreeyehm
fifth	**cinquième**	sangkyehm
sixth	**sixième**	seezyehm
seventh	**septième**	sehtyehm
eighth	**huitième**	weetyehm
ninth	**neuvième**	nurvyehm
tenth	**dixième**	deezyehm

| once/twice | **une fois/deux fois** | ewn fwah/dur fwah |
| three times | **trois fois** | trwah fwah |

a half	**une moitié**	ewn mwahtyay
half a ...	**un/une demi-**	ang/ewn dermee
half of ...	**la moitié de ...**	lah mwahtyay der
half (adj.)	**un/une demi-**	ang/ewn dermee
a quarter/one third	**un quart/un tiers**	ang kahr/ang tyehr
a pair of	**une paire de**	ewn pehr der
a dozen	**une douzaine**	ewn doozehn

| one per cent | **un pour cent** | ang poor sahng |
| 3.4% | **3,4%** | trwah veergwel kahtr poor sahng |

1981	**mille neuf cent quatre-vingt-un**	meel nurf sahng kahtr vang ang
1992	**mille neuf cent quatre-vingt-douze**	meel nurf sahng kahtr vang dooz
2003	**deux mille trois**	dur meel trwah

Year and age *Année et âge*

year	**l'an/l'année**	lahng/lahnay
leap year	**l'année bissextile**	lahnay beessehxteel
decade	**la décennie**	lah dayssehnee
century	**le siècle**	ler syehkl

this year	**cette année**	seht ahnay
last year	**l'année dernière**	lahnay dohrnyehr
next year	**l'année prochaine**	lahnay proshehn
each year	**chaque année**	shahk ahnay

2 years ago	**il y a 2 ans**	eel ee ah 2 zahng
in one year	**dans un an**	dahng zang nahng
in the eighties	**dans les années quatre-vingts**	dahng lay zahnay kahtr vang
the 16th century	**le seizième siècle**	ler sehzyehm syehkl
in the 20th century	**au vingtième siècle**	oa vangtyehm syehkl

How old are you?	Quel âge avez-vous?	kehl ahzh ahvay voo
I'm 30 years old.	J'ai trente ans.	zhay trahngt ahng
He/She was born in 1960.	Il/Elle est né(e) en mille neuf cent soixante.	eel/ehl eh nay ahng meel nurf sahng swahsssahngt
What is his/her age?	Quel âge a-t-il/elle?	kehl ahzh ahteel/ehl
Children under 16 are not admitted.	Les enfants de moins de seize ans ne sont pas admis.	lay zahngfahng der mwang der sehz ahng ner sawng pah zahdmee

Seasons *Saisons*

spring/summer	le printemps/l'été	ler prangtahng/laytay
autumn/winter	l'automne/l'hiver	loaton/leevehr
in spring	au printemps	oa prangtahng
during the summer	pendant l'été	pahngdahng laytay
in autumn	en automne	ahng noaton
during the winter	pendant l'hiver	pahngdahng leevehr
high season	haute saison	oat sehzawng
low season	basse saison	bahss sehzawng

Months *Mois*

January	janvier*	zhahngvyay
February	février	fayvreeyay
March	mars	mahrs
April	avril	ahvreel
May	mai	may
June	juin	zhwang
July	juillet	zhweeyeh
August	août	oot
September	septembre	sehptahngbr
October	octobre	oktobr
November	novembre	novahngbr
December	décembre	dayssahngbr
in September	en septembre	ahng sehptahngbr
since October	depuis octobre	derpwee oktobr
the beginning of January	le début (de) janvier	ler daybew (der) zhahngvyay
the middle of February	la mi-février	lah mee fayvreeyay
the end of March	la fin (de) mars	lah fang (der) mahrs

*The names of months aren't capitalized in French.

Days and Date *Jours et date*

What day is it today?	**Quel jour sommes-nous?**	kehl zhoor som noo
Sunday	**dimanche***	deemahngsh
Monday	**lundi**	langdee
Tuesday	**mardi**	mahrdee
Wednesday	**mercredi**	mehrkrerdee
Thursday	**jeudi**	zhurdee
Friday	**vendredi**	vahngdrerdee
Saturday	**samedi**	sahmdee
It's ...	**Nous sommes ...**	noo som
July 1	**le 1er juillet**	ler prermyay zhweeyeh
March 10	**le 10 mars**	ler dee mahrs
in the morning	**le matin**	ler mahtang
during the day	**pendant la journée**	pahngdahng lah zhoornay
in the afternoon	**l'après-midi**	lahpreh meedee
in the evening	**le soir**	ler swahr
at night	**la nuit**	lah nwee
the day before yesterday	**avant-hier**	ahvahng tyehr
yesterday	**hier**	yehr
today	**aujourd'hui**	oazhoordwee
tomorrow	**demain**	dermang
the day after tomorrow	**après-demain**	ahpreh dermang
the day before	**la veille**	lah vehy
the next day	**le lendemain**	ler lahngdermang
two days ago	**il y a deux jours**	eel ee ah dur zhoor
in three days' time	**dans trois jours**	dahng trwah zhoor
last week	**la semaine passée**	lah sermehn pahssay
next week	**la semaine prochaine**	lah sermehn proshehn
for a fortnight (two weeks)	**pendant quinze jours**	pahngdahng kangz zhoor
birthday	**l'anniversaire**	lahneevehrsehr
day off	**le jour de congé**	ler zhoor der kawngzhay
holiday	**le jour férié**	ler zhoor fayryay
holidays/vacation	**les vacances**	lay vahkahngss
week	**la semaine**	lah sermehn
weekend	**le week-end**	ler ''weekend''
working day	**le jour ouvrable**	ler zhoor oovrahbl

---

* The names of days aren't capitalized in French.

Public holidays *Jours fériés*

While there may be additional regional holidays, only national holidays in France (F), Belgium (B) and Switzerland (CH) are cited below.

January 1	**Nouvel An**	New Year's Day	F	CH	B
January 2				CH*	
May 1	**Fête du Travail**	Labour Day	F		B
July 14	**Fête Nationale**	Bastille Day	F		
July 21	**Fête Nationale**	National Day			B
August 1	**Fête Nationale**	National Day		CH*	
August 15	**Assomption**	Assumption Day	F		B
November 1	**Toussaint**	All Saints Day	F		B
November 11	**Armistice**	Armistice Day	F		B
December 25	**Noël**	Christmas	F	CH	B
December 26	**Saint-Etienne**	St. Stephen's Day		CH*	
Movable dates:	**Vendredi-Saint**	Good Friday	F	CH*	
	Lundi de Pâques	Easter Monday	F	CH*	B
	Ascension	Ascension Thursday	F	CH	B
	Lundi de Pentecôte	Whit Monday	F	CH	B

* Most cantons.

Merry Christmas!	**Joyeux Noël!**	zhwahyur noehl
Happy New Year!	**Bonne année!**	bon ahnay
Happy Easter!	**Joyeuses Pâques!**	zhwahyurz pahk
Happy birthday!	**Bon anniversaire!**	bawng nahneevehrsehr
Best wishes!	**Mes/Nos meilleurs vœux!**	may/noa mehyurr vur
Congratulations!	**Félicitations!**	fayleesseetahssyawng
Good luck/ All the best!	**Bonne chance!**	bon shahngss
Have a good trip!	**Bon voyage!**	bawng vwahyahzh
Have a good holiday!	**Bonnes vacances!**	bon vahkahngss
Best regards from ...	**Meilleures salutations de ...**	mehyurr sahlewtahssyawng der
My regards to ...	**Mes amitiés à ...**	may zahmeetyay ah

What time is it? *Quelle heure est-il?*

Excuse me. Can you tell me the time?	Pardon. Pouvez-vous m'indiquer l'heure?	pahrdawng. poovay voo mangdeekay lurr
It's ...	Il est ...	eel eh
five past one	une heure cinq*	ewn urr sangk
ten past two	deux heures dix	dur zurr deess
a quarter past three	trois heures un quart	trwah zurr ang kahr
twenty past four	quatre heures vingt	kahtr urr vang
twenty-five past five	cinq heures vingt-cinq	sangk urr vangt sangk
half past six	six heures et demie	see zurr ay dermee
twenty-five to seven	sept heures moins vingt-cinq	seht urr mwang vangt sangk
twenty to eight	huit heures moins vingt	weet urr mwang vang
a quarter to nine	neuf heures moins un quart	nurv urr mwang zang kahr
ten to ten	dix heures moins dix	dee zurr mwang deess
five to eleven	onze heures moins cinq	awngz urr mwang sangk
twelve o'clock (noon/midnight)	douze heures (midi/minuit)	dooz urr (meedee/meenwee)
in the morning	du matin	dew mahtang
in the afternoon	de l'après-midi	der lahpreh meedee
in the evening	du soir	dew swahr
The train leaves at ...	Le train part à ...	ler trang pahr ah
13.04 (1.04 p.m.)	treize heures quatre*	trehz urr kahtr
0.40 (0.40 a.m.)	zéro heure quarante	zayroa urr kahrahngt
in five minutes	dans cinq minutes	dahng sank meenewt
in a quarter of an hour	dans un quart d'heure	dahng zang kahr durr
half an hour ago	il y a une demi-heure	eel ee ah ewn dermee urr
about two hours	environ deux heures	ahngveerawng dur zurr
more than 10 minutes	plus de dix minutes	plew der dee meenewt
less than 30 seconds	moins de trente secondes	mwang der trahngt sergawngd
The clock is fast/slow.	L'horloge avance/a du retard.	lorlozh ahvahngss/ah dew rertahr

---

* In ordinary conversation, time is expressed as shown here. However, official time uses a 24-hour clock which means that after noon hours are counted from 13 to 24.

Common abbreviations   *Abréviations courantes*

apr. J.-C.	après Jésus-Christ	A.D.
av. J.-C.	avant Jésus-Christ	B.C.
bd, boul.	boulevard	boulevard
c.-à-d.	c'est-à-dire	that is to say, i.e.
c/c	compte courant	current account
CCP	compte de chèques postaux	postal account
CEE	Communauté Economique Européenne	European Economic Community
CFF	Chemins de Fer Fédéraux	Swiss Federal Railways
ch	chevaux-vapeur	horsepower
Cie, Co.	Compagnie	Co.
CRS	Compagnies Républicaines de Sécurité	French order and riot police
CV	chevaux-vapeur	horsepower
E.U.	Etats-Unis	U.S.A.
exp.	expéditeur	sender
h	heure	hour, o'clock
hab.	habitants	inhabitants, population
M./MM.	Monsieur/Messieurs	Mr./Messrs.
Mlle	Mademoiselle	Miss
Mme	Madame	Mrs.
ONU	Organisation des Nations Unies	United Nations Organization
PDG	président-directeur général	chairman (president) of the board
p.ex.	par exemple	for instance, e.g.
p.p.	port payé	postage paid
RATP	Régie Autonome des Transports Parisiens	Paris transport authority
RN	route nationale	national road
s/	sur	on
SA	société anonyme	Ltd., Inc.
S.à.R.L.	société à responsabilité limitée	limited liability company
SI	Syndicat d'Initiative	tourist office (France)
SNCB	Société Nationale des Chemins de Fer Belges	Belgian National Railways
SNCF	Société Nationale des Chemins de Fer Français	French National Railways
s.v.p.	s'il vous plaît	please
T.T.C.	Toutes taxes comprises	all taxes included
T.V.A.	Taxe à la Valeur Ajoutée	VAT, value-added tax

Signs and notices   *Ecriteaux*

A louer	For hire/For rent/To let
Ascenseur	Lift (elevator)
Attention	Caution
Attention au chien	Beware of the dog
A vendre	For sale
Caisse	Cash desk
Chaud	Hot
Chemin privé	Private road
Chiens interdits	Dogs not allowed
Complet	Full/No vacancies
Dames	Ladies
Danger (de mort)	Danger (of death)
Défense de ...	... forbidden
Défense d'entrer sous peine d'amende	Trespassers will be prosecuted
Défense de fumer	No smoking
Entrée	Entrance
Entrée interdite	No entrance
Entrée libre	Admission free
Entrez sans frapper	Enter without knocking
Fermé	Closed
Fermez la porte	Close the door
Froid	Cold
Fumeurs	Smoking allowed
Haute tension	High voltage
Hommes	Men
Hors service	Out of order
Libre	Vacant
Messieurs	Gentlemen
Ne pas déranger	Do not disturb
Ne pas toucher, s.v.p.	Do not touch
Occupé	Occupied
Ouvert de ... à ...	Open from ... to ...
Peinture fraîche	Wet paint
Piste cyclable	Cycle path
Poussez	Push
Privé	Private
Renseignements	Information
Réservé	Reserved
Soldes	Sale
Sonnez, s'il vous plaît	Please ring
Sortie	Exit
Sortie de secours	Emergency exit
Tirez	Pull

Emergency *Urgences*

Call the police	**Appelez la police**	ahperlay lah poleess
DANGER	**DANGER**	dahngzhay
FIRE	**AU FEU**	oa fur
Gas	**Gaz**	gahz
Get a doctor	**Appelez un médecin**	ahperlay ang maydssang
Go away	**Allez-vous-en**	ahlay voo zahng
HELP	**AU SECOURS**	oa serkoor
Get help quickly	**A l'aide, vite**	ah lehd veet
I'm ill	**Je suis malade**	zher swee mahlahd
I'm lost	**Je me suis perdu(e)**	zher mer swee pehrdew
Leave me alone	**Laissez-moi tranquille**	lehssay mwah trahngkeel
LOOK OUT	**ATTENTION**	ahtahngssyawng
POLICE	**POLICE**	poleess
Quick	**Vite**	veet
STOP	**ARRÊTEZ**	ahrehtay
Stop that man/ woman	**Arrêtez cet homme/ cette femme**	ahrehtay seht om/ seht fahm
STOP THIEF	**AU VOLEUR**	oa volurr

Emergency telephone numbers *Numéros d'urgence*

	Belgium	France	Switzerland
Fire	900	18	118
Ambulance	900	17	117
Police	901	17	117

Lost! *En cas de perte ou de vol*

Where's the ...?	**Où est ...?**	oo eh
lost property (lost and found) office?	**le bureau des objets trouvés**	ler bewroa day zobzheh troovay
police station	**le poste de police**	ler post der poleess
I want to report a theft.	**Je voudrais déclarer un vol.**	zher voodreh dayklahray ang vol
My ... has been stolen.	**On m'a volé ...**	awng mah volay
I've lost my ...	**J'ai perdu ...**	zhay pehrdew
handbag	**mon sac à main**	mawng sahk ah mang
passport	**mon passeport**	mawng pahsspor
wallet	**mon portefeuille**	mawng portfury

CAR ACCIDENTS, see page 78

157

Conversion tables

Centimetres and inches

To change centimetres into inches, multiply by .39.

To change inches into centimetres, multiply by 2.54.

	in.	feet	yards
1 mm.	0.039	0.003	0.001
1 cm.	0.39	0.03	0.01
1 dm.	3.94	0.32	0.10
1 m.	39.40	3.28	1.09

	mm.	cm.	m.
1 in.	25.4	2.54	0.025
1 ft.	304.8	30.48	0.305
1 yd.	914.4	91.44	0.914

(32 metres = 35 yards)

Temperature

To convert centigrade into degrees Fahrenheit, multiply centigrade by 1.8 and add 32.

To convert degrees Fahrenheit into centigrade, subtract 32 from Fahrenheit and divide by 1.8.

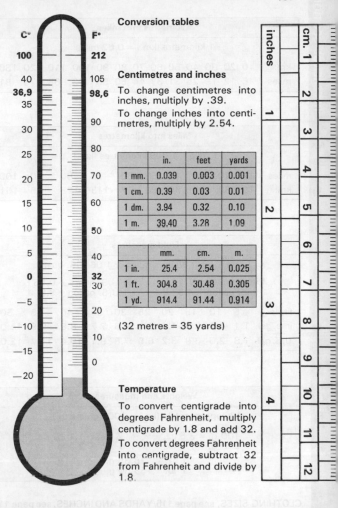

Kilometres into miles

1 kilometre (km.) = 0.62 miles

km.	10	20	30	40	50	60	70	80	90	100	110	120	130
miles	6	12	19	25	31	37	44	50	56	62	68	75	81

Miles into kilometres

1 mile = 1.609 kilometres (km.)

miles	10	20	30	40	50	60	70	80	90	100
km.	16	32	48	64	80	97	113	129	145	161

Fluid measures

1 litre (l.) = 0.88 imp. quart or 1.06 U.S. quart

1 imp. quart = 1.14 l.	1 U.S. quart = 0.95 l.
1 imp. gallon = 4.55 l.	1 U.S. gallon = 3.8 l.

litres	5	10	15	20	25	30	35	40	45	50
imp. gal.	1.1	2.2	3.3	4.4	5.5	6.6	7.7	8.8	9.9	11.0
U.S. gal.	1.3	2.6	3.9	5.2	6.5	7.8	9.1	10.4	11.7	13.0

Weights and measures

1 kilogram or kilo (kg.) = 1000 grams (g.)

100 g. = 3.5 oz.	½ kg. = 1.1 lb.
200 g. = 7.0 oz.	1 kg. = 2.2 lb.

| 1 oz. = 28.35 g. |
| 1 lb. = 453.60 g. |

CLOTHING SIZES, see page 115/YARDS AND INCHES, see page 112

Basic Grammar

Articles *Articles*

All nouns in French are either masculine or feminine.

1. Definite article (the):

masc. *le* **train**   the train   fem. *la* **voiture**   the car

Le and **la** are contracted to **l'** when followed by a vowel or a silent **h***.

*l'***avion**   the plane   *l'***hôtel**   the hotel

Plural (masc. and fem.):

les **trains**   *les* **voitures**   *les* **avions**

2. Indefinite article (a/an):

masc. *un* **timbre**   a stamp   fem. *une* **lettre**   a letter

Plural (masc. and fem.):

des **timbres**   stamps   *des* **lettres**   letters

3. Some/any (partitive)

Expressed by **de, du, de la, de l', des** as follows:

masc. **du** (= de + le)   **de l'** when followed by a
fem. **de la**   vowel or a silent **h***

Plural (masc. and fem.): **des** (= de + les)

du **sel**   some salt   *de la* **moutarde**   some mustard
*de l'***ail**   some garlic   *des* **oranges**   some oranges

In negatives sentences, **de** is generally used.

Il n'y a pas *de* **taxis.**   There aren't any taxis.
Je n'ai pas *d'***argent.**   I haven't any money.

Note the concentration **d'** before a vowel.

---

* In French the letter *h* at the beginning of a word is not pronounced. However, in several words the *h* is what is called "aspirate", i.e., no liaison is made with the word preceding it. E.g., *le héros*.

Nouns *Noms*

1. As already noted, nouns are either masculine or feminine. There are no short cuts for determining gender (though, note that most nouns ending in **-e, -té, -tion** are feminine). So always learn a noun together with its accompanying article.

2. The plural of the majority of nouns is formed by adding **s** to the singular. (The final **s** is not pronounced.)

3. To show possession, use the preposition **de** (of).

la fin *de* la semaine	the end of the week
le début *du* mois	the beginning of the month
le patron *de* l'hôtel	the owner of the hotel
les valises *des* voyageurs	the traveller's luggage
la chambre *de* Robert	Robert's room

Adjectives *Adjectifs*

1. Adjectives agree with the noun in gender and number. Most of them form the feminine by adding **e** to the masculine (unless the word already ends in **e**). For the plural, add **s**.

a. un grand magasin	a big shop	**des grands magasins**
b. une auto anglaise	an English car	**des autos anglaises**

2. As can be seen from the above, adjectives can come (a) before the noun or (b) after the noun. Since it is basically a question of sound and idiom, rules are difficult to formulate briefly; but adjectives more often follow nouns.

3. **Demonstrative adjectives:**

this/that	**ce** *(masc.)*
	cet *(masc. before a vowel or silent* h*)*
	cette *(fem.)*
these/those	**ces** *(masc. and fem.)*

4. **Possessive adjectives:** These agree in number and gender with *the noun they modify,* i.e., with the thing possessed and not the possessor.

	masc.	fem.	plur.
my	**mon**	**ma**	**mes**
your	**ton**	**ta**	**tes**
his/her/its	**son**	**sa**	**ses**
our	**notre**	**notre**	**nos**
your	**votre**	**votre**	**vos**
their	**leur**	**leur**	**leurs**

Thus, depending on the context:

son **fils**	can mean *his* son or *her* son
sa **chambre**	can mean *his* room or *her* room
ses **vêtements**	can mean *his* clothes or *her* clothes

Personal pronouns *Pronoms personnels*

	Subject	Direct object	Indirect object	After a preposition
I	**je**	**me**	**me**	**moi**
you	**tu**	**te**	**te**	**toi**
he/it (masc.)	**il**	**le**	**lui**	**lui**
she/it (fem.)	**elle**	**la**	**lui**	**elle**
we	**nous**	**nous**	**nous**	**nous**
you	**vous**	**vous**	**vous**	**vous**
they (masc.)	**ils**	**les**	**leur**	**eux**
they (fem.)	**elles**	**les**	**leur**	**elles**

Note: There are two forms for "you" in French: **tu** is used when talking to relatives, close friends and children (and between young people); **vous** is used in all other cases, and is also the plural form of **tu**.

Prepositions *Prépositions*

There is a list of prepositions on page 15. Be careful with **à** (to, at) and **de** (of, from).

à + le = au	**de + le = du**
à + les = aux	**de + les = des**

Adverbs *Adverbes*

Adverbs are generally formed by adding **-ment** to the feminine form of the adjective.

GRAMMAR

masc.:	fem.:	adverb:
lent (slow)	lente	lentement
sérieux (serious)	sérieuse	sérieusement

Verbs *Verbes*

Here we are concerned only with the infinitive and the present tense.

Learn these two **auxiliary verbs:**

être (to be)	**avoir** (to have)
je suis *(I am)*	j'ai *(I have)*
tu es *(you are)*	tu as *(you have)*
il/elle est *(he, she, it is)*	il/elle a *(he, she, it has)*
nous sommes *(we are)*	nous avons *(we have)*
vous êtes *(you are)*	vous avez *(you have)*
ils/elles sont *(they are)*	ils/elles ont *(they have)*

Il y a is equivalent to "there is/there are":

Il y a une lettre pour vous.	There's a letter for you.
Il y a trois colis pour elle.	There are three parcels for her.
Y a-t-il du courrier pour moi?	Is there any post for me?
Il n'y a pas de lettres pour vous.	There are no letters for you.

Regular verbs follow one of three patterns (conjugations) depending on the ending of the infinitive.

Infinitive	1 ends in **-er**	2 ends in **-ir**	3 ends in **-re**
	parler (to speak)	**finir** (to finish)	**attendre** (to wait)
je	parle	finis	attends*
tu	parles	finis	attends
il/elle	parle	finit	attend
nous	parlons	finissons	attendons
vous	parlez	finissez	attendez
ils/elles	parlent	finissent	attendent
Imperative	**parlez**	**finissez**	**attendez**

*j'attends: je is contracted before the following vowel

Grammaire

Irregular verbs: As in all languages, these have to be learned. Here are four you'll find useful.

Infinitive	pouvoir (to be able)	aller (to go)	voir (to see)	faire (to do/make)
je	peux	vais	vois	fais
tu	peux	vas	vois	fais
il/elle	peut	va	voit	fait
nous	pouvons	allons	voyons	faisons
vous	pouvez	allez	voyez	faites
ils/elles	peuvent	vont	voient	font
Imperative	–	allez	voyez	faites

Negatives *Négations*

Negatives are generally formed by putting **ne** before the verb and **pas** after it (**ne** is contracted to **n'** before a following vowel or a silent **h**).

Je parle français.	I speak French.
Je *ne* parle *pas* français.	I don't speak French.
Elle est riche.	She is rich.
Elle *n'*est *pas* riche.	She isn't rich.

Questions *Questions*

Questions may be formed in one of two ways:

1. by inverting the subject and the verb (putting the verb first, the subject second):

Est-elle riche?	Is she rich?
Avez-vous des enfants?	Have you any children?
Parle-t-il français?*	Does he speak French?

2. by using the expression **"est-ce que"** + the affirmative word order.

Est-ce que vous parlez français?	Do you speak French?

---

* t is inserted between the two vowels

Dictionary
and alphabetical index

English–French

| f feminine | m masculine | pl plural |

a un, une 159
abbey abbaye f 81
abbreviation abréviation f 154
able, to be pouvoir 163
about *(approximately)* environ 153
above au-dessus (de) 15, 63
abscess abcès m 145
absent absent(e) 136
absorbent cotton coton hydrophile
m 109
accept, to accepter 62, 102
accessories accessoires m/pl 116,
125
accident accident m 78, 139
accommodation logement m 22
account compte m 130, 131
ache douleur f 141
adaptor prise de raccordement f 119
address adresse f 21, 31, 76, 79, 102
address book carnet d'adresses m 104
adhesive autocollant(e) 105
admission entrée f 82, 89, 155
admitted admis(e) 150
Africa Afrique f 146
after après 15; au-delà de 77
afternoon après-midi m 151, 153
after-shave lotion lotion après
rasage f 110
age âge m 149, 150
ago il y a 149, 151
air conditioner climatiseur m 28
air conditioning climatisation f 23
airmail par avion 133
airplane avion m 65
airport aéroport f 16, 21, 65
alarm clock réveil m 121

alcoholic alcoolisé 59
Algeria Algérie f 146
allergic allergique 141, 143
allow, to autoriser 79
almond amande f 54
alphabet alphabet m 9
also aussi 15
alter, to *(garment)* retoucher 116
amazing étonnant 84
amber ambre m 122
ambulance ambulance f 79
American américain(e) 93, 105, 126
American plan pension complète f 24
amethyst améthyste f 122
amount montant m 62; somme f 131
amplifier amplificateur m 119
anaesthetic anesthésique m 144, 145
analgesic analgésique m 109
anchovy anchois m 44
and et 15
animal animal m 85
aniseed anis m 50
ankle cheville f 139
anorak anorak m 116
answer réponse f 136
antibiotic antibiotique m 143
antidepressant remontant m 143
antiques antiquités f/pl 83
antique shop antiquaire m 98
antiseptic antiseptique 109
antiseptic antiseptique m 140
any de, de la, du (pl des) 15
anyone quelqu'un 12
anything quelque chose 17, 25, 113
anywhere quelque part 89
aperitif apéritif m 56

appendicitis appendicite f 142
appendix appendice m 138
appetizer hors d'œuvre m 41
apple pomme f 54, 63
apple juice jus de pomme m 60
appliance appareil m 119
appointment rendez-vous m 30, 131, 137, 145
apricot abricot m 54
April avril m 150
archaeology archéologie f 83
architect architecte m 83
area code indicatif m 134
arm bras m 138, 139
arrival arrivée f 16, 65
arrive, to arriver 65, 68, 130
art art m 83
artery artère f 138
art gallery galerie d'art f 81, 98
artichoke artichaut m 49
artificial artificiel(le) 124
artist artiste m/f 83
ashtray cendrier m 27, 36
Asia Asie f 146
ask, to demander 25, 61, 136
asparagus asperge f 40
aspirin aspirine f 109
assorted varié(e) 41
asthma asthme m 141
at à 15
at least au moins 24
at once immédiatement 31
August août m 150
aunt tante f 93
Australia Australie f 146
automatic automatique 20, 122, 124
autumn automne m 150
available disponible 40
average moyen(ne) 91
awful horrible 84

B

baby bébé m 24, 111
baby food aliments pour bébés m/pl 111
babysitter garde d'enfants f 27
back dos m 138
backache mal de reins m 141
bacon bacon m 38; lard m 46
bacon and eggs œufs au bacon m/pl 38
bad mauvais(e) 14, 95
bag sac m 18, 103

baggage bagages m/pl 18, 26, 31, 71
baggage cart chariot à bagages m 18, 71
baggage check consigne f 67, 71
baggage locker consigne automatique f 18, 67, 71
baked au four 45, 47
baker's boulangerie f 98
balance (account) position f 131
balcony balcon m 23
ball (inflated) ballon m 128
ballet ballet m 88
ball-point pen stylo à bille m 104
banana banane f 54, 63
bandage bandage m 109
Band-Aid sparadrap m 109
bangle bracelet m 121
bangs frange f 30
bank (finance) banque f 98, 129
bank card carte d'identité bancaire f 130
banknote billet m 130; coupure m 130
bar bar m 33, 67; (chocolate) plaque f 64
barber's coiffeur m 30, 98
bass (fish) bar m 44
bath (hotel) salle de bains f 23, 25, 27
bath essence bain de mousse m 110
bathing cap bonnet de bain m 116
bathing hut cabine f 91
bathing suit costume de bain m 116
bathrobe peignoir (de bain) m 116
bathroom salle de bains f 27
bath salts sels de bain m/pl 110
bath towel serviette de bain f 27
battery pile f 119, 121, 125; (car) batterie f 75, 78
bay leaf laurier m 50
be, to être 161; se trouver 11
beach plage f 90
beach ball ballon de plage m 128
bean haricot m 49
beard barbe f 31
beautiful beau, belle 14, 84
beauty salon salon de beauté m 30; institut de beauté m 98
bed lit m 24, 144
bed and breakfast chambre avec petit déjeuner f 24
bedpan bassin m 144
beef bœuf m 46
beer bière f 56, 63
beet(root) betterave f 49

before *(place)* devant 15; *(time)* avant 15, 151
begin, to commencer 80, 87, 88
beginner débutant(e) *m/f* 91
beginning début *m* 150
behind derrière 15, 77
beige beige 113
Belgian belge 18
Belgium Belgique *f* 146
bell *(electric)* sonnette *f* 144
bellboy chasseur *m* 26
below au-dessous (de) 15
belt ceinture *f* 117
bend *(road)* virage *m* 79
berth couchette *f* 69, 70, 71
best meilleur(e) 152
better meilleur(e) 14, 113; mieux 25, 101
between entre 15
bicycle bicyclette *f* 74
big grand(e) 14, 101
bilberry myrtille *f* 54
bill note *f* 31; addition *f* 62; facture *f* 102; *(banknote)* billet *m* 130; coupure *f* 130
billion *(Am.)* milliard *m* 148
binoculars jumelles *f/pl* 123
bird oiseau *m* 85
birth naissance *f* 25
birthday anniversaire *m* 151, 152
biscuit *(Br.)* biscuit *m* 63
bitter amer, amère 61
black noir(e) 113
blackberry mûre *f* 54
blackcurrant cassis *m* 54
bladder vessie *f* 138
blade lame *f* 110
blanket couverture *f* 27
bleach décoloration *f* 30
bleed, to saigner 139, 145
blind *(window)* store *m* 29
blister ampoule *f* 139
block, to boucher 28
blood sang *m* 142
blood pressure tension *f* 141
blood transfusion transfusion (sanguine) *f* 144
blouse chemisier *m* 116
blow-dry brushing *m* 30
blue bleu(e) 113
blueberry myrtille *f* 54
boar *(wild)* sanglier *m* 48; *(young)* marcassin *m* 48
boarding house pension *f* 19, 22
boat bateau *m* 74

bobby pin pince à cheveux *f* 111
body corps *m* 138
boil furoncle *m* 139
boiled bouilli(e) 47
boiled egg œuf à la coque *m* 38
bone os *m* 138
book livre *m* 12, 104
book, to réserver 69
booking office bureau de réservation *m* 19, 67
booklet carnet *m* 72
bookshop librairie *f* 98, 104
boot botte *f* 118
born né(e) 150
botanical gardens jardin botanique *m* 81
botany botanique *f* 83
bottle bouteille *f* 17, 59
bottle-opener ouvre-bouteilles *m* 106
bottom bas *m* 145
bowels intestins *m/pl* 138
bow tie nœud papillon *m* 116
box boîte *f* 120
boxing boxe *f* 89
boy garçon *m* 112, 128
boyfriend ami *m* 93
bra soutien-gorge *m* 116
bracelet bracelet *m* 121
braces *(suspenders)* bretelles *f/pl* 116
braised braisé *f* 47
brake frein *m* 78
brandy cognac *m* 60
bread pain *m* 36, 38, 64
break, to casser 29, 119, 123, 145; se casser 139, 145
break down, to être en panne 78
breakdown panne *f* 78
breakdown van dépanneuse *f* 78
breakfast petit déjeuner *m* 24, 34, 38
breast sein *m* 138
breathe, to respirer 141
bridge pont *m* 85
briefs slip *m* 116
brill barbue *f* 44
bring, to apporter 13
bring down, to descendre 31
British britannique 93
broken cassé(e) 29, 119, 140
brooch broche *f* 121
brother frère *m* 93
brown brun(e) 113
bruise contusion *f* 139
brush brosse *f* 111

Brussels sprouts choux de Bruxelles *m/pl* 49
bucket seau *m* 106, 128
buckle boucle *f* 117
build, to construire 83
building bâtiment *m* 81, 83
bulb ampoule *f* 28, 75, 119
burn brûlure *f* 139
burn out, to (bulb) sauter 28
bus bus *m* 18, 19, 65, 72, 73
business affaires *f/pl* 16, 131
business trip voyage d'affaires *m* 93
bus stop arrêt de bus *m* 72, 73
busy occupé(e) 96
butane gas butane *m* 32, 106
butcher's boucherie *f* 98
butter beurre *m* 36, 38, 64
button bouton *m* 29, 117
buy, to acheter 82, 104

C

cabana cabine *f* 91
cabbage chou *m* 49
cabin cabine *f* 74
cable télégramme *m* 133
cable car télécabine *f* 74
cable release déclencheur *m* 125
caffein-free décaféiné 38, 60
cake gâteau *m* 55, 64
calculator calculatrice *f* 105
calendar calendrier *m* 104
call (phone) appel *m* 135; communication *f* 136
call, to appeler 11, 78, 136, 156
call back, to rappeler 136
calm calme 90
cambric batiste *m* 114
camel-hair poil de chameau *m* 114
camera appareil de photo *m* 124, 125
camera case étui à appareil photo *m* 125
camera shop magasin de photos *m* 98
camp, to camper 32
campbed lit de camp *m* 106
camping camping *m* 32
camping equipment matériel de camping *m* 106
camp site camping *m* 32
can (of peaches) boîte *f* 120
can (to be able) pouvoir 12, 163
Canada Canada *m* 146
Canadian canadien(ne) 93
cancel, to annuler 65
candle bougie *f* 106

candy bonbon *m* 126
can opener ouvre-boîtes *m* 106
cap casquette *f* 116
caper câpre *f* 50
capital (finance) capital *m* 131
car voiture *f* 19, 20, 75, 76, 78
carat carat *m* 121
caravan caravane *f* 32
caraway cumin *m* 50, 64
carbon paper papier carbone *m* 104
carbonated gazeux(euse) 60
carburetor carburateur *m* 78
card carte *f* 93, 131
card game jeu de cartes *m* 128
cardigan cardigan *m* 116
car hire location de voitures *f* 20
carp carpe *f* 44
car park parking *m* 77
car racing courses d'autos *m/pl* 89
car radio autoradio *m* 119
car rental location de voitures *f* 20
carrot carotte *f* 49
carry, to porter 21
cart chariot *m* 18
carton (of cigarettes) cartouche (de cigarettes) *f* 17
cartridge (camera) chargeur *m* 124
case (instance) cas *m* 143; (cigarettes etc) étui *m* 121, 123, 125
cash, to toucher 130, 133
cash desk caisse *f* 155
cashier caissier *m* 103
cassette cassette *f* 119, 127
castle château *m* 81
catacomb catacombe *f* 81
catalogue catalogue *m* 82
cathedral cathédrale *f* 81
Catholic catholique 84
cauliflower chou-fleur *m* 49
caution attention *f* 79, 155
cave grotte *f* 81
cellophane tape ruban adhésif *m* 104
cemetery cimetière *m* 81
centimetre centimètre *m* 112
centre centre *m* 19, 21, 76, 81
century siècle *m* 149
ceramics céramique *f* 83
cereal céréales *f/pl* 38
certificate certificat *m* 144
chain (jewellery) chaînette *f* 121
chain bracelet gourmette *f* 121
chair chaise *f* 106
chamber music musique de chambre *f* 128

change *(money)* monnaie f 62, 77, 130

change, to changer 61, 65, 68, 73, 75, 123; *(money)* 18, 130

chapel chapelle f 81

charcoal charbon de bois m 106

charge tarif m 20, 32, 77, 89; note f 28; taxe f 136

charge, to faire payer 24; *(commission)* prendre 130

charm *(trinket)* breloque f 121

charm bracelet bracelet à breloques m 121

cheap bon marché 14, 24, 25, 101

check chèque m 130; *(restaurant)* addition f 62

check, to contrôler 75, 123; vérifier 75; *(luggage)* faire enregistrer 71

check book carnet de chèques m 131

check in, to *(airport)* enregistrer 65

check out, to partir 31

checkup *(medical)* bilan de santé m 142

cheers! à votre santé! 56

cheese fromage m 53, 64

chemist's pharmacie f 98, 108

cheque chèque m 130

cheque book carnet de chèques m 131

cherry cerise f 54

chervil cerfeuil m 50

chess échecs m/pl 93

chess set jeu d'échecs m 128

chest poitrine f 138, 141

chestnut marron m 54

chewing gum chewing-gum m 126

chewing tobacco tabac à chiquer m 126

chicken poulet m 48, 63

chicken breast suprême de volaille m 49

chicory endive f 49; *(Am.)* chicorée f 49

chiffon mousseline f 114

child enfant m/f 24, 61, 82, 93, 139, 150

children's doctor pédiatre m/f 137

China Chine f 146

chips (pommes) frites f/pl 51, 63; *(Am.)* chips m/pl 51, 64

chives ciboulette f 50

chocolate chocolat m 120, 126, 127; *(hot)* chocolat chaud m 38, 60

chocolate bar plaque de chocolat f 64

choice choix m 40

chop côtelette f 46

Christmas Noël m 152

chromium chrome m 122

church église f 81, 84; *(Protestant)* temple m 84

cigar cigare m 126

cigarette cigarette f 17, 95, 126

cigarette case étui à cigarettes m 121, 126

cigarette holder fume-cigarette m 126

cigarette lighter briquet m 121

cine camera caméra f 124

cinema cinéma m 86, 96

cinnamon cannelle f 50

circle *(theatre)* balcon m 87

city ville f 81

clam palourde f 45

classical classique 128

clean propre 61

clean, to nettoyer 29, 76

cleansing cream crème démaquillante f 110

clear, to *(cheque)* vérifier 130

cliff falaise f 85

cloakroom vestiaire m 87

clock pendule f 121; horloge f 153

clock-radio radio-réveil m 119

close *(near)* proche 78, 98

close, to fermer 11, 82, 108, 132

closed fermé(e) 155

cloth toile f 118

clothes vêtements m/pl 29, 116

clothes peg pince à linge f 106

clothing habillement m 112

cloud nuage m 94

clove clou de girofle m 50

coach *(bus)* car m 72

coat manteau m 116

coconut noix de coco f 54

cod morue f 45; *(fresh)* cabillaud m 44

coffee café m 38, 60, 64

coin monnaie f 83

cold froid(e) 14, 25, 61, 94

cold *(illness)* rhume m 108, 141

cold cuts charcuterie f 64

colour couleur f 103, 112, 124, 125

colour fast grand teint 114

colour negative négatif couleurs m 124

colour rinse coloration f 30

colour shampoo shampooing colorant m 111

comb peigne m 111

come, to venir 36, 92, 95, 137, 146

comedy comédie f 86
commission commission f 130
common *(frequent)* courant(e) 154
compact disc disque compact m 127
compartment compartiment m 70
compass boussole f 106
complaint réclamation f 61
concert concert m 88
concert hall salle de concert f 81, 88
conductor *(orchestra)* chef d'orchestre m 88
confectioner's confiserie f 98
confirm, to confirmer 65
confirmation confirmation f 23
congratulation félicitation f 152
connection *(train)* correspondance f 65, 68
constipated constipé(e) 140
contact lens verre de contact m 123
contain, to contenir 37
contraceptive contraceptif m 109
control contrôle m 16
convent couvent m 81
cookie biscuit m 64
cool box glacière f 106
copper cuivre m 122
copperware's objets en cuivre m/pl 127
coral corail m 122
corduroy velours côtelé m 114
cork bouchon m 61
corkscrew tire-bouchons m 106
corn *(Am.)* maïs m 50; *(foot)* cor m 109
corner angle m 36; *(street)* coin de rue m 21, 77
corn plaster emplâtre pour les cors m 109
cost coût m 131; prix m 136
cost, to coûter 11, 133
cotton coton m 114
cotton wool coton hydrophile m 109
cough toux f 108, 141
cough, to tousser 142
cough drops pastilles contre la toux f/pl 109
counter guichet m 133
country pays m 93
countryside campagne f 85
court house palais de justice m 81
cousin cousin(e) m/f 93
cover charge couvert m 62
crab crabe m 44
cracker biscuit salé m 64
cramp crampe f 141

crayfish écrevisse f 44
crayon crayon de couleur m 104
cream crème f 55, 60, 110
credit crédit m 130
credit, to créditer 130, 131
credit card carte de crédit f 20, 31, 62, 102, 130
crepe crêpe f 114
crisps chips m/pl 51, 64
crockery vaisselle f 106, 107
cross croix f 121
cross-country skiing ski de fond m 91
crossing *(by sea)* traversée f 74
crossroads carrefour m 77
cruise croisière f 74
crystal cristal m 122, 127
cuckoo clock coucou m 121, 127
cucumber concombre m 49
cuff link bouton de manchette m 121
cup tasse f 36, 60, 107
curler bigoudi m 111
currency monnaie f 129
currency exchange office bureau de change m 18, 67, 129
current courant m 90
curtain rideau m 28
curve *(road)* virage m 79
customs douane f 16, 102
cut *(wound)* coupure f 139
cut, to couper 135
cut glass cristal taillé m 122
cuticle remover produit pour enlever les cuticules m 110
cutlery couverts m/pl 106, 107, 121; coutellerie f 127
cutlet escalope f 46
cycling cyclisme m 89
cystitis cystite f 142

D

dairy laiterie f 98
dance, to danser 88, 96
danger danger m 155, 156
dangerous dangereux(euse) 90
dark sombre 25; foncé(e) 101, 112, 113
date date f 25, 151; *(fruit)* datte f 54
daughter fille f 93
day jour m 16, 20, 24, 32, 80, 151; journée f 151
daylight lumière du jour f 124
day off jour de congé m 151
death mort f 155
decade décennie f 149

December décembre m 150
decision décision f 25, 102
deck *(ship)* pont m 74
deck-chair chaise longue f 91, 106
declare, to déclarer 17
delay retard m 69
delicatessen charcuterie f, traiteur m 98
delicious délicieux 62
deliver, to livrer 102
delivery livraison f 102
denim toile de coton f 114
dentist dentiste m/f 98, 145
denture dentier m 145
deodorant déodorant m 110
department *(museum)* département m 83; *(shop)* rayon m 100
department store grand magasin m 98
departure départ m 65
deposit *(car hire)* caution f 20; *(bank)* dépôt m 130
deposit, to *(bank)* déposer 130
dessert dessert m 37, 55
detour *(traffic)* déviation f 79
develop, to développer 124
diabetic diabétique 141
diabetic diabétique m/f 37
dialling code indicatif m 134
diamond diamant m 122, 127
diaper couche f 111
diarrhoea diarrhée f 140
dictionary dictionnaire m 104
diesel gas-oil m 75
diet régime m 37
difficult difficile 14
difficulty difficulté f 28, 102, 141; peine f 141
digital digital(e) 122
dining-car wagon-restaurant m 66, 68, 71
dining-room salle à manger f 27
dinner dîner m 34, 94
direct direct(e) 65
direct, to indiquer 13
direction direction f 76
director *(theatre)* metteur en scène m 86
directory *(phone)* annuaire m 134
disabled handicapé(e) 82
disc disque m 77, 127
discotheque discothèque f 88, 96
disease maladie f 142
dish plat m 37

dishwashing detergent produit (à) vaisselle m 106
disinfectant désinfectant m 109
dislocate, to disloquer 140
display case étalage m 100
dissatisfied mécontent(e) 103
district *(town)* quartier m 81
disturb, to déranger 155
diversion *(traffic)* déviation f 79
dizzy pris(e) de vertige 140
do, to faire 163
doctor médecin m 79, 137, 144; docteur m 145
doctor's office cabinet (de consultation) m 137
dog chien m 155
doll poupée f 128
dollar dollar m 18, 130
door porte f 155
double bed grand lit m 23
double room chambre pour deux personnes f 19, 23
down en bas 15
downhill skiing ski de piste m 91
downstairs en bas 15
down there là-bas 77
downtown centre m 81
dozen douzaine f 120, 149
draught beer bière pression f 56
drawing paper papier à dessin m 104
drawing pin punaise f 104
dress robe f 116
dressing gown peignoir m 116
drink boisson f 40, 59, 60, 61; verre m 95
drink, to boire 35, 36
drinking water eau potable f 32
drip, to *(tap)* fuire 28
drive, to conduire 21, 76
driving licence permis de conduire m 20, 79
drop *(liquid)* goutte f 109
drugstore pharmacie m 98, 108
dry sec, sèche 30, 59, 111
dry cleaner's teinturerie f 29, 98
dry shampoo shampooing sec m 111
Dublin bay prawn langoustine f 44
duck canard m 48
duckling caneton m 48
dull *(pain)* sourd(e) 140
dummy tétine f 111
during pendant 15, 150, 151
duty *(customs)* droits de douane m/pl 17

duty-free shop magasin hors-taxe *m* 19
dye teinture *f* 30, 111

E

each chaque 149
ear oreille *f* 138
earache mal aux oreilles *m* 141
ear drops gouttes pour les oreilles *f/pl* 109
early tôt 14
earring boucle d'oreille *f* 121
east est *m* 77
Easter Pâques *f/pl* 152
easy facile 14
eat, to manger 36, 144
eat out, to aller au restaurant 33
eel anguille *f* 44
egg œuf *m* 38, 64, 120
eggplant aubergine *f* 49
eight huit 147
eighteen dix-huit 147
eighth huitième 149
eighty quatre-vingts 148
elastic élastique 109
elastic bandage bandage élastique *m* 109
Elastoplast sparadrap *m* 109
electrical électrique 119
electrical appliance appareil électrique *m* 119
electrician électricien *m* 98
electricity électricité *f* 32
electronic électronique 125, 128
elevator ascenseur *m* 27, 100
eleven onze 147
embankment *(river)* quai *m* 81
embarkation embarquement *m* 74
emerald émeraude *f* 122
emergency urgence *f* 156
emergency exit sortie de secours *f* 27, 99, 155
emery board lime à ongles *f* 110
empty vide 14
enamel émail *m* 122
end fin *f* 150
endive chicorée *f* 49; *(Am.)* endive *f* 49
engine *(car)* moteur *m* 78
England Angleterre *f* 146
English anglais(e) 12, 80, 84, 104
enjoyable agréable 31
enjoy oneself, to s'amuser 96
enlarge, to agrandir 125

enough assez 15
enter, to entrer 155
entrance entrée *f* 67, 99, 155
entrance fee entrée *f* 82
envelope enveloppe *f* 27, 105
equipment équipement *m* 91; matériel *m* 106
eraser gomme *f* 105
escalator escalier mécanique *m* 100
espresso coffee express *m* 60
estimate estimation *f* 131
Europe Europe *f* 146
evening soir *m* 87, 95, 96, 151, 153; soirée *f* 95
evening dress tenue de soirée *f* 88; *(woman)* robe du soir *f* 116
everything tout 31
examine, to examiner 139
exchange, to échanger 103
exchange rate cours du change *m* 18, 130
excursion excursion *f* 80
excuse, to excuser 11
exercise book cahier *m* 105
exhaust pipe pot d'échappement *m* 78
exhibition exposition *f* 81
exit sortie *f* 67, 79, 99, 155
expect, to attendre 130
expensive cher, chère 14, 19, 24, 101
exposure *(photography)* pose *f* 124
exposure counter compte-poses *m* 125
express par exprès 133
expression expression *f* 10
expressway autoroute *f* 76
extension cord/lead prolongateur *m* 119
external externe 109
extra supplémentaire 27
extract, to *(tooth)* arracher 145
eye œil *m* (*pl* yeux) 138, 139
eye drops gouttes oculaires *f* 109
eye pencil crayon pour les yeux *m* 110
eye shadow fard à paupières *m* 110
eyesight vue *f* 123
eye specialist oculiste *m/f* 137

F

face visage *m* 138
face-pack masque de beauté *m* 30
face powder poudre *f* 110
factory usine *f* 81
fair foire *f* 81

fall chute f 139; *(autumn)* automne m 150
family famille f 93,
fan ventilateur m 28
fan belt courroie de ventilateur f 75
far loin 14, 100
fare tarif m 21; prix m 68, 73
farm ferme f 85
fashion mode f 127
fast *(film)* ultrarapide 124
fat *(meat)* gras m 37
father père m 93
faucet robinet m 28
fawn fauve 113
February février m 150
fee *(doctor)* honoraires m/pl 144
feeding bottle biberon m 111
feel, to *(physical state)* se sentir 140
felt feutre m 114
felt-tip pen crayon feutre m 105
fennel fenouil m 50
ferry ferry m 74
fever fièvre f 140
few peu de 14; *(a)* quelques 14
field champ m 85
fifteen quinze 147
fifth cinquième 149
fifty cinquante 147
fig figue f 54
file *(tool)* lime f 110
fill in, to remplir 26, 144
filling *(tooth)* plombage m 145
filling station station-service f 75
film film m 86, 124, 125
film winder levier d'avancement m 125
filter filtre m 125
filter-tipped avec filtre 126
find, to trouver 11, 12, 100, 137
fine *(OK)* d'accord 25
fine arts beaux-arts m/pl 83
finger doigt m 138
finish, to finir 162
fire feu m 156
first premier(ère) 68, 73, 149
first-aid kit trousse de premiers secours f 106
first class première classe f 69
first course entrée f 40
first name prénom m 25
fish poisson m 44
fish, to pêcher 90
fishing pêche f 90
fishing tackle attirail de pêche m 106

fishmonger's poissonnerie f 98
fit, to aller 115, 116
fitting room cabine d'essayage f 115
five cinq 147
fix, to réparer 75, 145
fizzy *(mineral water)* gazeux(euse) 60
flannel flanelle f 114
flash *(photography)* flash m 125
flash attachment glissière du flash f 125
flashlight lampe de poche f 106
flat plat(e) 118
flat tyre crevaison f 75, 78
flea market marché aux puces m 81
flight vol m 65
flight number numéro de vol m 65
flippers palmes f/pl 128
floor étage m 27
floor show spectacle de cabaret m 88
flour farine f 37
flower fleur f 85
flower shop fleuriste m 98
flu grippe f 142
fluid liquide m 75
fog brouillard m 94
folding chair chaise pliante f 106
folding table table pliante f 107
folk music musique folklorique f 128
food nourriture f 37; aliment m 111
food box boîte à conservation f 106
food poisoning intoxication alimentaire f 142
foot pied m 138
football football m 89
foot cream crème pour les pieds f 110
footpath sentier m 85
for pour 15; pendant 143
forbid, to défendre 155
forecast prévision f 94
foreign étranger(ère) 56
forest forêt f 85
forget, to oublier 61
fork fourchette f 36, 61, 107, 127
form *(document)* formule f 133; fiche f 25, 26
fortnight quinze jours m/pl 151
fortress forteresse f 81
forty quarante 147
foundation cream fond de teint m 110
fountain fontaine f 81
fountain pen stylo m 105
four quatre 147
fourteen quatorze 147
fourth quatrième 149

fowl volaille f 49
frame (glasses) monture f 123
France France f 146
free libre 14, 70, 82, 96, 155
French français(e) 11, 18, 95, 114
French bean haricot vert m 49
french fries (pommes) frites f/pl 51, 63
fresh frais, fraîche 54, 61
Friday vendredi m 151
fried frit(e) 45, 47
fried egg œuf au plat m 38
friend ami(e) m/f 93, 95
fringe frange f 30
frog grenouille f 44
from de 15
front avant 75
frost gel m 94
fruit fruit m 54
fruit cocktail salade de fruits f 54
fruit juice jus de fruits m 38, 60
frying-pan poêle f 106
full plein(e) 14; complet(ète) 155
full board pension complète f 24
full insurance assurance tous risques f 20
furniture meubles m/pl 83
furrier's fourreur f 98

G

gabardine gabardine f 114
gallery galerie f 81, 98
game jeu m 128; (food) gibier m 48
garage garage m 26, 78
garden jardin m 85
gardens jardin public m 81
garlic ail m 50
gas gaz m 71
gasoline essence f 75, 78
gastritis gastrite f 142
gauze gaze f 109
gem pierre précieuse f 121
general général(e) 27, 100
general delivery poste restante f 133
general practitioner généraliste m/f 137
gentleman monsieur m 155
genuine véritable 118
geology géologie f 83
Germany Allemagne f 146
get, to (find) trouver 11, 19, 21, 32; (call) appeler 31, 137; (obtain) obtenir 108, 134; se procurer 90; (go) se rendre 100

get back, to être de retour 80
get off, to descendre 73
get to, to aller à 19; arriver à 70
get up, to se lever 144
gherkin cornichon m 49, 64
gin and tonic gin-tonic m 60
ginger gingembre m 50
girdle gaine f 116
girl fille f 112; (child) fillette f 128
girlfriend amie f 93, 95
give, to donner 13, 123, 135
give way, to (traffic) céder le passage 79
glad (to know you) enchanté(e) 92
gland glande f 138
glass verre m 36, 59, 60, 61, 143
glasses lunettes f/pl 123
gloomy sombre 84
glossy (finish) brillant(e) 125
glove gant m 116
glue colle m 105
go, to aller 96, 162
go away, to s'en aller 156
gold or m 121, 122
golden doré(e) 113
gold plate plaqué or m 122
golf golf m 89
golf course terrain de golf m 89
good bon(ne) 14, 101
good-bye au revoir 10
Good Friday Vendredi-Saint m 152
goods articles m/pl 16
goose oie f 48
gooseberry groseille à maquereau f 54
gram gramme m 120
grammar book grammaire f 105
grape raisin m 54, 64
grapefruit pamplemousse m 54
grapefruit juice jus de pamplemousse m 38, 60
gray gris(e) 113
graze éraflure f 139
greasy gras(se) 30, 111
great (excellent) formidable 95
Great Britain Grande-Bretagne f 146
green vert(e) 113
green bean haricot vert m 49
greengrocer's primeur m 98
green salad salade verte f 42
greeting salutation f 10
grey gris(e) 113
grilled grillé(e) 45, 47

DICTIONARY

grocery magasin d'alimentation *m* 98, 120; épicerie *f* 98
groundsheet tapis de sol *m* 106
group groupe *m* 82
guide guide *m/f* 80
guidebook guide (de voyage) *m* 82, 104
guinea fowl pintade *f* 48
gum *(teeth)* gencive *f* 145
gynaecologist gynécologue *m/f* 137

H

haddock aiglefin *m* 44
hair cheveux *m/pl* 30, 111
hairbrush brosse à cheveux *f* 111
haircut coupe de cheveux *f* 30
hairdresser's coiffeur *m* 30, 98; salon de coiffure *m* 27
hair dryer sèche-cheveux *m* 119
hairgrip pince à cheveux *f* 111
hair lotion lotion capillaire *f* 111
hairpin èpingle à cheveux *f* 111
hairspray laque *f* 30, 111
half moitié *f* 149
half a day demi-journée *f* 80
half a dozen demi-douzaine *f* 120
half an hour demi-heure *f* 153
half board demi-pension *f* 24
half price *(ticket)* demi-tarif *m* 69
hall *(large room)* salle *f* 81, 88
hall porter concierge *m* 26
ham jambon *m* 38, 46, 63, 64
ham and eggs œufs au jambon *m/pl* 38
hamlet hameau *m* 85
hammer marteau *m* 106
hammock hamac *m* 106
hand main *f* 138
handbag sac à main *m* 116, 156
hand cream crème pour les mains *f* 110
handicrafts artisanat *m* 83
handkerchief mouchoir *m* 116
handmade fait(e) à la main 113
hanger cintre *m* 27
hangover gueule de bois *f* 108
happy heureux 152
harbour port *m* 81
hard dur(e) 123
hard-boiled *(egg)* dur 38
hardware shop quincaillerie *f* 98
hare lièvre *m* 48
hat chapeau *m* 116
have, to avoir 161; posséder 130; *(meal)* prendre 38
haversack musette *f* 106

hayfever rhume des foins *m* 108, 141
hazelnut noisette *f* 54
he il 161
head tête *f* 138, 139
headache mal de tête *m* 141
headlight phare *m* 79
headphones casque à écouteurs *m* 119
head waiter maître d'hôtel *m* 61
health santé *f* 56
health food shop magasin de diététique *m* 98
health insurance assurance maladie *f* 144
health insurance form feuille maladie *f* 144
heart cœur *m* 138
heart attack crise cardiaque *f* 141
heat, to chauffer 90
heating chauffage *m* 23, 28
heavy lourd(e) 14, 101
heel talon *m* 118
helicopter hélicoptère *m* 74
hello! *(phone)* allô! 135
help aide *m* 156
help! au secours! 156
help, to aider 13, 21, 71, 100, 134; *(oneself)* se servir 120
her son, sa *(pl ses)* 161
herbs fines herbes *f/pl* 50
herb tea tisane *f* 60
here ici 14; voici 14
herring hareng *m* 44
high haut(e) 90; *(blood pressure)* élevé(e) 141
high season haute saison *f* 150
high-speed ultrarapide 124
high tide marée haute *f* 90
hill colline *f* 85
hire location *f* 20, 74
hire, to louer 19, 20, 74, 90, 91, 119, 155
his son, sa *(pl ses)* 161
history histoire *f* 83
hitchhike, to faire l'auto-stop 74
hold on! *(phone)* ne quittez pas! 136
hole trou *m* 29
holiday jour férié *m* 151
holidays vacances *f/pl* 16, 151
home address lieu de domicile *m* 25
honey miel *m* 39
horse racing courses (de chevaux) *f/pl* 89
horseradish raifort *m* 50

Dictionnaire

hospital hôpital *m* 99, 144
hot chaud(e) 14, 25, 38, 94
hotel hôtel *m* 19, 21, 22
hotel guide guide des hôtels *m* 19
hotel reservation réservation d'hôtel *f* 19
hot water eau chaude *f* 23, 28
hot-water bottle bouillotte *f* 27
hour heure *f* 153
house maison *f* 83, 85
hovercraft aéroglisseur *m* 74
how comment 11
how far à quelle distance 11, 76, 85
how long combien de temps 11, 24
how many combien 11
how much combien 11, 24, 101
hundred cent 148
hungry, to be avoir faim 13, 35
hurry (to be in a) être pressé(e) 21
hurry up! dépêchez-vous! 13
hurt, to faire mal 139, 145; *(oneself)* se blesser 139
husband mari *m* 93
hydrofoil hydroptère *m* 74

I
I je 161
ice glace *f* 94
ice-cream glace *f* 55, 64
ice cube glaçon *m* 27
iced tea thé glacé *m* 60
ice pack cartouche réfrigérante *f* 106
ill malade 140, 156
illness maladie *f* 140
important important(e) 13
imported importé(e) 113
impressive impressionnant(e) 84
in dans 15
include, to comprendre 20, 24, 31, 32, 62, 80
included compris(e) 40, 62
India Inde *f* 146
indigestion indigestion *f* 141
inexpensive bon marché 35, 124
infect, to infecter 140
infection infection *f* 141
inflammation inflammation *f* 142
inflation inflation *f* 131
inflation rate taux d'inflation *m* 131
influenza grippe *f* 142
information renseignement *m* 67, 155
injection piqûre *f* 142, 144
injure, to blesser 139
injured blessé(e) 79, 139

injury blessure *f* 139
ink encre *f* 105
inn auberge *f* 22, 33
inquiry renseignement *m* 68
insect bite piqûre d'insecte *f* 108, 139
insect repellent crème anti-insecte *f* 109
insect spray bombe insecticide *f* 109
inside dedans 15
instead à la place 37
instrumental *(music)* instrumental(e) 128
insurance assurance *f* 20, 79, 144
interest intérêt *m* 80, 131
interested, to be s'intéresser 83, 96
interesting intéressant(e) 84
international international 133, 134
interpreter interprète *m* 131
intersection carrefour *m* 77
introduce, to présenter 92
introduction présentation *f* 92, introduction *f* 130
investment investissement *m* 131
invitation invitation *f* 94
invite, to inviter 94
invoice facture *f* 131
iodine teinture d'iode *f* 109
Ireland Irlande *f* 146
Irish irlandais(e) 92
iron *(laundry)* fer à repasser *m* 119
iron, to repasser 29
ironmonger's quincaillerie *f* 99
Italy Italie *f* 146
its son, sa *(pl ses)* 161
ivory ivoire *m* 122

J
jacket veston *m* 116
jam confiture *f* 38, 63
jam, to coincer 28; bloquer 125
January janvier *m* 150
jar pot *m* 120
jaundice jaunisse *f* 142
jaw mâchoire *f* 138
jeans jeans *m/pl* 116
jersey tricot *m* 116
jewel bijou *m* 121
jewel box coffret à bijoux *m* 121
jeweller's bijouterie *f* 99, 121
joint articulation *f* 138
journey trajet *m* 72
juice jus *m* 38, 41, 60
July juillet *m* 150
jumper *(sweater)* chandail *m* 116
June juin *m* 150

K

keep, to garder 62
kerosene pétrole m 106
key clé f 27
kidney rein m 138
kilogram kilogramme m 120
kilometre kilomètre m 20, 78
kind aimable 95
kind (type) genre m 140
knapsack sac à dos m 106
knee genou m 138
knife couteau m 36, 61, 107
knock, to frapper 155
know, to savoir 16, 24; connaître
    96, 114

L

label étiquette f 105
lace dentelle f 114, 127
lady dame f 155
lake lac m 81, 85, 90
lamb agneau m 46
lamp lampe f 29, 106, 119
landmark point de repère m 85
landscape paysage m 92
lane (traffic) piste f 79
lantern lanterne f 106
large grand(e) 101, 118; gros(se) 130
lark alouette f 48
last dernier(ère) 14, 68, 73, 149;
    passé(e) 151
last name nom (de famille) m 25
late tard 14
laugh, to rire 95
launderette laverie automatique f 99
laundry (place) blanchisserie f 29,
    99; (clothes) linge m 29
laundry service blanchisserie f 23
laxative laxatif m 109
leap year année bissextile f 149
leather cuir m 114, 118
leave, to partir 31, 68, 74, 95; lais-
    ser 156; (deposit) déposer 26, 71
leek poireau m 50
left gauche 21, 63, 69, 77
left-luggage office consigne f 67, 71
leg jambe f 138
lemon citron m 37, 38, 54, 60, 64
lemonade limonade f 60
lemon juice citron pressé m 60
lens (glasses) verre m 123; (camera)
    objectif m 125
lens cap capuchon d'objectif m 125
lentil lentille f 50

less moins 15
lesson leçon f 91
let, to (hire out) louer 155
letter lettre f 132
letter box boîte aux lettres f 132
lettuce laitue f 50
level crossing passage à niveau m 79
library bibliothèque f 81, 99
licence (permit) permis m 20, 79
lie down, to s'étendre 142
life belt ceinture de sauvetage f 74
life boat canot de sauvetage m 74
lifeguard maître nageur m 90
lift ascenseur m 27, 100
light lumière f 28, 124; (cigarette)
    feu m 95
light léger(ère) 14, 55, 59, 101,
    128; (colour) clair(e) 101, 112, 113
lighter briquet m 126
lighter fluid essence à briquet f 126
lighter gas gaz à briquet m 126
light meter cellule photoélectrique f
    125
lightning éclair m 94
like, to vouloir 13, 20, 23; aimer 61,
    96, 112; désirer 103; plaire 25,
    92, 102
line ligne f 73
linen (cloth) lin m 114
lip lèvre f 138
lipsalve beurre de cacao m 110
lipstick rouge à lèvres m 110
liqueur liqueur f 60
liquid liquide m 123
listen, to écouter 128
litre litre m 59, 75, 120
little (a) un peu 14
live, to vivre 83
liver foie m 46, 138
lobster homard m 44
local local(e) 36, 59
London Londres m 130
long long(ue) 116, 117
long-sighted presbyte 123
look, to regarder 100; voir 123
look for, to chercher 13
look out! attention! 156
loose (clothes) large 116
lorry camion m 79
lose, to perdre 123, 156
loss perte f 131
lost perdu(e) 13, 156
lost and found office bureau des
    objets trouvés m 67, 156

DICTIONARY

lost property office bureau des objets trouvés m 67, 156
lot (a) beaucoup 14
lotion lotion f 110
loud (voice) fort(e) 135
love, to aimer 95
lovely beau, belle 94
low bas(se) 90, 141
lower inférieur(e) 69, 71
low season basse saison f 150
low tide marée basse f 90
luck chance f 135, 152
luggage bagages m/pl 18, 26, 31, 71
luggage locker consigne automatique f 18, 67, 71
luggage trolley chariot à bagages m 18, 71
lump (bump) bosse f 139
lunch déjeuner m 34, 80, 94
lung poumon m 138

M

machine machine f 114
mackerel maquereau m 45
magazine revue f 105
magnificent splendide 84
maid femme de chambre f 26
mail, to mettre à la poste 28
mail courrier m 28, 133
mailbox boîte aux lettres f 132
make, to faire 131, 162
make up, to faire 28; préparer 108
make-up remover pad disque démaquillant m 110
man homme m 115, 155
manager directeur m 26
manicure manucure f 30
many beaucoup de 15
map carte f 76, 105; plan m 105
March mars m 150
marinated mariné(e) 45
market marché m 81, 99
marmalade marmelade f 38
married marié(e) 93
mass (church) messe f 84
mat (finish) mat(e) 125
match allumette f 106, 126; (sport) match m 89
match, to (colour) s'assortir à 112
material (cloth) tissu m 113
mattress matelas m 106
May mai m 150
may (can) pouvoir 12, 163

meadow pré m 85
meal repas m 24, 34, 62, 143
mean, to vouloir dire 11; signifier 26
measles rougeole f 142
measure, to prendre les mesures 114
meat viande f 46, 47, 61
meatball boulette f 46
mechanic mécanicien m 78
mechanical pencil porte-mine m 105, 121
medical médical(e) 144
medicine médecine f 83; (drug) médicament m 143
medium (meat) à point 47
medium-sized moyen(ne) 20
meet, to rencontrer 96
melon melon m 54
memorial monument m 81
mend, to réparer 75; (clothes) raccommoder 29
menthol (cigarettes) mentholé(e) 126
menu menu m 37, 39; (printed) carte f 36, 39, 40
merry joyeux(euse) 152
message message m 28, 136
methylated spirits alcool à brûler m 106
metre mètre m 112
mezzanine (theatre) balcon m 87
middle milieu m 69, 87, 150
midnight minuit m 153
mileage kilométrage m 20
milk lait m 38, 60, 64
milkshake frappé m 60
million million m 148
mineral water eau minérale f 60
minister (religion) pasteur m 84
mint menthe f 50
minute minute f 153
mirror miroir m 115, 123
miscellaneous divers(e) 127
Miss Mademoiselle f 10
miss, to manquer 18, 29, 61
mistake erreur f 31, 61, 62, 102
mixed salad salade mêlée f 42
modified American plan demi-pension f 24
moisturizing cream crème hydratante f 110
moment moment m 136
monastery monastère m 81
Monday lundi m 151
money argent m 129, 130, 156
money order mandat m 133

month mois *m* 16, 150
monument monument *m* 81
moon lune *f* 94
moped vélomoteur *m* 74
more plus 15
morning matin *m* 151, 153
Morocco Maroc *m* 146
mortgage hypothèque *f* 131
mosque mosquée *f* 84
mosquito net moustiquaire *f* 106
mother mère *f* 93
motorbike moto *f* 74
motorboat canot à moteur *m* 91
motorway autoroute *f* 76
mountain montagne *f* 85
moustache moustache *f* 31
mouth bouche *f* 138
mouthwash gargarisme *m* 109
move, to bouger 139
movie film *m* 86
movie camera caméra *f* 124
movies cinéma *m* 86, 96
Mr. Monsieur *m* 10
Mrs. Madame *f* 10
much beaucoup 14
mug grosse tasse *f* 107
mulberry mûre *f* 54
muscle muscle *m* 138
museum musée *m* 81
mushroom champignon *m* 49
music musique *f* 83, 128
musical comédie musicale *f* 86
music box boîte à musique *f* 121
mussel moule *f* 45
must, to devoir 31, 37, 61; falloir 95
mustard moutarde *f* 37, 50, 64
my mon, ma *(pl* mes*)* 161

N

nail *(human)* ongle *m* 10
nail brush brosse à ongles *f* 110
nail clippers coupe-ongles *m* 110
nail file lime à ongles *f* 110
nail polish vernis à ongles *m* 110
nail polish remover dissolvant *m* 110
nail scissors ciseaux à ongles *m/pl*
  110
name nom *m* 23, 25, 79, 85, 92
napkin serviette *f* 36, 105, 106
nappy couche *f* 111
narrow étroit(e) 118
nationality nationalité *f* 25, 92
natural naturel(le) 83
nauseous nauséeux(euse) 140

near près 14; près de 15
nearby à proximité 77
nearest le(a) plus proche 78, 98
neat *(drink)* sec 56, 60
neck cou *m* 138; *(nape)* nuque *f* 30
necklace collier *m* 121
need, to avoir besoin de 90; falloir 29
needle aiguille *f* 27
negative négatif *m* 125
nephew neveu *m* 93
nerve nerf *m* 138
nervous nerveux(euse) 138
nervous system système nerveux *m*
  138
Netherlands Pays-Bas *m/pl* 146
never ne ... jamais 15
new nouveau, nouvelle 14
newspaper journal *m* 104, 105
newsstand kiosque à journaux *m* 19,
  67, 99, 104
New Year Nouvel An *m* 152
New Zealand Nouvelle-Zélande *f* 146
next prochain(e) 14, 65, 68, 73, 76,
  149, 151
next time la prochaine fois 95
next to à côté de 15, 77
nice beau, belle 94
niece nièce *f* 93
night nuit *f* 24, 151
nightclub boîte de nuit *f* 88
night cream crème de nuit *f* 110
nightdress chemise de nuit *f* 116
nine neuf 147
nineteen dix-neuf 147
ninety quatre-vingt-dix 148
ninth neuvième 149
no non 10
noisy bruyant(e) 25
nonalcoholic sans alcool 60
none aucun(e) 15
nonsmoker non-fumeurs *m/pl* 36, 70
noodle nouille *f* 51
noon midi *m* 31, 153
normal normal(e) 30
north nord *m* 77
North America Amérique du Nord *f*
  146
nose nez *m* 138
nosebleed saignement de nez *m* 141
nose drops gouttes nasales *f/pl* 109
not ne ... pas 15, 163
note *(banknote)* billet *m* 130;
  coupure *f* 130
notebook bloc-notes *m* 105

note paper papier à lettres m 105
nothing rien 15, 17
notice (sign) écriteau m 155
November novembre m 150
now maintenant 15
number numéro m 26, 65, 135, 136; nombre m 147
nurse infirmière f 144
nutmeg (noix) muscade f 50

O

occupation profession f 93
occupied occupé(e) 14, 70, 155
October octobre m 150
octopus poulpe f 45
offer, to offrir 95
office bureau m 19, 67, 99, 132, 133, 156
oil huile f 37, 75, 111
oily gras(se) 30, 111
old vieux, vieille 14; ancien(ne) 14
old town vieille ville f 81
olive olive f 41
omelet omelette f 42
on sur 15
once une fois 149
one un, une 147
one-way (ticket) aller m 65, 69
on foot à pied 76
onion oignon m 50
on request sur demande 73
on time à l'heure 68
only seulement 80
onyx onyx m 122
open ouvert(e) 14, 82, 155
open, to ouvrir 11, 17, 82, 108, 131, 132, 142
open-air en plein air 90
opera opéra m 88
opera house opéra m 81, 88
operation opération f 144
operator opérateur m, opératrice f 134
operetta opérette f 88
opposite en face 77
optician opticien(ne) m/f 99, 123
or ou 15
orange orange 113
orange orange f 54, 64
orange juice jus d'orange m 38, 60
orchestra orchestre m 88; (seats) parterre m 87
orchestral music musique symphonique f 128

order (goods, meal) commande f 40, 102
order, to (goods, meal) commander 61, 102, 103
oregano origan m 50
ornithology ornithologie f 83
our notre (pl nos) 161
out of order hors service 155
out of stock épuisé(e) 103
outlet (electric) prise f 27
outside dehors 15, 36
oval ovale 101
overalls salopette f 116
overdone trop cuit(e) 61
overheat, to (engine) chauffer 78
overnight (stay) d'une nuit 24
overtake, to doubler 79
owe, to devoir 144
owerwhelming imposant(e) 84
oyster huître f 44

P

pacifier tétine f 111
packet paquet m 120, 126
page (hotel) chasseur m 26
pail seau m 106, 128
pain douleur f 140, 141, 144
painkiller calmant m 140, 144
paint peinture f 155
paint, to peindre 83
paintbox boîte de couleurs f 105
painter peintre m 83
painting peinture f 83
pair paire f 116, 118, 149
pajamas pyjama m 116
palace palais m 81
pancake crêpe f 63
panties slip m 116
panty girdle gaine-culotte f 116
panty hose collant m 116
pants (trousers) pantalon m 116
paper papier m 105
paperback livre de poche m 105
paperclip trombone f 105
paper napkin serviette en papier f 105, 106
paraffin (fuel) pétrole m 106
parcel colis m 132
parents parents m/pl 93
park parc m 81
park, to garer 26, 77
parking stationnement m 77, 79
parking disc disque de stationnement m 77

parking meter parcomètre *m* 77
parliament parlement *m* 81
parsley persil *m* 50
part partie *f* 138
partridge perdrix *f* 48
party *(social gathering)* réception *f* 95
pass, to *(car)* doubler 79
passport passeport *m* 16, 17, 25, 26, 156
passport photo photo d'identité *f* 124
pass through, to être de passage 16
pasta pâtes *f/pl* 51
paste *(glue)* colle *f* 105
pastry pâtisserie *f* 64
pastry shop pâtisserie *f* 99
patch, to *(clothes)* rapiécer 29
path chemin *m* 85
patient patient *m* 144
pay, to payer 31, 62, 102
payment paiement *m* 102, 131
pea petit pois *m* 50
peach pêche *f* 54
peak sommet *m* 85
peanut cacahouète *f* 54
pear poire *f* 54
pearl perle *f* 122
pedestrian piéton *m* 79
peg *(tent)* piquet *m* 107
pen plume *f* 105
pencil crayon *m* 105
pencil sharpener taille-crayon *m* 105
pendant pendentif *m* 121
penicilline pénicilline *f* 143
penknife canif *m* 106
pensioner retraité(e) *m/f* 82
people gens *m/pl* 93
pepper poivre *m* 37, 38, 51, 64
per cent pour cent 149
perch perche *f* 45
per day par jour 20, 32, 89
perfume parfum *m* 110, 127
perfume shop parfumerie *f* 108
perhaps peut-être 15
per hour horaire 77; par heure 89
period *(monthly)* règles *f/pl* 141
period pains règles douloureuses *f/pl* 141
permanent wave permanente *f* 30
permit permis *m* 90
per night par nuit 24
per person par personne 32
person personne *f* 32, 36
personal personnel(le) 17

personal call communication avec préavis *f* 135
personal cheque chèque à ordre *m* 130
person-to-person call communication avec préavis *f* 135
per week par semaine 20, 24
petrol essence *f* 75, 78
pewter étain *m* 122
pheasant faisan *m* 48
phone téléphone *m* 28, 78, 79, 134
phone, to téléphoner 134
phone booth cabine téléphonique *f* 134
phone call appel *m* 135; communication *f* 136
phone number numéro de téléphone *m* 96, 134, 135
photo photo *f* 82, 124, 125
photocopy photocopie *f* 104, 131
photograph, to photographier, prendre des photos 82
photographer photographe *m/f* 99
photography photographie *f* 124
phrase expression *f* 12
pick up, to prendre 80, 96
picnic pique-nique *m* 63
picture tableau *m* 83; *(photo)* photo *f* 82
piece morceau *m* 120
pig cochon *m* 46
pigeon pigeon *m* 48
pike brochet *m* 44
pill pilule *f* 141, 143
pillow oreiller *m* 27
pin épingle *f* 110, 111, 121
pineapple ananas *m* 54
pink rose 113
pipe pipe *f* 126
pipe cleaner nettoie-pipe *m* 126
pipe tool cure-pipe *m* 126
place place *m* 25; endroit *m* 76
place of birth lieu de naissance *m* 25
plaice carrelet *m* 44; plie *f* 45
plane avion *m* 65
planetarium planétarium *m* 81
plaster plâtre *m* 140
plastic plastique *m* 107
plastic bag sac en plastique *m* 107
plate assiette *f* 36, 61, 107
platform quai *m* 67, 68, 69, 70
platinum platine *f* 122
play *(theatre)* pièce *f* 86
play, to jouer 86, 88, 89, 93

playground terrain de jeu *m* 32
playing card carte à jouer *f* 105
please s'il vous plaît 10
plimsolls tennis *m/pl* 118
plug *(electric)* fiche *f* 29
plum prune *f* 54
pneumonia pneumonie *f* 142
poached poché(e) 45
pocket poche *f* 117
point, to *(show)* montrer 12
poison poison *m* 109
poisoning intoxication *f* 142
pole *(ski)* bâton *m* 91
police police *f* 78, 156
police station poste de police *m* 99, 156
polish *(nails)* vernis *m* 110
pond étang *m* 85
pop music musique pop *f* 128
poplin popeline *f* 114
poppy pavot *m* 64
porcelain porcelaine *f* 127
pork porc *m* 46
port port *m* 74; *(wine)* porto *m* 60
portable portatif(ive) 119
porter porteur *m* 18, 71; *(hotel)* bagagiste *m* 26
portion portion *f* 37, 55, 61
possible possible 137
post *(letters)* courrier *m* 28, 133
post, to mettre à la poste 28
postage tarif (d'affranchissement) *m* 132
postage stamp timbre *m* 28, 126, 132
postcard carte postale *f* 105, 126, 132
post office bureau de poste *m* 99, 132
potato pomme de terre *f* 51
pothole nid de poule *m* 79
pottery poterie *f* 83, 127
poultry volaille *f* 48
pound *(money)* livre *f* 18, 130; *(weight)* livre *f* 120
powder poudre *f* 110
powder compact poudrier *m* 122
powder puff houppette *f* 110
prawns scampi *m/pl* 45
preference préférence *f* 101
pregnant enceinte 141
premium *(gasoline)* super *m* 75
preparation préparation *f* 51
prescribe, to prescrire 143
prescription ordonnance *f* 108, 143
press, to *(iron)* repasser à la vapeur 29

press stud bouton-pression *m* 117
pressure pression *f* 75
price prix *m* 24
priest prêtre *m* 84
print *(photo)* copie *f* 125
private privé(e) 91, 155
processing *(photo)* développement *m* 124
profession profession *f* 25
profit bénéfice *m* 131
programme programme *m* 87
prohibit, to interdire 79
pronunciation prononciation *f* 6
propelling pencil porte-mine *m* 105, 122
propose, to proposer 40
Protestant protestant(e) 84
provide, to procurer 131
prune pruneau *m* 54
public holiday jour férié *m* 152
pull, to tirer 155
pullover pull(over) *m* 117
puncture crevaison *f* 75
purchase achat *m* 131
pure pur(e) 114
purple violet(te) 113
push, to pousser 155
put, to mettre 24
pyjamas pyjama *m* 117

Q

quail caille *f* 48
quality qualité *f* 103, 113
quantity quantité *f* 14, 103
quarter quart *m* 149; *(part of town)* quartier *m* 81
quarter of an hour quart d'heure *m* 153
question question *f* 11
quick rapide 14; vite 156
quickly vite 137, 156
quiet tranquille 23, 25

R

rabbi rabbin *m* 84
rabbit lapin *m* 48
race course/track champ de courses *m* 90
racket *(sport)* raquette *f* 90
radiator radiateur *m* 78
radio *(set)* poste de radio *m* 23, 119; radio *f* 28
radish radis *m* 50
railroad crossing passage à niveau *m* 79

railway chemin de fer m 154
railway station gare f 19, 21, 67, 70
rain pluie f 94
rain, to pleuvoir 94
raincoat imperméable m 117
raisin raisin sec m 54
rangefinder télémètre m 125
rare *(meat)* saignant(e) 47, 61
rash éruption f 139
raspberry framboise f 54
rate tarif m 20; taux m 131
razor rasoir m 110
razor blade lame de rasoir f 110
reading-lamp lampe de chevet f 27
ready prêt(e) 29, 118, 123, 125, 145
real véritable 121
rear arrière 75
receipt quittance f 103, 144
reception réception f 23
receptionist réceptionnaire m 26
recommend, to recommander 35, 36; indiquer 35, 88, 137, 145; conseiller 80, 86
record *(disc)* disque m 127, 128
record player tourne-disque m 119
rectangular rectangulaire 101
red rouge 59, 113
redcurrant groseille f 54
red mullet rouget m 45
reduction réduction f 24, 82
refill recharge f 105
refund remboursement m 103
regards salutations f/pl, amitiés f/pl 152
register, to *(luggage)* faire enregistrer 71
registered mail recommandé(e) 133
registration enregistrement m 25
registration form fiche f 25, 26
regular *(petrol)* normale f 75
religion religion f 83
religious service service religieux m, culte m 84
rent, to louer 19, 20, 74, 90, 91, 119, 155
rental location f 20, 74
repair réparation f 125
repair, to réparer 29, 118, 119, 121, 123, 125, 145
repeat, to répéter 12
report, to déclarer 156
require, to exiger 88
reservation réservation f 19, 23, 65, 69

reservations office bureau de réservation m 19, 67
reserve, to réserver 19, 23, 36, 87
restaurant restaurant m 19, 32, 34, 35, 67
return *(ticket)* aller-retour m 65, 69
return, to *(give back)* rendre 103
reverse the charges, to téléphoner en P.C.V. 135
rheumatism rhumatisme m 141
rhubarb rhubarbe f 54
rib côte f 46, 138
ribbon ruban m 105
rice riz m 51
right droite 21, 63, 69, 77; *(correct)* juste 14
ring *(on finger)* bague f 122
ring, to sonner 155; téléphoner 134
river rivière f 85, 90; *(major)* fleuve m 85
road route f 76, 77, 85
road assistance assistance routière f 78
road map carte routière f 105
road sign panneau routier m 79
roast rôti(e) 47
roast beef rosbif m 46
roll *(bread)* petit pain m 38, 64
roller skate patin à roulettes m 128
roll film bobine f 124
roll-neck à col roulé 117
room chambre f 19, 23, 24, 25, 28; *(space)* place f 32
room service service d'étage m 23
rope corde f 107
rosary chapelet m 122
rosemary romarin m 51
rouge fard à joues m 110
round *(golf)* partie f 89
round rond(e) 101
round-neck à col rond 117
roundtrip *(ticket)* aller-retour m 65, 69
rowing-boat barque à rames f 91
royal royal(e) 82
rubber *(material)* caoutchouc m 118; *(eraser)* gomme f 105
ruby rubis m 122
rucksack sac de montagne m 107
ruin ruine f 81
ruler *(for measuring)* règle f 105
rum rhum m 60
running water eau courante f 23
rye seigle m 64

S

saddle selle f 46
safe (not dangerous) sans danger 90
safe coffre-fort m 26
safety pin épingle de sûreté f 110
saffron safran m 51
sage sauge f 51
sailing-boat voilier m 91
salad salade f 42
sale vente f 131; (bargains) soldes m/pl 100
sales tax T.V.A. f 24, 102
salmon saumon m 45
salt sel m 37, 38, 64
salty salé(e) 61
sand sable m 90
sandal sandale f 118
sanitary towel/napkin serviette hygiénique f 109
sapphire saphir m 122
Saturday samedi m 151
sauce sauce f 51
saucepan casserole f 107
saucer soucoupe f 107
sauerkraut choucroute f 47
sausage saucisse f 46, 64
sautéed sauté(e) 45, 47
scallop coquille St-Jacques f 45; (meat) escalope f 46
scampi langoustines f/pl 44
scarf foulard m 117
scarlet écarlate 113
scenic route route touristique f 85
school école f 79
scissors ciseaux m/pl 107, 110
Scotland Ecosse f 146
scrambled egg œuf brouillé m 38
screwdriver tournevis m 107
sculptor sculpteur m 83
sculpture sculpture f 83
sea mer f 23, 85, 90
sea bream daurade f 44
seafood fruits de mer m/pl 44
season saison f 40, 150
seasoning condiments m/pl 37
seat place f 69, 70, 87
seat belt ceinture de sécurité f 75
second deuxième 149
second seconde f 153
second class deuxième classe f 69
second hand trotteuse f 122
second-hand d'occasion 104
secretary secrétaire m/f 27, 131
see, to voir 12, 163

send, to envoyer 102, 103, 133; expédier 132
send up, to faire monter 26
sentence phrase f 12
separately séparément 62
September septembre m 150
seriously (wounded) grièvement 139
service service m 24, 62, 98, 100; (religion) culte m 84
serviette serviette f 36
set (hair) mise en plis f 30
set menu menu (à prix fixe) m 36, 40
setting lotion fixatif m 30, 111
seven sept 147
seventeen dix-sept 147
seventh septième 149
seventy soixante-dix 148
sew, to coudre 29
shade (colour) ton m 112
shallot échalote f 50
shampoo shampooing m 30, 111
shape forme f 103
share (finance) action f 131
sharp (pain) aigu(e) 140
shave, to raser 31
shaver rasoir (électrique) m 27, 119
shaving brush blaireau m 111
shaving cream crème à raser f 111
she elle 161
shelf étagère f 120
ship navire m 74
shirt chemise f 117
shivery pris(e) de frissons 140
shoe chaussure f 118
shoelace lacet m 118
shoemaker's cordonnerie f 99
shoe polish cirage m 118
shoe shop magasin de chaussures m 99
shop magasin m 98
shopping achats m/pl 97
shopping area quartier commerçant m 82, 100
shopping centre centre commercial m 99
short court(e) 30, 116, 117
shorts short m 117
short-sighted myope 123
shoulder épaule f 46, 138
shovel pelle f 128
show spectacle m 86, 87, 88
show, to montrer 13, 76, 100, 101, 103, 119, 124; indiquer 12
shower douche f 23, 32

shrimp crevette f 44
shrink, to rétrécir 114
shut fermé(e) 14
shutter (window) volet m 29; (camera) obturateur m 125
sick (ill) malade 140, 156
sickness (illness) maladie f 140
side côté m 30
sideboards/burns favoris m/pl 31
sightseeing visite touristique f 80
sightseeing tour visite guidée f 80
sign (notice) écriteau m 155; (road) panneau m 79
sign, to signer 26, 131
signature signature f 25
signet ring chevalière f 122
silk soie f 114
silver argenté(e) 113
silver argent m 121, 122
silver plate plaqué argent m 122
silverware argenterie f 122
since depuis 15, 150
sing, to chanter 88
single célibataire 93
single (ticket) aller m 65, 69
single room chambre pour une personne f 19, 23
sister sœur f 93
sit down, to s'asseoir 95
six six 147
sixteen seize 147
sixth sixième 149
sixty soixante 147
size format m 124; (clothes) taille f 114; (shoes) pointure f 118
skate patin m 91
skating rink patinoire f 91
ski ski m 91
ski, to faire du ski 91
ski boot chaussure de ski f 91
skiing ski m 89, 91
ski lift remonte-pente m 91
skin peau f 138
skin-diving plongée sous-marine f 91
skirt jupe f 117
ski run piste de ski f 91
sky ciel m 94
sled luge f 91
sleep, to dormir 144
sleeping bag sac de couchage m 107
sleeping-car wagon-lit m 66, 68, 69, 70
sleeping pill somnifère m 109, 143, 144
sleeve manche f 117

slice tranche f 120
slide (photo) diapositive f 124
slip jupon m 117
slipper pantoufle f 118
slow lent(e) 12, 14, 135
slow down, to ralentir 79
small petit(e) 14, 25, 101, 118, 130
smoke, to fumer 95
smoked fumé(e) 45
smoker fumeurs m/pl 70
snack casse-croûte m 63
snack bar buffet-express m 34, 67
snail escargot m 44
snap fastener bouton-pression m 117
sneakers tennis m/pl 118
snorkel tuba m 128
snow neige f 94
snow, to neiger 94
snuff tabac à priser m 126
soap savon m 27, 111
soccer football m 89
sock chaussette f 117
socket (outlet) prise m 27
soft drink boisson non alcoolisée f 64
soft-boiled (egg) mollet 28
sold out (theatre) complet 87
sole semelle f 118; (fish) sole f 45
soloist soliste m/f 88
some de, de la, du (pl des) 15
someone quelqu'un 95
something quelque chose 36, 55, 108, 112, 113, 125, 139
son fils m 93
song chanson f 128
soon bientôt 15
sore (painful) douloureux(euse) 145
sore throat mal de gorge m 141
sorry désolé(e) 11, 87; (I'm) excusez-moi 16
sort genre m 89; sorte f 120
sound-and-light show spectacle son et lumière m 86
soup soupe f, potage m 43
south sud m 77
South Africa Afrique du Sud f 146
souvenir souvenir m 127
souvenir shop magasin de souvenirs m 99
Soviet Union Union soviétique f 146
spade pelle f 128
Spain Espagne f 146
spare tyre roue de secours f 75
sparking plug bougie f 76
sparkling (wine) mousseux(euse) 59

spark plug bougie f 76
speak, to parler 12, 135, 162
speaker (loudspeaker) haut-parleur m 119
special spécial(e) 20, 37
special delivery par exprès 133
specialist spécialiste m/f 142
speciality spécialité f 40, 59
specimen (medical) prélèvement m 142
spectacle case étui à lunettes m 123
spell, to épeler 12
spend, to dépenser 101
spice épice f 50
spinach épinard m 49
spine colonne vertébrale f 138
spiny lobster langouste f 44
sponge éponge f 111
spoon cuillère f 36, 61, 107
sport sport m 89
sporting goods shop magasin d'articles de sport m 99
sports jacket veste de sport f 117
sprain, to fouler 140
spring (season) printemps m 150; (water) source f 85
square carré(e) 101
squid calmar m 44
stadium stade m 82
staff personnel m 26
stain tache f 29
stainless steel inox m 107, 122
stalls (theatre) parterre m 87
stamp (postage) timbre m 28, 126, 132
staple agrafe f 105
star étoile f 94
start, to commencer 80, 87, 88; (car) démarrer 78
starters hors-d'œuvre m 41
station (railway) gare f 19, 21, 67, 70; (underground, subway) station f 73
stationer's papeterie f 99, 104
statue statue f 82
stay séjour m 31, 92
stay, to rester 16, 24, 26; loger 93
steal, to voler 156
steamed cuit(e) à la vapeur 45
stew ragoût m 47
stewed à l'étouffée 47
stew pot marmite f 107
stiff neck torticolis m 141
still (mineral water) non gazeux (euse) 60

sting piqûre f 139
sting, to piquer 139
stitch, to (clothes) recoudre 29; (shoes) coudre 118
stock (in shop) stock m 103
stock exchange bourse f 82
stocking bas m 117
stomach estomac m 138
stomach ache maux d'estomac m/pl 141
stools selles f/pl 142
stop (bus) arrêt m 72, 73
stop, to s'arrêter 21, 68, 70, 72
stop thief! au voleur! 156
store magasin m 98
straight (drink) sec 56, 60
straight ahead tout droit 21, 77
strange étrange 84
strawberry fraise f 54
street rue f 25
streetcar tram m 72
street map plan de ville m 19, 105
string ficelle f 105
strong fort(e) 143
student étudiant(e) m/f 82, 93
study, to étudier 93
stuffed farci(e) 41
sturdy solide 101
subway (railway) métro m 73
suede daim m 114, 118
sugar sucre m 37, 63, 64
suit (man) complet m 117; (woman) tailleur m 117
suitcase valise f 18
summer été m 150
sun soleil m 94
sunburn coup de soleil m 108
Sunday dimanche m 151
sunglasses lunettes de soleil f/pl 123
sunny ensoleillé(e) 94
sunshade (beach) parasol m 91
sunstroke insolation f 141
sun-tan cream crème solaire f 111
sun-tan oil huile solaire f 111
super (petrol) super m 75
superb superbe 84
supermarket supermarché m 99
supplement supplément m 40
suppository suppositoire m 109
surfboard planche de surf f 91
surgery (consulting room) cabinet (de consultation) m 137
surname nom (de famille) m 25
surroundings environs m/pl 35

suspenders *(Am.)* bretelles *f/pl* 117
swallow, to avaler 143
sweater chandail *m* 117
sweatshirt sweatshirt *m* 117
sweet *(food)* sucré(e) 61; *(wine)* doux, douce 59
sweet bonbon *m* 126
sweet corn maïs *m* 50
sweetener édulcorant *m* 37
swell, to enfler 139
swelling enflure *f* 139
swim, to nager, se baigner 90
swimming natation *f* 89; baignade *f* 91
swimming pool piscine *f* 32, 90
swimming trunks maillot de bain *m* 117
swimsuit costume de bain *m* 117
Swiss suisse 18
switch interrupteur *m* 29
switchboard operator standardiste *m/f* 26
switch on, to *(light)* allumer 79
Switzerland Suisse *f* 146
swollen enflé(e) 139
synagogue synagogue *f* 84
synthetic synthétique 114
system système *m* 138

T

table table *f* 36, 107
tablet comprimé *m* 109
tailor's tailleur *m* 99
take, to prendre 18, 25, 72, 73, 102; porter 114
take away, to *(carry)* emporter 63, 102
talcum powder talc *m* 111
tampon tampon hygiénique *m* 109
tangerine mandarine *f* 54
tap *(water)* robinet *m* 28
tape recorder magnétophone *m* 119
tapestry tapisserie *f* 127
tarragon estragon *m* 50
tart tarte *f*, tartelette *f* 55
taxi taxi *m* 19, 21, 31
tea thé *m* 38, 60, 64
team équipe *f* 89
tear, to déchirer 140
tearoom salon de thé *m* 34
teaspoon cuillère à café *f* 107, 143
telegram télégramme *m* 133
telegraph office bureau du télégraphe *m* 99, 133

telephone téléphone *m* 28, 78, 79, 134
telephone, to téléphoner 134
telephone booth cabine téléphonique *f* 134
telephone call appel *m* 135; communication *f* 136
telephone directory annuaire téléphonique *m* 134
telephone number numéro de téléphone *m* 96, 135, 136
telephoto lens téléobjectif *m* 125
television *(set)* poste de télévision *m* 23; télévision *f* 28; téléviseur *m* 119
telex télex *m* 133
telex, to envoyer un télex 130
tell, to dire 13, 73, 136; indiquer 76, 153
temperature température *f* 90, 142; *(fever)* fièvre *f* 140
temporary provisoire 145
ten dix 147
tendon tendon *m* 138
tennis tennis *m* 89
tennis court court de tennis *m* 89
tennis racket raquette de tennis *f* 90
tent tente *f* 32, 107
tenth dixième 149
tent peg piquet de tente *m* 107
tent pole montant de tente *m* 107
term *(word)* terme *m* 131
terrace terrasse *f* 36
terrifying effrayant 84
terrycloth tissu-éponge *m* 114
tetanus tétanos *m* 140
than que 15
thank you merci 10
that ce, cette 160; cela 11, 100
the le, la *(pl* les) 159
theatre théâtre *m* 82, 86
theft vol *m* 156
their leur *(pl* leurs) 161
then ensuite 15
there là 14; voilà 14
thermometer thermomètre *m* 109, 144
these ces 160; ceux-ci 63
they ils, elles 161
thief voleur *m* 156
thigh cuisse *f* 138
thin mince 113
think, to penser 94; croire 62
third troisième 149
third tiers *m* 149
thirsty, to be avoir soif 13, 35
thirteen treize 147

thirty trente 147
this ce, cette 160, ceci 11, 100
those ces 160; ceux-là 63, 120
thousand mille 148
thread fil *m* 27
three trois 147
throat gorge *f* 138, 141
throat lozenge pastille pour la gorge *f* 109
through à travers 15
through train train direct *m* 68, 69
thumb pouce *m* 138
thumbtack punaise *f* 105
thunder tonnerre *m* 94
thunderstorm orage *m* 94
Thursday jeudi *m* 151
thyme thym *m* 51
ticket billet *m* 65, 69, 87, 89, 156; *(bus)* ticket *m* 72
ticket office guichet *m* 67
tide marée *f* 90
tie cravate *f* 117
tie clip pince à cravate *f* 122
tight *(clothes)* étroit(e) 116
tights collant *m* 117
time temps *m* 80; *(clock)* heure *f* 137, 153; *(occasion)* fois *f* 143
timetable horaire *m* 68
tin *(can)* boîte *f* 120
tinfoil papier d'aluminium *m* 107
tin opener ouvre-boîtes *m* 107
tint coloration *f* 111
tinted teinté 123
tire pneu *m* 75, 76
tired fatigué(e) 13
tissue *(handkerchief)* mouchoir en papier *m* 111
to à 15
toast pain grillé *m* 38
tobacco tabac *m* 126
tobacconist's bureau de tabac *m* 99, 126
today aujourd'hui 29, 151
toe orteil *m* 138
toilet paper papier hygiénique *m* 111
toiletry articles de toilette *m/pl* 110
toilets toilettes *f/pl* 27, 32, 37, 67
toilet water eau de toilette *f* 111
toll péage *m* 75, 79
tomato tomate *f* 50
tomato juice jus de tomate *m* 41, 60
tomb tombe *f* 82
tomorrow demain 29, 151
tongs pince *f* 107

tongue langue *f* 46, 138
tonic water Schweppes *m* 60
tonight ce soir 29, 86, 87, 96
tonsil amygdale *f* 138
too trop 15; *(also)* aussi 15
tooth dent *f* 145
toothache mal de dents *m* 145
toothbrush brosse à dents *f* 111, 119
toothpaste dentifrice *m* 111
top haut *m* 30, 145
torch *(flashlight)* lampe de poche *f* 107
torn déchiré(e) 140
touch, to toucher 155
tough dur(e) 61
tourist office syndicat d'initiative *m* 22, 80; office du tourisme *m* 80
tourist tax taxe de séjour *f* 32
towards vers 15
towel serviette *f* 27, 111
tower tour *f* 82
town ville *f* 19, 21, 76, 93, 105
town hall mairie *f* 82
tow truck dépanneuse *f* 78
toy jouet *m* 128
toy shop magasin de jouets *m* 99
tracksuit survêtement *m* 117
traffic circulation *f* 79
traffic light feu *m* 77
trailer caravane *f* 32
train train *m* 66, 68, 69, 70; *(underground, subway)* rame *f* 73
tram tram *m* 72
tranquillizer tranquillisant *m* 109, 143
transfer *(bank)* transfert *m* 131
transformer transformateur *m* 119
translate, to traduire 12
transport transport *m* 74
travel, to voyager 92
travel agency agence de voyages *f* 99
traveller's cheque chèque de voyage *m* 18, 62, 102, 130
travelling bag sac de voyage *m* 18
travel sickness mal du voyage *m* 108
treatment traitement *m* 143
tree arbre *m* 85
tremendous formidable 84
trim, to *(beard)* rafraîchir 31
trip voyage *m* 93, 152; trajet *m* 72
tripe tripes *f/pl* 47
trolley chariot *m* 18, 71
trousers pantalon *m* 117
trout truite *f* 45

DICTIONARY

truck camion *m* 79
truffle truffe *f* 50
try, to essayer 115; *(sample)* goûter 60
T-shirt teeshirt *m* 117
tube tube *m* 120
Tuesday mardi *m* 151
tuna thon *m* 45
Tunisia Tunisie *f* 146
tunny thon *m* 45
turbot turbot *m* 45
turkey dinde *f* 48
turn, to tourner 21, 77
turnip navet *m* 50
turquoise turquoise *f* 122
turtleneck à col roulé 117
tweezers pince à épiler *f* 111
twelve douze 147
twenty vingt 147
twice deux fois 149
twin bed lits jumeaux *m/pl* 23
two deux 147
typewriter machine à écrire *f* 27, 105
typing paper papier à machine *m* 105
tyre pneu *m* 75, 76

U

ugly laid (e) 14, 84
umbrella parapluie *m* 117; *(beach)* parasol *m* 91
uncle oncle *m* 93
unconscious évanoui(e) 139
under sous 15
underdone *(meat)* saignant(e) 47; pas assez cuit(e) 61
underground *(railway)* métro *m* 73
underpants caleçon *m*, slip *m* 117
undershirt maillot de corps *m* 117
understand, to comprendre 12, 16
undress, to déshabiller 142
United States Etats-Unis *m/pl* 146
university université *f* 82
unleaded sans plomb 75
until jusqu'à 15
up en haut 15
upper supérieur(e) 69
upset stomach indigestion *f* 108
upstairs en haut 15
urgent urgent(e) 13, 145
urine urine *f* 142
use usage *m* 17, 109
use, to utiliser 134; se servir de 78
useful utile 15
usual habituel(le) 143

V

vacancy chambre disponible *f* 23
vacant libre 14, 155
vacation vacances *f/pl* 151
vaccinate, to vacciner 140
vacuum flask thermos *m* 107
vaginal vaginal(e) 141
valley vallée *f* 85
value valeur *f* 131
value-added tax T.V.A. *f* 24, 102, 154
vanilla vanille *f* 55
VAT *(sales tax)* T.V.A. *f* 24, 102, 154
veal veau *m* 46
vegetable légume *m* 49
vegetarian végétarien *m* 37
vein veine *f* 138
velvet velours *m* 114
velveteen velours de coton *m* 114
venereal disease maladie vénérienne *f* 142
venison cerf *m*, chevreuil *m* 48
very très 15
vest maillot de corps *m* 117; *(Am.)* gilet *m* 117
video cassette vidéocassette *f* 119, 124, 127
video recorder magnétoscope *m* 119
view vue *f* 23, 25
village village *m* 76, 85
vinegar vinaigre *m* 37
vineyard vignoble *m* 85
visit visite *f* 92
visit, to visiter 84
visiting hours heures de visite *f/pl* 144
vitamin pills vitamines *f/pl* 109
V-neck à col en V 117
volleyball volley-ball *m* 89
voltage voltage *m* 27, 119
vomit, to vomir 140

W

waistcoat gilet *m* 117
wait, to attendre 21, 95, 162
waiter garçon *m* 26, 36
waiting-room salle d'attente *f* 67
waitress serveuse *f* 26; mademoiselle *f* 36
wake, to réveiller 27, 71
Wales Pays de Galles *m* 146
walk, to marcher 74; aller à pied 85
wall mur *m* 85
wallet portefeuille *m* 156
walnut noix *f* 54

Dictionnaire

want, to *(wish)* vouloir, désirer 13
warm chaud(e) 94
wash to laver 20, 114
washable lavable 114
wash-basin lavabo *m* 28
washing powder lessive *f* 107
watch montre *f* 121, 122, 127
watchmaker's horlogerie *f* 99, 121
watchstrap bracelet de montre *m* 122
water eau *f* 23, 28, 32, 38, 75, 90
watercress cresson *m* 49
waterfall chute d'eau *f* 85
water flask gourde *f* 107
watermelon pastèque *f* 54
water-ski ski nautique *m* 91
wave vague *f* 90
way route *f*, chemin *m* 76
we nous 161
weather temps *m* 93
weather forecast prévisions météo *f/pl* 94
wedding ring alliance *f* 122
Wednesday mercredi *m* 151
week semaine *f* 16, 20, 24, 80, 151
weekend week-end *m* 151
well *(healthy)* bien 10, 140
well-done *(meat)* bien cuit(e) 47
west ouest *m* 77
what quoi, que, comment 11; quel(e) 20, 21
wheel roue *f* 78
when quand, à quelle heure 11
where où 11
which lequel, laquelle 11
whipped cream crème Chantilly *f* 55
whisky whisky *m* 17, 60
white blanc, blanche 59, 113
whitebait blanchaille *f* 44
whiting merlan *m* 45
Whit Sunday Pentecôte *f* 152
who qui 11
why pourquoi 11
wick mèche *f* 126
wide large 118
wide-angle lens grand-angulaire *m* 125
wife femme *f* 93
wig perruque *f* 111
wild boar sanglier *m* 48; *(young)* marcassin *m* 48
wind vent *m* 94
window fenêtre *f* 28, 36, 69; *(shop)* vitrine *f* 100, 112
windscreen/shield pare-brise *m* 76

wine vin *m* 57, 59, 61
wine list carte des vins *f* 59
wine merchant marchand de vin *m* 99
winter hiver *m* 150
winter sports sports d'hiver *m/pl* 91
wiper essuie-glace *m* 76
wish vœu *m* 152
with avec 15
withdraw, to *(bank)* retirer 131
without sans 15
woman femme *f* 115
wonderful merveilleux(euse) 96
wood bois *m* 85
wood alcohol alcool à brûler *m* 107
woodcock bécasse *f* 48
woodgrouse coq de bruyère *m* 48
wool laine *f* 114
word mot *m* 12, 15, 133
work, to *(function)* fonctionner 28, 119
working day jour ouvrable *m* 151
worse pire 14
worsted peigné *m* 114
wound blessure *f* 139
wrinkle resistant infroissable 114
write, to écrire 12, 101
writing pad bloc *m* 105
writing-paper papier à lettres *m* 27
wrong faux, fausse 14, 135

X

X-ray *(photo)* radio *f* 140

Y

year an *m*, année *f* 149
yellow jaune 113
yes oui 10
yesterday hier 151
yet encore 15
yield, to *(traffic)* céder le passage 79
yoghurt yaourt *m*, yoghourt *m* 38, 64
you tu, vous 161
young jeune 14
your ton, ta *(pl* tes) 161; votre *(pl* vos) 161
youth hostel auberge de jeunesse *f* 22, 32

Z

zero zéro *m* 147
zip(per) fermeture-éclair *f* 117
zoo jardin zoologique *m* 82
zoology zoologie *f* 83
zucchini courgette *f* 49

Index français